# HISTORY OF CEYLON

# HISTORY OF CEYLON

REVISED AND ENLARGED

L. E. BLAZE

GYAN

*Published by*

GYAN

Gyan Publishing House
5, Ansari Road
Daryaganj, New Delhi-110002
Phone: 011-47034999, 9811692060
E-mail: books@gyanbooks.com

*Distribution Network*
gyanbooks.com
India, USA, Canada, UK, Australia, France



ISBN : 978-81-212-3513-6 (PB)
First Published, Colombo, 1933

2nd Impression 2020

*Printed at:* Gyan Press, Delhi.



**History of Ceylon**
Author: L. E. Blaze

# HISTORY

# OF

# CEYLON

BLAZE

*(Revised and Enlarged Edition)*

---

The Christian Literature Society
for India & Africa,
Ceylon Branch—COLOMBO

1933

# CONTENTS.


| Chapter | | | Page |
|---|---|---|---|
| I | Introductory | ... | 1 |
| II | Vijaya the Conqueror | ... | 5 |
| III | From Vijaya's death to Mutasiva | ... | 11 |
| IV | Buddha and Buddhism | ... | 16 |
| V | Devanampiya Tissa | ... | 19 |
| VI | The First Tamil Invasion | ... | 24 |
| VII | The Kings of Ruhuna | ... | 27 |
| VIII | The Triumph of Gemunu | ... | 31 |
| IX | Dutugemunu's Buildings | ... | 34 |
| X | Valagam Ba | ... | 38 |
| XI | The Cholians | ... | 42 |
| XII | The Last of the Mahavansa Kings | ... | 46 |
| XIII | The Gupta Period in India | ... | 50 |
| XIV | Progress in Arts and Literature | ... | 53 |
| XV | Two Famous Visitors | ... | 57 |
| XVI | Sigiriya | ... | 58 |
| XVII | Growth of Tamil Influence | ... | 63 |
| XVIII | The Rise of Polonnaruva | ... | 70 |
| XIX | Civil Strife among the Sinhalese | ... | 77 |
| XX | Ancient Trade of Ceylon | ... | 80 |
| XXI | Vijaya Bahu I. | ... | 85 |
| XXII | A Time of Disorder | ... | 90 |
| XXIII | Parakrama's Early Life | ... | 93 |
| XXIV | How Parakrama became King of Lanka | | 96 |
| XXV | The Reign of Parakrama | ... | 99 |
| XXVI | Another Tamil Invasion | ... | 104 |
| XXVII | Pandita Parakrama Bahu | ... | 109 |
| XXVIII | The Last Phase I. | ... | 111 |
| XXIX | The Last Phase II. | ... | 117 |
| XXX | The Arrival of the Portuguese | ... | 121 |
| XXXI | The Discovery of Ceylon | ... | 124 |
| XXXII | Extension of Portuguese Influence | ... | 128 |
| XXXIII | The Kandyan Kingdom | ... | 133 |
| XXXIV | Dutch Trade with India | ... | 139 |

| Chapter | | Page |
|---|---|---|
| XXXV | The Last Years of Portuguese Rule ... | 147 |
| XXXVI | Robert Knox in Ceylon ... | 161 |
| XXXVII | Beginnings of Dutch Rule ... | 170 |
| XXXVIII | The First Dutch Period ... | 173 |
| XXXIX | The Dutch Government of Ceylon ... | 177 |
| XL | Conciliation and Economy ... | 181 |
| XLI | The Dutch take Kandy ... | 185 |
| XLII | The End of Dutch Rule ... | 190 |
| XLIII | Results of Dutch and Portuguese Rule | 194 |
| XLIV | Early Troubles of British Rule ... | 199 |
| XLV | War Against Kandy, 1803 ... | 209 |
| XLVI | The Ehelapola Tragedy ... | 213 |
| XLVII | The End of Independence ... | 215 |
| XLVIII | The Rebellion of 1817—1818 ... | 219 |
| XLIX | Peace and Progress ... | 223 |
| L | From A.D. 1837 to 1850 ... | 228 |
| LI | From A.D. 1850 to 1865 ... | 233 |
| LII | From A.D. 1865 to 1877 ... | 238 |
| LIII | From A.D. 1877 to 1931 ... | 243 |


## TABLES


| | |
|---|---|
| Kings of the Mahavansa ... | 258 |
| Kings of the Lower Dynasty ... | 260 |
| Portuguese Governors ... | 263 |
| Dutch Governors ... | 264 |
| British Governors ... | 265 |
| Index ... | 266 |



*[This History was first published in 1900. Second Edition 1903. Third Edition 1912. Fourth Edition 1913. Fifth Edition 1923. Sixth Edition 1927. Seventh Edition 1929. Eighth Edition 1931. Ninth Edition 1934.*

# A HISTORY OF CEYLON

CHAPTER I.

## Introductory

THE object of this little book is to tell in simple language the story of Ceylon :—of its fame in early times, and of the people who, so far as we know, then lived in it ; of its conquest by the Sinhalese, the Portuguese, and the Dutch, in turn ; and of how it came to be, as it is now, under British rule. It is necessary that we should have some knowledge of these matters, for Ceylon is the land in which we live, and to nearly all of us it is our native country. No one can be a lover of his country who does not know something of its peoples, and how they came into it.

But even apart from this, the history of Ceylon is full of interest. No island in the world has been so long famous, and famous among so many different nations. It is the sacred land of three religions. The Hindus reverence it as the place where Rama, once honoured as one of their princes, and then worshipped as one of their gods, fought to get back his bride who had been cruelly carried away from her home in India. The Muhammadans declare that when Adam and Eve were driven out of Paradise, Ceylon was given to them to console them for their loss. The Buddhists regard it as the centre of their faith, the land which the Buddha loved, which he is said to have thrice visited. The fertility of its soil, the loveliness of its scenery, its delightful climate, its valuable commercial products, the wealth that lay hidden in the heart of its mountains and in the sands of its rivers, —all these advantages united to give the land a strange, irresistible charm that was felt by every traveller who was so fortunate as to visit its shores. To the Brahman this land was *Lanka* the shining land ; to the Siamese, *Tewa Lanka* " Lanka the divine " ; to the Indian Buddhist, the "pearl upon the brow of India" ; to the Chinese, the " island of jewels " ; to the Greek and the Persian, the " land of the hyacinth and the ruby " ; to the Tamil of South India, *I'lam,* the land of gold ; to the Sinhalese, the " island of the lion-race " ; to the modern European, the " Eden of the Eastern Wave."

It was first known in Europe as *Taprobane** a name which the English poet, Milton, has preserved in one of his great poems. In Arabic writings it is spoken of as *Serendib.* And this is how the island was described by an English traveller three centuries ago :—" The heavens with their dews, the air with a pleasant wholesomeness and fragrant freshness ; the waters in their many rivers and fountains, the earth diversified in aspiring hills, lowly vales, equal and indifferent plains, filled in her inward chambers with metals and jewels, in her outward court and upper face stored with whole woods of the best cinnamon that the sun seeth ;

* Pronounced *Ta—prob—a—ne.*

# Map of Ceylon's Surroundings

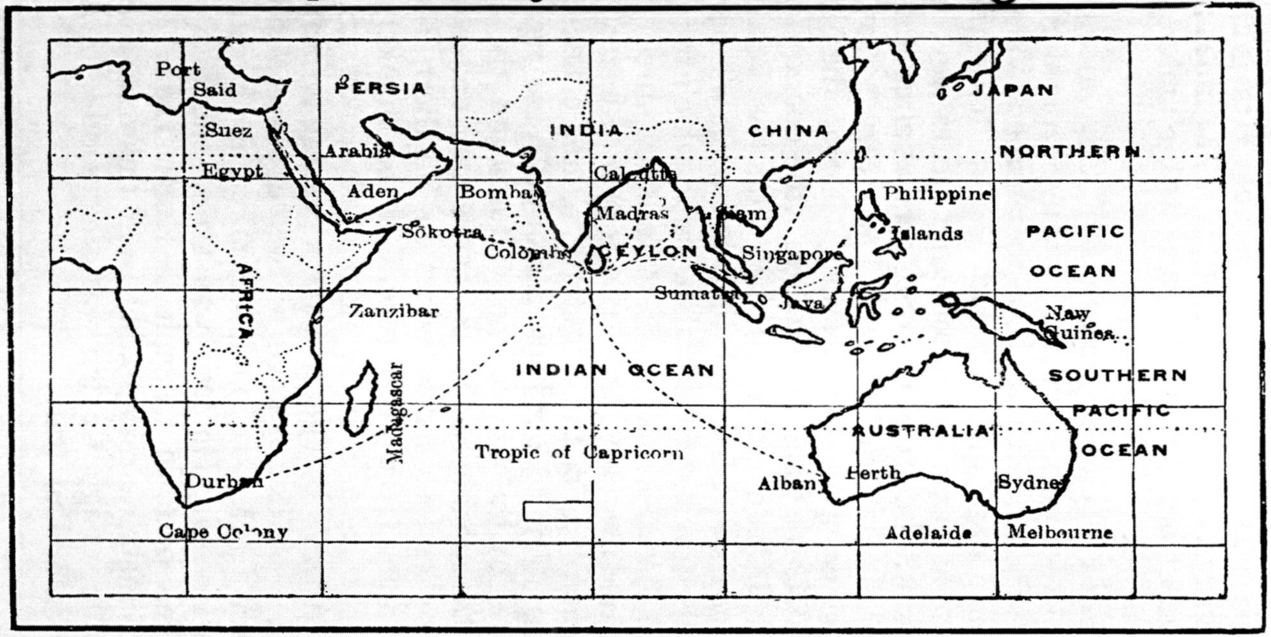

India sixty-one times, as large. Its greatest length from north to south is 271½ miles; its greatest breadth, 137½ miles; its circumference, about 760 miles.

For the earliest mention of Ceylon in old books we must turn to an Indian poem called the *Rāmāyana*, written by a poet named Valmiki. This poem is about events said to have taken place at least three thousand years ago, and cannot, of course, be considered as altogether a record of actual facts. The story* may be summed up in a few words. Rama, the eldest son of the king of Ayodhya (the country now called Oudh, in India), had won the beautiful princess Sitā for his bride; but while wandering in the forests of Central India, to which the pair had been banished, Sitā was captured and carried away to Lanka (Ceylon) by Rāvana, the demon king of this country. Rama collected a large army to get back his bride. He was assisted by the king of the vultures and the king of the monkeys; that is, as we may understand it, by various native tribes in Southern India. Hanuman, the chief general of the monkeys, is said to have built the ridge of sand now known as Adam's Bridge, to make a passage for Rama's army. After a siege of twelve years, Lankapura, Ravana's capital, was taken and burnt, the demon king himself was slain, and Sitā was taken back in triumph to North India. The main fact we may gather from this narrative is that ages ago Ceylon was successfully invaded by an Indian army.

---

* For a fuller account see "The Story of Lanka." (C.L.S.)

CHAPTER II.

## Vijaya the Conqueror

THE regular history of Ceylon may be said to begin with the arrival of Vijaya in the island. According to the Sinhalese historians this event took place on the very day of the Buddha's death, and the year B.C. 543 is usually given as the date of both occurrences. But those who have looked into these matters carefully are of opinion that this date is too early, and that the Buddha's death took place about B.C. 483.

Vijaya was the eldest son of Sinha-bahu, the king of Lala, a district near Magadha (now Bihar) in Northern India. The mother of Sinha-bahu was a princess of Vanga (Bengal). She is said to have married a lion. This would mean that she married a man of lower rank, or of a different race, who was known as *Siha or Sinha*, i.e., *lion*. In Sinhapura, the capital of Lala, prince Vijaya became the leader of a band of lawless men who committed numberless acts of mischief and violence. The people complained of this to the king, who on two occasions severely censured his son. But when these acts of oppression still went on, the people angrily demanded that Vijaya should be put to death. The king then resolved on banishing the offenders. Vijaya and seven hundred (that is to say, a large number) of his followers were placed on board a large ship and sent adrift.

---

B.C. 538 Decree of Cyrus for the return of the Jews from Babylon.

,, 535—446 Pythagoras, Anacreon, Aeschylus, Pindar.

,, 480 Battles of Thermopylae and Salamis.

In another vessel the king sent away the wives of these men, and in a third vessel their children. The men, women, and children, drifting in different directions, landed and settled in different countries. Vijaya landed at first at a port on the east (but some think it was on the west) coast of India; but here, fearing lest the people of that place should be roused against him by the rash deeds of his lawless followers, he re-embarked, and sailed on till he came to Ceylon.

Vijaya's route from India to Ceylon has been a matter of much controversy. There are also doubts as to the situation of Lala, where Vijaya lived. Some authorities are of opinion that Lala was not near Bihar but was Guzerat, a district of north-west India, north of Bombay. The port Supparaka, which Vijaya is said to have touched at on his voyage from India, is believed to be the modern Sopara. There are many difficulties in the old records; but while it is interesting to try to solve these difficulties, it must not be forgotten that the whole story of Vijaya is more legend than history. There were probably several bands of invaders from India at various times, before and after Vijaya, and the old writers have tried to combine the different traditions into one narrative.

The island was at this time inhabited by a race, or races, about whom very little indeed is known They may have been originally the same people as the hill tribes of the neighbouring coast of Southern India, but they were much less civilized and less powerful than the invaders from Northern India, who easily overcame the feeble resistance offered to them. The Indian conquerors gave these people the names *Yakkhas* (demons) and *Nagas* (snakes), either in contempt, or because the conquered races worshipped demons and snakes, or, it may be, for both reasons. The Yakkhas lived in the central portions of the island, and had a capital named Lankapura. The Nagas lived in the northern and western districts, and gave the name *Nagadipa* (the Isle of Serpents) to the whole of their possessions. There was a Naga king of Kelaniya, and there were two other kings in Nagadipa who once fought for a gem-set throne, which each king claimed as belonging to himself.

Among these people Vijaya and his seven hundred followers, believed to be Aryans by race, descended. They landed at a point on the north-western coast, near to where Puttalam now stands.* Weary and faint after their long voyage they came out of their ship, and threw themselves on the welcome beach. There is a story that when they rose from the ground they found that the palms of their hands were stained by the red-brown soil on which they had rested: and that therefore they gave the name *Tambapanni* (copper-coloured) to the place. This name, whether it was so derived or not, was afterwards given to the whole island, and from it is derived the name *Taprobane* used by Greek writers.

* Opinion is divided as to the place of landing; Tamankaduwa and a port on the south coast have also been suggested. But several "invasions" or settlements might have taken place.

Shortly after the invaders landed, one of them saw a dog and followed it into the country. "Where there are dogs," he argued, "there must be a village also." Instead of a village however, the dog led him to a tank near which what appeared to be a devotee (a very religious person) was seated spinning thread. Seeing a human being, as he took her to be, he was encouraged to bathe in the tank and to collect for food some of the roots that grew in it. But while he was thus occupied, the devotee (who was really a Yakkha princess, named Kuveni) started up, seized the astonished man, and flung him into a cave. One by one the followers of Vijaya were in this way imprisoned, and at last Vijaya himself came to the place. Seeing that all the footprints led into the tank and none out of it, he suspected that the Yakkhini had imprisoned the men there. In his rage he caught her by the neck, and would have killed her but that she instantly submitted, and restored his followers to him, feeding them on the rice taken from ships which had been wrecked on the coast. Vijaya afterwards took Kuveni for his wife, and with her aid gradually became master of the country round about. The neighbouring Yakkha chiefs were subdued, and a capital, named Tammana Nuwara was built a few miles east of Puttalam.

Vijaya was now in fact, if not in name, the chief ruler of the island. We may therefore now begin to speak of him and his followers as the *Sinhalese*, the lion-race; for it will be remembered that Vijaya's father was Sinhabahu, the lion-arm. The island itself afterwards

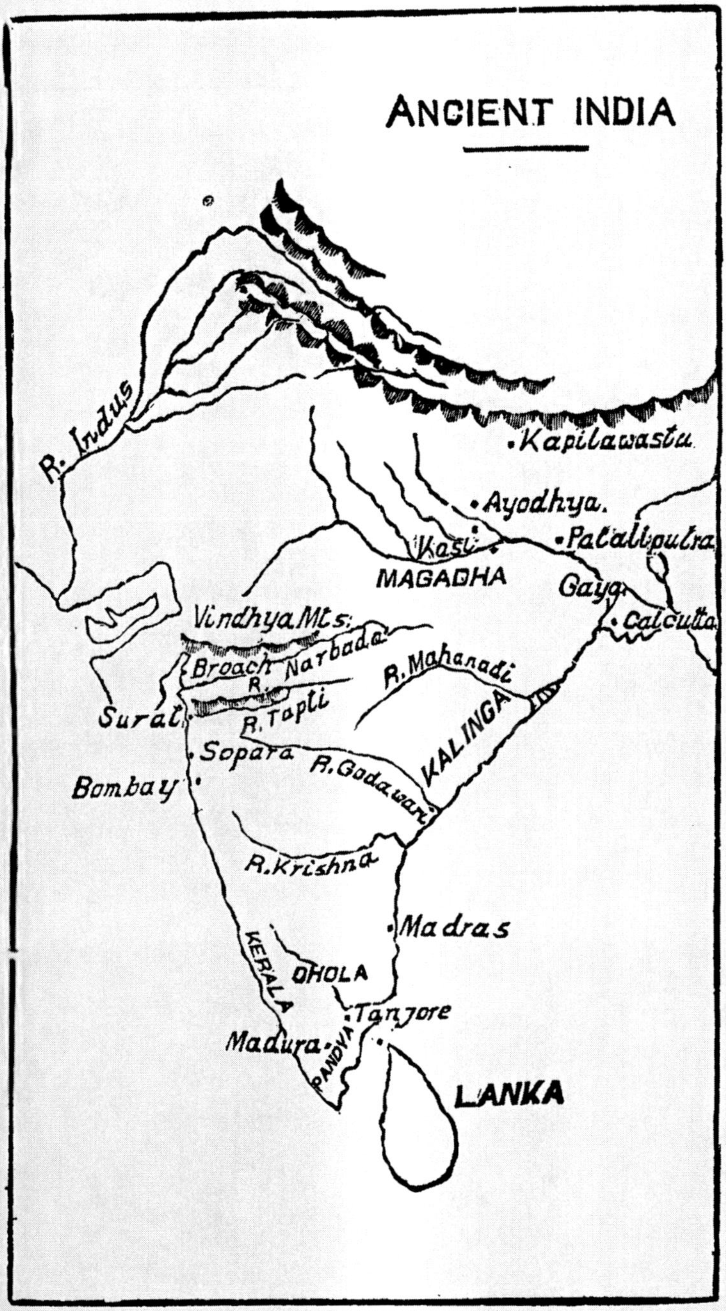
ANCIENT INDIA
R. Indus
Kapilawastu
Ayodhya.
Kasi
Patalipulra
MAGADHA
Gaya
Calcutta
Vindhya Mts.
Broach
R. Narbada
R. Mahanadi
Surat
R. Tapti
KALINGA
Sopara
R. Godawari
Bombay
R. Krishna
Madras
KERALA
CHOLA
Tanjore
Madura
PANDYA
LANKA

took the conqueror's name. It was called *Sinhala-dipa,* the Island of the Sinhalese. From this were formed the various names *Serendiva, Serendib, Ceilao, Zeilan, Ceylan,* and lastly *Ceylon*, though to the Sinhalese people it is always *Lanka.*

It took many years before the native Yakkhas and Nagas were finally subdued, and we shall sometimes find them mentioned in our history as having separate chiefs, cities, and armies of their own Vijaya's followers established themselves in various parts of the country, forming petty chieftaincies over which they ruled. One of them went north and settled where Anuradhapura now stands. Another went farther north and founded the settlement of Upatissa. A third founded Vijitapura on the east. Then these chiefs decided that it was time their leader took upon himself the rank and office of a king. But Vijaya refused to do this until he could marry a queen of his own rank. Thereupon the chiefs sent an embassy to Madura (the capital of the kingdom of Pandya * in South India) to ask for the king's daughter to be Vijaya's queen. The request was readily granted, and seven hundred daughters of the principal nobles of Madura came with the princess to Ceylon. The princess married king Vijaya, whose "inauguration," or coronation, was then celebrated with great splendour, while the seven

* *See, map p. 8.* The kingdom of Pandya extended southward from about Point Calimere to Cape Comorin. It had the kingdom of Chola on its north, and the Chera or Kerala kingdom on its west.

hundred other ladies were bestowed on the king's ministers, "according to their grades or castes" This is the first time castes are mentioned in Sinhalese history, though the caste system must have been previously brought by Vijaya to Ceylon. Workmen of various sorts, such as goldsmiths, carpenters, etc., came also at this time.

But what of Kuveni—the Yakkha princess who had been Vijaya's wife till now, who had borne him two children (a son and a daughter), and with whose assistance he had made himself master of the country? She was put away by Vijaya, and he made a strange excuse for doing so. "A king's daughter," said he, meaning the Indian princess who was now his queen, "is a timid being. Thou must therefore leave thy children, and go from my house." "But whither can I go?" pleaded Kuveni; "On thy account I fought against and killed mine own people. I dread their revenge; and now thou too turnest me away. Whither shall I go?" Vijaya offered to provide a shelter for her within his own dominions; but the proud, broken-hearted woman indignantly refused the offer, and with her children sought to rejoin her tribe. They, of course, remembering the wrong she had done, put her to death, and the children saved themselves by flight. They fled to the nighbourhood of Adam's Peak, and under the protection of the king founded a numerous race. The people called Veddas are supposed to be their descendants. There is little doubt, however, that the Veddas represent the aborigines, or earliest inhabitants of the island.

For thirty-eight years (B.C. 543-505) Vijaya reigned at Tammana Nuwara (Tambapanni) over Ceylon. Nothing of importance took place after his coronation. He is believed to have visited Jaffna; but towards the end of his reign, he was troubled with anxiety as to who should succeed him, for his Indian queen bore him no son He resolved to invite Sumitta, one of his brothers, from Sinhapura. A letter was accordingly sent to Northern India; but long before the letter reached its destination, Vijaya departed this life and "went to the world of the devas."

CHAPTER III.

## From Vijaya's Death to Mutasiva

UPATISSA, the leading chief among the Sinhalese, now took up the government, and acted as king for one year, during which he made his own city, Upatissa Nuwara, the capital. When Vijaya's letter reached Sinhapura. Sumitta had already succeeded his father as king of that country. As he himself was thus prevented from coming, he sent **Panduvasu-deva,** the youngest of his three sons, to rule over the new kingdom that Vijaya had won; and on his arrival at Upatissa Nuwara the government was at once given over to him.

Panduvasu-deva's reign was not uneventful. Like his uncle, Vijaya, he married an Indian

B.C. 444—359. Aristophanes and Xenophon.

princess, and she was a relative of Gautama Buddha. Six of her brothers afterwards came to Ceylon, and distributed themselves over the country, forming settlements from which they took, or to which they gave, their names. Thus we find *Ramagona Ruhuna*, *Dighayu*, *Uruvela*, *Anuradha*, and *Vijitagama*.* Anuradha in his settlement caused a great tank to be built, the first about which there is any record in the old books. About this time also the island was divided into three great provinces, the names and boundaries of which were roughly :—

I. *Pihiti Rata or Raja Rata*—all the country north of the Mahaveli Ganga and the Deduru Oya; bounded on the west, north, and east by the sea. Anuradhapura and Polonnaruwa were its chief cities in later years. It may be presumed that Sinhalese influence was strongest here.

II. *Maya Rata*—bounded on the north by the Deduru Oya; east by the Mahaveli Ganga; south by the Kalu Ganga; west by the sea.

III. *Ruhuna Rata*—All the country south of the Mahaveli Ganga and the Kalu Ganga. *Malaya* was the central mountain region of Ceylon.

After a reign of thirty years Panduvasu died, and was succeeded by **Abhaya**, the eldest of his ten sons. Abhaya appears to have been

---

* cf. p. 9.

LANKA
(ANCIENT CEYLON)
Jaffna
ADAMS
BRIDGE
Mantota
Mannar
GIANT'S TANK
Ilpatissa
Aruvi Aru
RAJA RATA
Kuderamalai
Trincomalie
OR
Anuradhapura
Kala
Mihintale
RITIGALA
Vijitapura
Puttalam
KALAWEWA
MINNERIYA TANK
Polonnaruwa
PIHITI
Dambulla
Dedurn Oya
Batticaloa
Aluwihara
Chilaw
Dambadeniya
MAYA
Mahaweli
Kandy
Mahiyangana
RATA
Badulla
Kelaniya
Colombo
Kotta
ADAM'S PEAK
Kalu Ganga
Kalutara
RUHUNA
Kataragama
Beruwala
Tissamaharama
Magama
Rawana's Fort
(GREAT BASSES)
Hambantota
Galle
Matara
Dewi Nuwara

a weak and indulgent ruler, and his reign is noted only for a rebellion caused by his nephew Pandukabhaya. It had been foretold that Pandukabhaya would kill his uncles and take the kingdom. His uncles therefore sought to put him to death, but he escaped, and lived with a wealthy Brahman who taught him every accomplishment necessary for a king, and in the end provided him with money and troops to fight for his kingdom. Getting together a large force he took up a strong position near the Mahaveli Ganga, and for some years resisted all the efforts of his uncles to dislodge him. When king Abhaya heard of his nephew's success, he sent a letter to the prince secretly conferring on him the rule of all the country south of the river. This was really sharing the sovereignty of Ceylon with Pandukabhaya. The king's brothers were naturally very angry when they heard of this. They dethroned Abhaya (who had already reigned twenty years) and set up **Tissa,** one of themselves, to rule in his place.

There was now no king in Ceylon acknowledged by all the Sinhalese as supreme. For seventeen years (B.C. 454—437) the war lasted between Pandukabhaya and his eight uncles—for, of the ten, Abhaya and another were on his side. Pandukabhaya at last called in the aid of the Yakkhas whom he had fought and brought under his rule, and many more of

---

B. C.—437—427 Plato.

B. C. 384—322 Aristotle and Demosthenes.

his own people began to join him. With this larger army he occupied the Arittha mountain (Ritigala, about midway between Anuradhapura and Polonnaruva) and when his eight uncles came up, he fell upon them vigorously, slew them, and dispersed their forces.

**Pandukabhaya** was thirty-seven years old when he gained possession of the throne. He spared the lives of the two uncles who had befriended him. To them, and to the son of the Brahman who had sheltered him in his youth, he gave offices of great trust and responsibility, Abhaya being appointed ruler of the city during the night, with the title *Nagara-guttika,* guardian of the city. The Yakkhas who had fought for him were treated with great consideration, and were assigned quarters in and about the capital. He even ordered that offerings should be provided annually for the gods worshipped by the Yakkhas. Indeed, the king was very indulgent in matters of religion; he "provided a residence for five hundred persons of various foreign faiths."

Up to this time Upatissa Nuwara had been the capital of the Sinhalese kings. Pandukabhaya preferred Anuradhapura, removed to that place, and made the city worthy of a king's capital, which it continued to be for more than a thousand years afterwards. Two great tanks, the *Jaya-veva* and the *Abhaya-veva,* were made by the king's orders. Four suburbs were added to the city, a cemetery and "a place of execution and torture" were constructed, and arrangements were made for keeping the city clean and healthy by wise sanitary measures. In the twelfth year of his reign (*i e.*, B.C. 425) the king "fixed the boundaries of the villages in all parts of Lanka." His entire reign extended to seventy years, and it is interesting to note how much progress was made in establishing a settled rule in the new Sinhalese kingdom.

**Mutasiva**, the son of Pandukabhaya, succeeded to the throne, and is said to have reigned for sixty years.* His reign was one of unbroken peace, and the only act recorded of him is that he built the famous pleasure-garden at Anuradhapura. It was named *Mahamegha* (the great cloud), from a heavy fall of rain which took place unexpectedly when the garden was being laid out. We shall hear of this garden again presently.

The king died B.C. 307 [B.C. 247] and was succeeded by his son Tissa, afterwards known as **Devanampiya Tissa**, in whose reign a great change was made in the religion of the people.

---

* According to the Sinhalese historians Pandukabhaya must have been 107 years old when he died ; for he was 37 years old when he began to reign, and he reigned 70 years. Mutasiva succeeds and reigns 60 years. There is a difficulty in allowing two such long reigns in succession. One writer suggests that there was a reign between the two reigns in question, thus :—

| | |
|---|---|
| Pandukabhaya ... ... ... | 70 years. |
| Ganatissa (son of Pandukabhaya) ... ... | 13 ,, |
| Mutasiva (son of Ganatissa) ... ... | 47 ,, |

A later theory is that reigns of Pandukabhaya and Mutasiva are said to be longer than they really were in order that the day of Vijaya's arrival might be made to agree with the day of the Buddha's death.

## CHAPTER IV

# Buddha and Buddhism

SOME years before the landing of Vijaya in Ceylon, a king of an Aryan people called the Sakyas reigned at Kapilavastu, a town in North India,—in Oudh, or in Nepal. This king had a son named Siddartha, a youth of a quiet and reserved disposition. He was brought up in all princely accomplishments and was happily married. In his twenty-ninth year, however, he renounced all pleasures, comforts, and worldly honours, and gave himself up entirely to religious meditation. What troubled the prince most was that there existed around him so much pain and suffering which could not be relieved. For six years he wandered from place to place and sought in various ways to find a remedy by which man could overcome pain and suffering. He followed the directions of priests and religious teachers, he studied different religions, he lived a hermit's life of loneliness and self-denial, he suffered penances, but all in vain. He had now come near to the city of Gaya (in Bihar), and sat under a bo-tree, meditating on the problems for which he sought a solution, and fighting against the temptations which crowded into his mind. At last it seemed to him that he had found the remedy It was the mind of man which had to be taught and trained. Pain was caused by unsatisfied desire; every man should therefore seek to get rid of desire. When desire is extinguished, there will be deliverance from suffering. This was the chief teaching of the new religion, and round it clustered other teachings, all collectively known as the teaching of *Buddhism*.

Gautama—tne prince Siddartha is often so named from the tribe or clan to which he belonged—had now become the *Buddha*, or the enlightened one. For forty-five years he preached his doctrines, and a great part of Northern India adopted the new Buddhist creed.

During these years the Buddha is said to have visited Ceylon three times, knowing that "Lanka would be the place where his religion would be most glorified." His first appearance was at Bintenne, in the present Province of Uva, on a great plain where the Yakkhas were accustomed to meet. He terrified them with rains and darkness, and drove them to the hills. The Mahiyangana dagaba was afterwards built on this plain. The second visit was in the fifth year of his Buddhahood, when he came to Naga-dipa (the northern, or north-western, portion of Ceylon) to settle a dispute regarding a gem-set throne which two Naga kings claimed. The third visit was three years later. The Naga king of Kelaniya, near Colombo, invited him to come over and preach Buddhism. It was during this visit that the Buddha is said to have left the impression of his foot on Adam's Peak, and to have visited the place new called Anuradhapura.

After Gautama Buddha's death three great Councils were held in India. The first was at Rajagaha, the capital of Magadha (Bihar), in the year after the Buddha's death. But the spread of Buddhism brought with it unavoidable difficulties. A number of sects sprang up, and teachings different from those preached by the Buddha were widely taught. To settle the points in dispute, to decide clearly what were true Buddhist teachings, and what were not, the second Council was called. It was held about one hundred years after the first, about year B C. 443 [B.C. 383.]

Meanwhile, the great emperor of India known sometimes as *Asoka* (the sorrowless), and sometimes as *Piyadāsa* (the beholder of delight), and referred to in the Sinhalese writings as *Dharmasoka* (Asoka the righteous), became a convert to Buddhism. He was the ruler of Magadha, but in a short time he had extended his empire throughout the whole of India, except a small portion of the south. He ruled also over Afghanistan and Beluchistan. His chief city was Pataliputra (Patna). Asoka is chiefly known by his *Edicts*, which are thirty or more inscriptions on stone pillars or rocks. They are found in the most distant parts of his empire, and they are valuable records of Buddhist teaching and of historical facts. He was a devoted follower of the Buddha, a zealous believer, anxious to spread the faith everywhere. Buddhism became the State religion, and "Jambudipa [India] glittered

---

**B. C. 264—244 First Punic War.**

with yellow robes." In the seventeenth year of his reign, and in the third century after the Buddha's death, a third Council was held [B. C. 247] for the same purpose as the second, to settle disputed doctrines. But the third Council did something more; it decided to send preachers of Buddhism to foreign countries, and one country chosen for this purpose was Lanka. For Lanka, indeed, one of the greatest of Buddhist teacners was set apart,—Mahinda, the son (though some take him to be the younger brother) of Asoka. Mahinda had already founded a Buddhist monastery in the Tanjore district, then known as the kingdom of Chola; and now he and other four leading disciples were waiting for a suitable opportunity to take Buddhism into Ceylon.

## CHAPTER V

## Devanampiya Tissa

WE must return to the kings of Ceylon. When Tissa became king great wonders are said to have occurred. Precious metals and gems that had long lain buried in the earth rose to the surface. Treasures from ships which had been wrecked round the coast, and pearls from the depths of the sea, came up and cast themselves upon the shore. Near Anuradhapura three large graceful necklaces appeared. One, shining like silver, had on it beautiful creepers which gleamed like gold. Another was bright with full-blown flowers of various hues. The third shewed birds and beasts of divers colours.

The priests who wrote Tissa's history said all this in Tissa's praise, because the king became the friend and patron of the Buddhist priesthood. Indeed, the king is spoken of by them as *Devanampiya Tissa,* " Tissa the delight of the gods."

In some way or other, Tissa and the great Asoka of India, though the two kings never met, were friends of long standing. Tissa resolved to strengthen this friendship by sending an embassy with rich presents to Asoka. The presents included " the three kinds of gems, the three chariot-like necklaces, a chank with the whorls to the right, [i.e. winding to the right] and the eight descriptions of pearls." We must bear in mind that the Sinhalese were at this time followers of the Brahman or Hindu religion ; and at the head of Tissa's embassy went the king's nephew, Maha Arittha.

It is possible that the embassy was suggested not only by friendship but also by rumours which had come to Ceylon already of the new religion. From Anuradhapura the embassy went northwards, embarked at a port near where Jaffna now stands, disembarked at Tamalitti (now Tamluk), then at the mouth of the Ganges, and in seven days more reached Pataliputra (Patna), where they delivered their presents to Asoka. That monarch was very pleased with the rich gifts brought to him. He conferred high honours on the leaders of the embassy, and sent them back accompanied by ambassadors from himself, bearing valuable gifts. Among these gifts were water from the Ganges and other articles necessary for the anointing and consecration of a king. Nor did Asoka miss this opportunity of advancing the religion which he himself followed so earnestly. A "gift of pious advice" was added to the sword and crown and other substantial presents sent to Tissa. "I," said Asoka to the king of Lanka, "I have taken refuge in Buddha, his religion, and his priesthood.* Ruler of men, turn thou thy mind to belief in these supreme blessings, and with true faith do thou also seek refuge in this salvation."

Now Tissa had been already "consecrated." or crowned king, and he is always spoken of as Asoka's equal in rank, not his inferior. But Asoka claimed to be king of Ceylon as well as of vast regions in India; and if Ceylon adopted Buddhism, the island would, in a certain sense, be subject to him. Tissa accepted the advice sent by the Indian monarch. He favoured the introduction of the new religion, and was duly consecrated a second time.

Mahinda, the royal missionary appointed for Ceylon, arrived in the island about the year B.C. 307, [B.C. 246] His first interview with king Tissa took place on a mountain near Anuradhapura which was known afterwards as Mahinda's mountain, or, as it is now called, Mihintale. He was welcomed gladly and received with great reverence. The king soon became a convert to Buddhism, and the people

---

* Alluding to the threefold formula—

"I take refuge in the Buddha.
I take refuge in the Law.
I take refuge in the Order (of priests)."

followed his example in large numbers; for the sermons of the new preacher, as well as his fame and the austerity of his life, drew crowds to him wherever he went, and made a deep impression on those who listened. Buddhism was established at the capital, and the royal garden, Mahamega, was given over to Mahinda and the priests.

It seemed as if the king could not do too much for the new religion. His time, his energies, his treasures, were all freely spent in schemes for the comfort and advantage of the priests. He marked out and set apart for the service of Buddhism a large tract of ground which included the capital itself. Within this he built a vihara, or monastery, known since then as the Maha Vihara, which grew into "a great seat of learning and the home of great men." He built numerous other viharas too, and among them one with thirty-two cells cut out of the rock on the Mihintale mountain. Observing that there were no relics of the Buddha in the island, Mahinda advised that a request should be made to Asoka for the right collar-bone of the great teacher. This, it is said, was immediately sent, and with it the alms-bowl which had been used by the Buddha, and a number of other relics, which were all reverently deposited in a shrine on the mountain which was therefore called the Cetiya *(Shrine)* mountain. Over the collar-bone was erected in Anuradhapura the Thuparama dagaba, the first dagaba built in Ceylon (B.C. 306) [B.C. 245].

Women also were converted to Buddhism through Mahinda's preaching, and the princess Anula, the wife of the king's younger brother, with five hundred ladies of her company, asked for admission into the priesthood. Mahinda said that the rules of Buddhism did not allow him to ordain females; they might, however, apply to Asoka to send Sanghamitta (Mahinda's younger sister), who had become a priestess and was renowned for her learning, to Ceylon for this purpose. At the same time they were to ask for a branch of the sacred bo-tree under the shade of which Gautama had found Buddhahood.

The request was made, and, though Asoka did all he could to discourage her, Sanghamitta at once decided to leave her home for Ceylon. When the king pleaded that he would be left comfortless and alone in his old age, she replied that her brother's appeal must not be disregarded, since those in Ceylon who wished to be ordained were many. So, taking a branch of the sacred bo-tree given to her by the king, she came to this island accompanied be eleven other priestesses. The branch was planted with great ceremony in the Mahamega garden, and large numbers of women—Anula among them—were ordained priestesses by Sanghamitta. For her the king built a separate vihara in a cool and secluded place where, with her community of nuns, she spent the remainder of her life.

When Tissa died, after a long and eventful reign of forty years, he left his kingdom converted to the religion of "the vanquisher."

CHAPTER VI

## The First Tamil Invasion

**Uttiya,** the younger brother of Tissa, succeeded to the throne. In the eighth year of his reign [B.C. 199] the priest Mahinda died. The funeral of the noble Buddhist preacher was attended with every mark of honour. The rich coffin in which his remains lay embalmed was taken with solemn ceremonies to the Maha Vihara, and after seven days, during which frequent offerings were made, it was placed on the funeral pile, to which king Uttiya himself applied the torch. Sanghamitta died in the year following, and her body was burned with similar honours.

Mahinda and Sanghamitta well deserved the respect paid to their memory. They lived useful and unselfish lives, giving up the comforts and privileges of their royal home at Magadha to live among strangers, and to teach the highest truths they knew. They did not weary of their task; they sought no temporal reward; and they died in a strange land in the midst of their labours.

**Mahasiva,** the younger brother and successor of Uttiya, did nothing more noteworthy than build a fine vihara for a priest who happened to please him. But in the regin of the next king, **Sura Tissa** (a brother of the three previous kings) we come upon the beginnings of a new trouble from which the Sinhalese were to suffer for many centuries. In their anxiety to extend the Buddhist religion, and to gain " merit " for themselves after death by the building of innumerable viharas and dagabas the kings of Ceylon failed to take proper measures for the protection of the country, both from foreign invasion and from the revolts of their own ambitious chiefs. The king's army was neglected, and the Sinhalese people were setting down as peaceful tillers of the soil. Many of them were employed on the various buildings which the kings had in hand. These buildings were chiefly in the northern part of the island, especially near Anuradhapura, the capital. But all the time the Sinhalese chieftains were forming settlements of their own in the southern and western districts—settlements which gradually became more and more independent of the king's authority. Two Tamils, named **Sena** and **Guttaka**, sons of a Malabar trader in horses, soon discovered the weak state of the country, and resolved to rule over it themselves. They brought over a Tamil army, treacherously murdered the king, and kept the government in their hands for no fewer than twenty-two years, when they were defeated and put to death by **Asela**, who is said to be the ninth of Mutasiva's ten sons, though this is improbable.

Asela's reign lasted ten years. But the Tamils in India had by this time found out how easy it was to take possession of the island, and in B.C. 205 [B.C. 145] the first noteworthy Tamil invasion occurred. The Tamils were led by **Elara**, a prince of the kingdom of Chola* in South India. He landed on the east coast at the mouth of the Mahaveli Ganga, and marched victoriously to Anuradhapura where he defeated and slew Asela. All Ceylon north of the Great River he brought wholly under his rule; and though the chiefs of Maya-rata and Ruhuna-rata were allowed to govern their own provinces, they were compelled to acknowledge Elāra's supremacy and to pay him tribute. Of Ruhuna we shall hear again presently.

Elāra built thirty-two forts to make himself secure in his new kingdom. Mantota, a village near Mannar, where in after times new bands of Tamil invaders landed, is said to have been founded by him. His justice and impartiality are noted by the historian, and the people seem to have been satisfied, or at any rate patient, under his rule. He caused a bell with a long rope to be hung over the head of his bed so that anyone who thought himself injured was able to bring his complaint to the king himself. Though a Hindu, the king gained the favour of the Buddhist priests by offering them his protection and by supporting their institutions. There are some, however, who assert that Elāra, was a violent

---

* *See map, p. 6.* The kingdom of Chola or *Sola*, extended from Nellore on the north to Pudukattai, or a little below Point Calimere, where it met the kingdom of Pandya. On the west it reached to Coorg. Tanjore was its capital, but there was an older capital, Uraiyar, near Trichinopoly. The name *Coromandel* is a corruption of *Chola-mandalam*, the country of the Cholas.

enemy of Buddhism, that he pulled down the viharas, and sought to force his own religion on the Sinhalese. This cannot be altogether true, though it is probable that in the capital, and in the northern part of the island, Buddhism did suffer to some extent, while the Hindu religion made great progress.

CHAPTER VII

## The Kings of Ruhuna

THUS Elara the Tamil continued to reign for forty-four years. But south of the great river the native chiefs ruled undisturbed, and Buddhism still prevailed. In Ruhuna the sovereign power was held by a member of the Vijaya family, and to this southern province we must now give some attention.

When Devanampiya Tissa was king of Lanka, Mahanaga, his younger brother, held the office of " sub-king." The queen of Tissa was afraid that this Mahanaga would, on his brother's death, take the kingdom, as Tissa's son was but a child; she tried to kill him. While Mahanaga was engaged in the building of a tank she sent him a jar of mangoes in which the uppermost mango contained poison. Tissa's son, who was with Mahanaga at the time, happened to eat this fruit and died. Upon this, afraid of what might follow, Mahanaga fled from Anuradhapura to Ruhuna, and there established himself, making Mahagama (now Magama, east of Hambantota) his capital, and building viharas and dagabas for the Buddhist religion. He was succeeded by his son, Yatthala Tissa, who made Kelaniya his capital, and built there the Kelaniya dagaba, on the spot where the Buddha is said to have visited the Naga king. The story goes that Kelaniya was then sixteen miles distant from the sea. King Tissa mistakenly suspecting the high priest of the dagaba of a crime, ordered him and others to be killed and their bodies to be flung into the sea. To avenge this wrong, the gods caused the sea to overflow the land, and were scarcely pacified when the king's daughter was sacrificed to them. This "pious and beautiful daughter," named Devi was placed in a richly-furnished boat and sent adrift on the sea. The winds and currents brought her to Mahagama near the Mudu vihara at Kirinde, built by Mahanaga. Hence she was known as *Vihara-Devi*.

When Elāra reigned at Anuradhapura, the king of Ruhuna was Yatthala Tissa's grandson, named Kavan Tissa. His wife was Vihara Devi, the gentle and pious princess of Kelaniya. She bore him two sons—Gemunu and Tissa—who were carefully brought up in the Buddhist faith. But Gëmunu, the elder son, was from his youth vexed at the usurpation of the Tamils, and eager to drive them out of the island. He made no secret of his intention to expel them as soon as he was able. On one occasion when Gëmunu was twelve and Tissa ten years old, the king placed three portions of boiled rice before them. "Eat this portion," said he, pointing to the first, "vowing you will never do injury to the priests." Again, pointing to the next portion, he said "Eat this, vowing that you two brothers will ever live in friendship." Both the boys ate their portions "as if," says the record, "they had consisted of celestial food." Then pointing to the third portion of the food, the king bade them eat it vowing, "Never to make war against the Tamils." This the boys angrily refused to do. They flung the food from them, and Gëmunu retiring to his bed laid himself on it with his hands and feet drawn up. His mother followed him to his room, and caressing him enquired, "My boy, why do you not stretch yourself on your bed and lie down at ease?" "How can I?" he replied; "shut in on one side by the Tamils beyond the river, and by the ocean on the other, how can I lie down with limbs outstretched?"

Gemunu spent his youth in preparing for a great war against the Tamils. First he trained himself in all warlike exercises. He learnt to use the bow and to manage the elephant and the horse. Then as his personal attendants he gathered round him a band of ten powerful warriors, each famous for some notable feat of strength or daring, and all taught to be loyal to their leader and their country. Their names and exploits are carefully celebrated in the Sinhalese histories. Nandimitta came from the capital itself, from Anuradhapura, where he fearlessly slew any Tamil whom he found dishonouring any building sacred to the Buddhists. Suranimila could make wonderfully quick journeys between places very far apart. Mahasona and Gothayimbra could uproot young palms and trees. Thera-putta-bhaya, who afterwards became a priest, like his father, could fell a palmyra or a coconut palm with a huge staff sixteen cubits long. Bharana was swift of foot, like the deer or the hare. Velusumana, on a charger which no other man could even mount, whirled along at full speed in the ring, so that there was "the appearance of one continuous horse in every part of the circus." Kanjadeva, the deformed of foot, could kill wild buffaloes by lifting them with his hands, and dashing them on the ground. Phussadeva, the chank-blower and lightning archer (for he could hit his mark by the flash of lightning) could shoot either through a horsehair held as a target, or through a cart filled with sand. Vasabha, the handsome one, could throw about huge baskets of earth which ten stout labourers could together scarcely raise from the earth. These, each "possessing the strength of ten elephants," were the ten heroes who followed Gëmunu, and by their means a large army was raised. Each hero enlisted ten others, each of these again ten more, and so on, till the prince commanded 11,110 men in all.

Gëmunu was now satisfied that he was able to carry on a successful war against the Tamils, but the king, his father, would not hear of it. Three times permission to begin the fight was asked and refused. Kavan Tissa thought only of the danger to his son in war against so experienced a warrior as Elāra, but he knew that the war must come, and he had even made preparations for it. These refusals, however, irritated Gëmunu so much that he insolently sent to his father a trinket worn by women, and said to his friends, "If my father were a man, he would not say No. Let him, therefore, wear this." Then, to avoid his father's anger, he fled to the mountains, and was ever after known as *Dutu Gémunu*—Gëmunu the disobedient.

The hills of Kotmale are supposed to have been Gëmunu's place of refuge. Legends are still told there of his stay in the district, and there he is said to have fallen in love with a beautiful maiden whom he married, but who did not belong to the royal caste.

CHAPTER VIII.

## The Triumph of Gemunu.

ON the death of Kavan Tissa, prince Tissa seized the throne, and a conflict took place between him and his elder brother. Two great battles were fought, in the second of which Tissa was defeated, but he was afterwards forgiven by Gëmunu at the intercession of the priests. Then at the head of a united army, and with the blessing of the priests, Gëmunu began the great war which had been the chief desire of his youth. One by one the Tamil chiefs in the neighbouring districts were overcome. Crossing the Great River, Gëmunu advanced upon Vijitapura, near the Kalaveva, where all the Tamils who had escaped slaughter along the banks of the river were now collected. The city held out for four months. It was defended by three lines of trenches and lofty battlements. The entrance into it was by a massive iron gate, against which Kandula, the king's powerful elephant, charged in vain; for, as he charged, the defenders poured melted resin on his back, and the maddened animal would rush into the nearest pond to soothe his pain. A covering of buffalo hides was provided for him when his wounds were healed, and again he returned to his task. At last the gate was burst open. Through this, and through breaches made in the wall, the besiegers entered, destroyed the fortifications, and slew the panic-stricken Tamils.

After taking several other forts of less importance, Gemunu prepared for the final assault on Anuradhapura. He took up a strong position near the city, and made it stronger still by erecting round it no fewer than thirty-two well-fortified redoubts, within the innermost of which he stationed himself. Elāra decided to begin the attack, and advanced against the enemy. He was mounted on his elephant, and was accompanied by the valiant Dighajantu, his chief general. The latter distinguished himself that day by a reckless valour that made the Tamils victorious wherever he led them. One by one the redoubts were taken, and the Tamil army at length approached the position defended by Gëmunu himself. But the daring warrior's successful course was there checked, and he fell a victim to the sword of Suranimila. The Tamil army now gave way, and a fierce slaughter took place, till Elārā himself advanced and rallied his men. Gëmunu, mounted on Kandula, immediately sought his rival. The two kings met in single combat near the southern gate of the capital. The old Tamil warrior hurled his spear at his young foe, who avoided it, and urged Kandula to an attack on the elephant that Elāra rode. As the two animals rushed on each other Gëmunu hurled his javelin at the Tamil king, and both Elāra and his elephant fell dead together. (B.C. 161) [B.C. 101.]

So ended "the solitary tale of Ceylon chivalry." Dutu-Gemunu was a really brave man, for he was able to respect courage in others, even in his enemies. Elāra's dead body was not treated like that of a foreign usurper, but was burnt with all due honour on the spot where he fell, and a tomb was built over the ashes. More than that, the king made a decree that any who passed that tomb, were it even the king of Lanka himself in grand procession, should silence all music and pass on foot. The rule was strictly observed. Nearly two thousand years later—in A.D. 1818 —a notable Kandyan chief was attempting to escape after an unsuccessful attempt at rebellion. As he came near the reputed tomb of Elāra, he "alighted from his litter, although weary and almost incapable of exertion; and, not knowing the precise spot, walked on, until assured that he had passed far beyond this ancient memorial."

## CHAPTER IX.

## Dutu-Gëmunu's Buildings.

THE Sinhalese dynasty was now restored, and **Dutu-Gëmunu** reigned for twenty-five years sole sovereign over Lanka. A week after Elāra's cremation, a Tamil army from India, commanded by Elāra's nephew, attempted to regain possession of the island; but the invaders were easily defeated, and henceforth Dutu-Gëmunu's reign was one of unbroken peace. The king's wars were over. But when he thought upon these wars and the numerous lives sacrificed in them, peace of mind was denied him. To make amends for the suffering he had caused, he determined to do all he could for the advancement of the religion of the Buddha; and if good works could in themselves quiet the reproaches of conscience, and atone for wrong, Dutu-Gëmunu might have been happy; for to the end of his life he faithfully observed the resolution he had made. He was first the patron of the priests, and then their slave. He gave them abundance of food and garments. For them he built viharas and dagabas whose very ruins now compel admiration. He built and furnished hospitals for the sick and infirm. He celebrated religious festivals with regularity. But no one can read the story of his later days without feeling that all these acts did not quite satisfy him or bring to his mind the comfort of which he had need.

Of Dutu-Gëmunu's many buildings at Anuradhapura there are two worth special notice—the *Lôvā Mahā Pāya* and the *Ruanveli Séya*. The Lovā Mahā Pāya, or Brazen Palace, was built to accommodate the large and increasing number of priests in the capital. It stood on sixteen hundred columns of granite, each column consisting of a single stone. These stones may still be seen, some of them rising twelve feet above the ground. The palace that stood on them was about 250 feet long, 250 feet broad, and 250 feet high. It was roofed with sheets of brass, whence its name, the Brazen Palace. In it were nine storeys, each divided into a hundred richly-decorated apartments. The priests of highest rank occupied the uppermost storey, the lowest in rank lived on the first floor. In the middle of the palace there was a hall supported on gilt pillars representing lions and other animals. In the centre of this inner hall was placed a beautiful ivory throne on which rested an ivory fan of exquisite beauty; while above the throne glittered the white umbrella-shaped canopy which was the Sinhalese emblem of royal power and authority.

The Ruanveli Dagaba, known also as the Maha Thupa, was begun by Dutu-Gëmunu, but he did not live to see it completed. No forced labour was employed in this work or in building the Brazen Palace. The people had suffered so severely from the taxes required by the war against the Tamils, that the king saw he could not ask more from them. He therefore ordered that all the workmen should be paid for the work they did. This dagaba was about 270 feet high and about a thousand feet in circumference. The foundations for so massive a building were made very strong, and the foundation stone, or "festival-brick," was laid with great ceremony. Both the capital and the road leading to it were decorated ; crowds assembled from the city and the provinces ; thousands of priests, among them many from India, were present ; and the pious king went to the place in full state, robed in his royal apparel, and accompanied by his officers, guards, and musicians.

In the middle of the dagaba was built a relic-chamber in the centre of which was placed a bo-tree made of the precious metals, and an image of the Buddha, round which were groups of figures representing various events in the life of the Buddha.

The building of the spire and the plastering of the dagaba alone remained to be done when king Dutu-Gëmunu fell ill. As the king wished to see how the work would appear when completed, his brother Saddha Tissa had the building covered with white cloth, and put up a temporary spire made of bamboos, so that

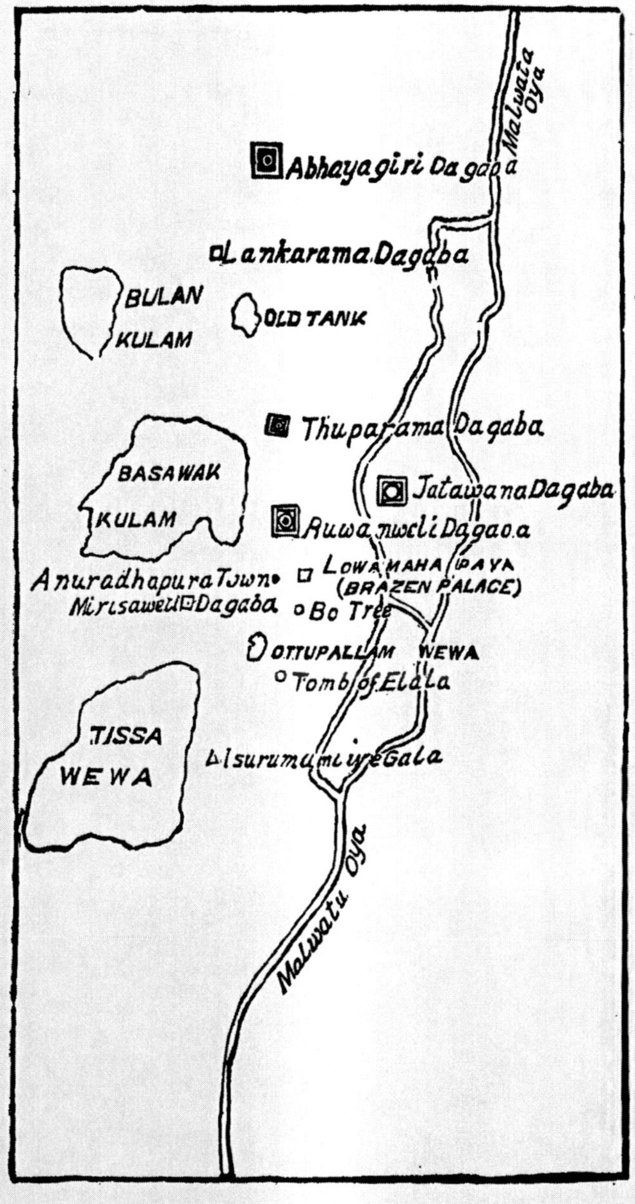

Malwatu Oya
Abhayagiri Dagaba
Lankarama Dagaba
BULAN KULAM
OLD TANK
Thuparama Dagaba
BASAWAK KULAM
Jatawana Dagaba
Ruwanweli Dagaba
Anuradhapura Town
LOWA MAHA PAYA (BRAZEN PALACE)
Mirisawetti Dagaba
Bo Tree
OTTUPALLAM WEWA
Tomb of Elala
TISSA WEWA
Isurumuniye Gala
Malwatu Oya

the king's last wishes might be gratified. Dutu-Gëmunu was then carried round the dagaba to which he reverently bowed in worship. Then, as he lay on a carpet which had been spread on the ground, his eyes rested on the Maha Thupa which stood on one side of him, and again on the Brazen Palace that stood on the other side. "In times past," he said to the priest Théraputtabhaya, who had been one of his ten heroes, "I was supported by you in war; now single handed must I begin my fight with Death. This enemy I shall not be permitted to overcome." To which the priest replied, "Ruler of men, the power of Death cannot be overcome unless the enemy Sin is first subdued. Call to mind your many acts of piety, and comfort shall surely be given you." The secretary read to him a record of the king's pious deeds, but when the list was finished all that the king remarked was. "All these things were given when I was prosperous. The thought of them brings me no relief. Only two offerings made when I was in adversity bring comfort to my mind."

He directed his brother Saddha Tissa to complete all that remained to be done at the Maha Thupa; to continue the offerings he had been accustomed to make; and in no respect to be wanting in attention to the priesthood. Then, gazing on the dagaba which had been the last work of his eventful life, the heroic king closed his eyes and passed away to the abode of the gods.

## CHAPTER X.

# Valagam Ba

DUTU-GËMUNU left a son, Sali; but this prince had married a woman of a lower caste, and was therefore excluded from the throne. However, the romance of prince Sali's love for *Asoka-mala*, the flower maiden, is still the theme of many a tale and of many a song. **Saddha Tissa,** the brother of Dutu-Gemunu, now became king, and reigned eighteen years. He completed the Ruanveli Dagaba and built a number of viharas. In this reign the Brazen Palace caught fire and was burnt down. The king had it rebuilt, but reduced the number of storeys from nine to seven

Three kings followed Saddha Tissa, of whom nothing more need be said than that they encouraged Buddhism and added to the beauty of the Buddhist buildings in Anuradhapura. But, thirty-three years after Dutu-Gemunu's death, **Valagam Ba,** a son of Saddha Tissa, ascended the throne. A few months after his accession the next great Tamil invasion took place. Seven Tamil chiefs landed in the island and made their way to Anuradhapura, where they attacked and defeated the king. His queen Somadevi was taken prisoner and Valagam Ba saved himself by flight. For nearly fifteen years he wandered in concealment in the forests south of Anuradhapura

---

* *Ba* is a contraction of *Abhaya* or *Abha*, the Pali form of the king's name being Vatta-Gamini-Abhaya. *Bahu* (as in Parakrama Bahu) means *arm*, denoting strength.

and afterwards in the Malaya district, while the Tamils ruled over the country. Two of the Tamil chiefs returned to India, and the remaining five attempted to govern Lanka. Each after a short reign was murdered by his successor, and the last was put to death by Valagam Ba, who then resumed his sovereignty, but probably not over the whole island; for it may have been about this time that the Tamils established themselves in the north, and began the kingdom of Jaffna.

Valagam Ba celebrated his restoration in the usual way, by building temples and monasteries. He was the first king of Ceylon to set apart lands for the support of the priesthood. The king had previously been accustomed to confer personal gifts on the priests, but when Valagam Ba was a fugitive he had no gifts at command. In his gratitude, however, to a priest who had befriended him, the king made the priest a grant, inscribed on the leaf of a tree, of certain lands, and the practice once begun was extensively carried on afterwards by succeeding rulers.

Of Valagam Ba's viharas the most famous is that at Dambulla, where once the king hid from his enemies. It is a large cave made into a temple, and richly decorated with figures of the Buddha and of the king himself, while pictures of scenes in the history of Ceylon (such as the landing of Vijaya, and the fight between Elara and Dutu-Gëmunu) are painted on the walls The Somarama monastery was built to commemorate the recovery of his queen Soma Devi from the Tamils. North of the Ruanveli dagaba the king built what is now known as the Lankarama Dagaba. But more notable was the Abhayagiri Dagaba (412 feet high) built at Anuradhapura. B.C. 87. It was so named after the king (*Vatta-Gamini-Abhaya*) and *Giri*, an Indian monk who had his temple where the dagaba was afterwards built. The new monastery caused a division in Buddhism. Its priests, who, on account of the king's favour to them, had grown numerous, taught certain doctrines which the priests of the Maha Vihara rejected. It happened at this time that the Maha Vihara priests expelled one of their number who had broken one of the monastic laws. A pupil of the expelled priest was offended at this, and went over to the Abhayagiri Vihara, where he was admitted as a member of the community. The Maha Vihara, therefore ceased to recognize the new establishment, which now became a separate sect. This sect itself broke up a short time after into two parties.

The Maha Vihara priests did one thing more to mark their opposition to the new sect. From the time of Mahinda, son of Asoka, the Buddhist doctrines were committed to memory by the priests and handed down orally. It was now determined to record these doctrines in writing, and by this method to give less opportunity for doubt and mistake as to what the Buddha taught. An assembly of five hundred priests met at Aluvihara, near Matale, and there the *Tripitaka*, or "Threefold Collection," with the Commentaries or Notes on them, were written down. This happened about the year 85 B.C. [B. C. 26]. Valagam Ba died B. C. 76 [B C. 17] after a reign of twelve years, having also reigned five months before the Tamils drove him from the throne.

The next king was **Mahachula**, a nephew of Valagam Ba. During his reign of fourteen years (which were devoted entirely to the service of the priesthood) Naga, the son of Valagam Ba, was leading the life of a robber, going about from place to place plundering where he could. For this reason he was called **Chora Naga**, Naga the marauder. On Mahachula's death he became king, but twelve years later was poisoned by his queen Anula, a woman notorious for her wickedness. **Kuda Tissa**, the eldest son of Mahachula, succeeded, and was also poisoned by Anula, after a reign of three years. Then from B.C. 47 to B.C. 42, **Anula** herself ruled over Ceylon, its first reigning queen. Within these five years she married in succession no fewer than four others. Raising them to the sovereignty she got rid of each by poison when she tired of him. For the last four months she reigned without the advice of ministers, and was then put to death by **Makalan** or **Kutakanna Tissa**, the second son of Mahachula. The new king, who died B.C. 22, built a rampart, about 16 feet high, round Anuradhapura.

## CHAPTER XI

# The Cholians

BHATIYA TISSA I., the son and successor of Makalan Tissa, was noted for his piety and his devotion to the priesthood. He repaired the sacred buildings, and set apart the revenues trom certain lands to meet the cost of keeping these buildings in good order. This monarch appears to have been very fond of flowers. He not only planted extensive gardens, but adorned the Ruvanveli Dāgaba with flowers. He is said to have completely covered the dāgaba on one occasion with a great heap of flowers, and then to have poured over them, as an offering, water brought by means of machinery from the tank.

We must pause here to note an event of the greatest importance that occurred in another part of Asia, during this reign, if we take B.C. 543 as the date of Vijaya's arrival in Ceylon. At Bethlehem, in the land of Palestine, a country smaller than Ceylon, JESUS CHRIST, the Founder and Head of the Christian religion, was born. The year of His birth is reckoned the first of the Christian era—that is, it is the period from which Christian nations date all historical events. It is the year A.D. I, the letter "A.D." standing for the Latin words *Anno Domini*, in the year of our Lord. All events that took place before this birth are said to have occurred " B.C "., *Before Christ;*

---

B.C. 55. Julius Cæsar's invasion of Britain.

all events after this are dated " A.D." Bhātiya's reign, for instance, began B.C. 20, and ended A.D. 9 ; or more fully, it began 20 years before Jesus Christ was born, and ended in the ninth year after that event. The dates in this history book will from this time be marked A.D. If, however, we accept B.C. 483 as the date of Vijaya's arrival, the Christian era began in the reign of Chora Naga, which would be from B.C. 3 to A.D. 9.

The next king, **Mahadeliya Mana,** the younger brother of Bhatiya I, also greatly encouraged the cultivation of flowers for religious purposes, but even the priests were obliged to protest against the excesses of his piety. He celebrated a splendid festival at a dagaba (the Ambatthala *thupa*) which he had caused to be built on the Mihintale mountain, on the plain where the meeting between Mahinda and king Tissa took place. He built several viharas in Ruhuna, and dedicated lands for their maintenance. In these matters he did nothing more than other kings before him had done. But when he dedicated himself, his horse, and his state elephant, as slaves to the priesthood, the priests themselves reproved him, and he had afterwards to be released from his vow by the payment of a large sum of money.

The next three kings may be briefly noticed, **Ada-Gemunu** forbade the killing of animals, and caused melons and other fruits to be grown for food in various places. He built the Ridi Vihara (the Silver Vihara) near Kurunegala

A.D. 25—29. A king of Kashmir is said to have visited Ceylon about this time.

and 55 miles South of Anuradhapura. He was put to death by **Kanirajanu Tissa**, his younger brother, who at the same time seized sixty priests on a charge of conspiring against the throne, and imprisoned them in a cave in the Mihintale mountain. **Chulabhaya** son of Ada Gëmunu, succeeded, and after a short reign gave place to **Sivali**, his sister, and the second reigning queen of Ceylon. She reigned four months only, and was deposed by **Ila Naga**, a nephew of Ada Gëmunu.

In the first year of Ila Naga's reign an insurrection took place. The Lambakannas, a royal caste, happened to displease the king, and as a punishment he ordered that they themselves should work to make a road leading to the Ruanveli dagaba ; and over them he placed overseers of a lower caste. Enraged at this the Lambakannas rebelled and made the king a prisoner. He, however, escaped to the north coast, and remained beyond the seas. gathering an army to recover his throne. After three years he returned, landing at a port in Ruhuna, and with his foreign troops and his own army he defeated the rebels and severely punished their leaders. The Tissamaharama, one of the largest dagabas in the south-east of Ceylon, was built by him.

Illa Naga was succeeded, after a further reign of six years, in A.D. 44 [A.D. 101] by his son **Sandamuhunu Siva** who built a tank and gave it over to the Issurumuniya Vihara.

---

A.D. 41—54 Claudius I Emperor of Rome. Embassy from Ceylon to Rome ?

A.D. 59—60 S. Paul in Rome.

This king was murdered by his younger brother **Yasalalaka Tissa**, who afterwards met his death in a curious way. A young gate porter, named Subha, bore a close personal resemblance to the king. The king would often in a merry mood change places with the porter. The latter, wearing the royal robes, would then be seated on the throne, while the real king, Yasalalaka Tissa, would stand at the palace gate with the porter's staff in his hand. The king found great amusement in watching the ministers of state paying respect to the mock king. One day, however, the jest was turned to earnest. **Subha**, the porter on the throne, used his temporary authority to order the real king to be put to death, and then he himself reigned for six years, when he was slain by **Vasabha,** a descendant of the Vijayan house, and a member of the Lambakanna clan.

Among the many pious deeds of Vasabha it is recorded that he built a roof over the Ruanveli dagaba, formed eleven tanks, and made twelve canals for purposes of irrigation. He did not neglect to take measures for the better protection of the capital, for he raised the wall round it to a height of 41 feet, that is 25 feet higher than it had been made by Makalan Tissa. Vasabha reigned 44 years and was succeeded by his son **Vankanasika Tissa** in whose reign (A.D., 110-113) another Tamil invasion is said to have occurred.* The Cholians

* Rajavaliya; the Mahavansa says nothing of it, or of Gaja Bahu's expedition.

A.D. 79. Pompeii and Herculaneum destroyed by an eruption of Vesuvius.

plundered the country, and went back taking 12,000 Sinhalese with them as prisoners. In the next reign, however, **Gaja Bahu,** the son of Vankanasika, avenged this outrage. He crossed over to India with an army, plundered the Chola country, and brought back not only the Sinhalese who had been taken away, but also the same number of Cholians, to whom he gave lands at Harispattu, Tumpane, and Alutkuru Korale. The descendants of these settlers even now bear traces of their Indian origin. To celebrate this victory over the Cholians a Perahera procession was annually celebrated at Anuradhapura.

CHAPTER XII

## The Last of the Mahavansa Kings

PASSING over the next six kings, we come to **Voharika Tissa,** A.D. 215, who abolished torture as a punishment. Early in the king's reign there was another conflict between the Maha Vihara and the Abhayagiri Vihara. The priests of the latter taught certain strange doctrines which they had learnt from an Indian named Vaitulya. These doctrines were probably those taught by the "Northern" Buddhists in Tibet, Kashmir, China, etc., as distinguished from the "Southern" Buddhism of Ceylon, Burma, and Siam. The king promptly put down this teaching, but, as we shall see, the heresy was revived not long after.

Voharika Tissa reigned twenty-two years and was then put to death by his younger brother, **Abhaya Naga,** who, with the aid of a Tamil army, seized the throne. On his death, Voharika Tissa's son and grandson respectively occupied the throne. In the reign of the latter, three men of the Lambakanna caste formed a conspiracy, slew the king, and reigned in succession. The first, **Sanga Tissa**, reigned for four years. In the reign of the second, **Siri Sangabo I**, who reigned two years, a terrible drought occurred, as also a plague which chiefly affected the eyes. It is said that the practice of *Bali* offerings and devil-dancing was established at this time, to keep off the red-eyed demon to whom the plague was attributed. The king was a very superstitious ruler. In consequence of certain Buddhist vows that he had taken he would not allow the execution of criminals who had been condemned to death. Robbers were seized, and brought to trial; but they were afterwards privately set free, and the corpses of persons who had died natural deaths were burned in their stead. The king's weak folly encouraged the prime minister to form a plot against his rule. To avoid bloodshed, Sangabo secretly left the capital, unaccompanied by attendants, and taking with him only his water-strainer, lest in drinking water he should cause the death of the little animals in it. He was soon discovered and slain by a peasant at Attanagalla, and his head was taken to Gothabhaya, third of the Lambakannas, who now became king.

**Gothabhaya** began his rule by attempting to purify the Buddhist religion. The Vaitulyan heresy had quietly spread in spite of the efforts made by Voharika Tissa to destroy it, and the heretics had become "thorns unto the religion of the vanquisher." Sixty of them—who were priests of the Abhayagiri Vihara—were excommunicated and banished to India. A Vaitulyan, named Sangha Mitta, afterwards came secretly over to Ceylon, and contrived to win the favour of king Gothabhaya, who appointed him to be tutor to his two sons. But while the younger prince, Maha Sena, was easily converted by the teaching of Sangha Mitta, the elder, Jettha Tissa, disliked his teacher, who fled to India when this prince became king. **Jettha Tissa I** reigned ten years, and strongly supported the Maha Vihara priests. But when on his death (A.D. 277) **Maha Sena** his younger brother succeeded, Sangha Mitta came back, and the older monastery suffered. Prompted by Sangha Mitta, Maha Sena forbade the giving of alms to any priest of the Maha Vihara. These priests accordingly went in their distress to the Ruhuna district, and for nine years the Great Vihara remained untenanted. The Vaitulyan then declared that unclaimed property belonged to the king, and the vihara was in consequence pulled down, and its materials were carried away to adorn the Abhayagiri Vihara. Over three hundred religious buildings were in this way destroyed, and even the great Brazen Palace was pulled down. These proceedings gave great offence to the people, and the king's chief minister retired to Ruhuna and collected a force to rise against the king. But before there was any fighting, the king seems to have thought better of it, and gave way. He renounced his errors, and as Sangha Mitta happened to be assassinated about this time, Maha Sena did all he could to atone for his previous misconduct. He began to rebuild the Brazen Palace, and repaired many damaged religious buildings throughout the island. He destroyed some of the devalas (Hindu temples), and erected viharas in their place. He built also the Jetavanarama dagaba, about 321 feet high, much to the annoyance of the Maha Vihara Priests, for it stood within their boundaries; and he built a *thupa* or temple for a Yakkha chief. This shews us that the original inhabitants of the island were still of some importance, and were employed together with the Sinhalese in the various works that Maha Sena undertook.

But it is by his tanks, made for the purpose of helping and extending cultivation, that Maha Sena will be best remembered. Of these he built sixteen, the largest being the Minneriya tank. It was from fifteen to twenty miles in circumference, and was formed by building a dam across the Kara Ganga. It lies between Dambulla and Trincomalee.

Maha Sena died A. D. 304 [A. D. 352], and "having performed during the whole course of his existence, acts both of piety and impiety, his destiny after death was according to his merits." This was the verdict of the priests, who could not forget that at the beginning of his reign the king persecuted them and pulled down their sacred places. But the people remembered only the benefits conferred on them by the great tanks which Maha Sena had formed. At Minneriya, a temple was erected in his honour, and he was worshipped as a god.

With Maha Sena ends the *Mahavansa* or Great Dynasty. The kings that followed Maha Sena are said to belong to the *Suluvansa*, or lower dynasty, either because they were not of unmixed descent, or because the island was not so prosperous in their times. We shall see, however, that considerable interest in literature and the arts was shewn during the rule of the kings of the lower line, and that one of them, at least, earned as much military glory as any of his predecessors.

## CHAPTER XIII.

## The Gupta Period in India

THE new period in Ceylon begins at a specially brilliant time in the history of India, and to this country we must turn our attention to explain the happenings in Ceylon.

About six hundred years after king Asoka, there ruled in Northern India a dynasty of kings called the *Guptas*. Their capital was first at Pataliputra (Patna), and then at Ayodhya (Oudh). Their empire, which began A. D. 320, included nearly all the territory, from the western to the eastern sea, which was watered by the Ganges and the Jumna. It was the strongest power in India till about A. D. 467, when the White Huns, a tribe from Central Asia, overcame it; but Gupta kings continued to reign over the eastern districts of their empire till near the end of the fifth century, and "later Guptas," as they are called, reigned in Magadha to the middle of the seventh century. This "Gupta Period" of North Indian history thus extended from the fourth to the seventh century, that is, from the reign of our Siri Sangabo to the troublous times of Agbo II.

It was a time of brilliant achievements in war, in literature, and in the arts; and we have to take note of these achievements because they influenced Ceylon as well as other eastern countries. There was a vigorous intellectual awakening in Ceylon, as in India, and because of India. The large number of tanks built in Maha Sena's reign shews how much activity there was among the people. The disputes between the Maha Vihara and the Abhayagiri Vihara shew that religious questions were keenly studied and debated. Traces of Gupta architecture are shewn in some of the Ceylon temples, and the rock-fortress of Sigiriya (see chapter xvi) was built during this period. Marks of Gupta sculpture are seen at the Issurumuniya Temple in Anuradhapura, and Gupta painting has survived in the frescoes painted at Sigiriya.

In India, Sanskrit, which had long been the sacred language of the Brahmans and their religion, now began to be used more freely by the people, and this may have helped to make Buddhism less popular than it was in Asoka's time. Many poems were now composed in Sanskrit, and the greatest of Sanskrit poets was *Kalidasa,* who is often spoken of as "the Shakespeare of the East." His most famous play was named *Sakuntala*, and it tells us of a beautiful girl who loses the ring given to her by her husband, and of her sufferings in lonely wanderings till the ring is found and she is reunited to her husband. The exact dates of Kalidasa's birth and death are not known, but it is most likely that he lived during the first half of the fifth century.

The customs of the Brahmans of Northern India are described in an important book called the *Code*, or *Laws*, *of Manu*, and this was compiled about the beginning of the fourth century, when also the *Mahabharata* and the *Ramayana* are believed to have taken the form in which they are now read. It was a Gupta king who, in the second half of the fifth century, built the splendid monastery at Nalanda in India, near Buddha-Gaya, which soon became a great Buddhist university.

The explanation of this remarkable intellectual awakening is that during the Gupta period peace and order prevailed so largely that the people had leisure to cultivate the arts and literature. What they thus knew was added to by the frequent communication which took place with foreign nations such as China on the east, and Rome on the west. The influence of both these countries is noticeable in the coins, sculpture, painting, architecture, and scientific writings of the time. As Ceylon was closely in touch with India, Ceylon could not fail to be influenced also in a considerable measure.

CHAPTER XIV

## Progress in Arts and Literature

THE reign of **Siri Meghavanna** or **Kit Siri Mevan,** son and successor of Maha Sena, is notable in the history of Buddhism. He profited by his father's mistakes, and took the part of the Maha Vihara priests. He completed the restoration of the Brazen Palace and the Jetavanarama dagaba, and built numerous viharas and tanks.

That there was communication all this time between India and Ceylon is shewn by the fact that Siri Meghavanna sent two priests to India to visit a monastery which Asoka had built near the sacred bo-tree at Buddha-Gaya. On their return to Ceylon the priests complained that there was no place in India where they could stay with comfort, for they had been coldly received in that country. The reason for this is that Buddhism was losing its hold in North India. The Gupta kings, of whom we have read in the previous chapter of this book were strict Hindus. Siri Meghavanna sought and obtained from the Indian king (Samudragupta) permission to build in India a monastery for pilgrims from Ceylon, and shortly afterwards a splendid vihara accommodating a thousand priests, was built at Budha-Gaya.

The story of Mahinda who brought Buddhism into Ceylon interested the king greatly, and when he had informed himself of all that there was to be known of the Buddhist missionary's life he caused a golden statue of Mahinda to be made, and then, conveying it in solemn procession through the city, he placed it with due honour in a building near the palace.

More important than this was the bringing to Ceylon of the famous relic known as the Buddha's tooth. This happened about A.D. 313 [A.D. 360], in the ninth year of Siri Meghavanna's reign.

After the Buddha's death this tooth had been kept safe in Kalinga* in India. It is believed that Kalinga was at that time a Buddhist country. A neighbouring king made war against Kalinga to get possession of the relic and, fearing defeat, the king of Kalinga gave it to his daughter to be brought to Ceylon. She and her husband disguised themselves as religious ascetics and came to Ceylon with the relic safely hidden in the folds of the princess's hair. Siri Meghavanna received it with reverence, and placing it in a valuable casket, kept it in the royal park in a house thenceforward known as the House of the Tooth.

**Jettha Tissa II,** the younger brother of the king, succeeded Siri Meghavanna and reigned nine years. He was skilled in sculpture and carving and painting, and established schools where these arts were taught. There was about this time a beginning, or it may be a revival, of interest in the fine arts, and in

---

* Kalinga is the district in the middle east of India between the Mahanadi and Godavari rivers. It is now known as Orissa. See Map, page 8.

Sinhalese as well as Pali literature, due to the spread of the Gupta culture in India.

His son, **Buddha-dasa** (the "Slave of the Buddha," was exceedingly devout and benevolent. The priests spoke of him "as a mine of virtue and an ocean of riches." He was famous also as a physician and surgeon. It was his practice to carry a case of surgical instruments in his waist cloth, and he was thus able to give prompt relief to many sufferers who came under his notice.

From the anecdotes mentioned in the Sinhalese records one may be selected to show that the king could cure diseases of the mind as well as diseases of the body. There seems to be no reason why we should doubt the general truth of this incident. One day, while going in procession through the city, he noticed a leper who behaved in a very unseemly fashion when the king passed in his place in the procession. He struck the earth with his hand and with a stick which he carried; and he loudly abused the king in insulting language. Observing this, the king sent a messenger to find out the reason for this extraordinary behaviour, and learnt that the leper had conceived a strange hatred against the king, and was even determined to kill him. Here was evidently a case of insanity, and the royal physician took the case in hand. He gave full instructions to one of his attendants how the disease was to be treated. Following out these instructions, the king's messenger went to the leper, pretended that he himself had long wished to put the king to death, but could find no one to help him; and he succeeded at last in persuading the madman that they could work out their plans more easily by living together in the messenger's house. There the madman was lodged very comfortably, and treated with the utmost care and attention, till his health improved and he became more manageable. After some time, when food and dainties were, as usual, placed before him, the messenger let him know that these gifts had come from no less a benefactor than the king. The leper was at first very angry to learn that he had been dependent on the kindness of one whom he hated; but he gradually yielded to his friend's arguments, and in time became an attached subject of the king; so attached, indeed, was he, that when he heard a false rumour of the king's death, he was so saddened that he actually died of grief.

The king's skill in medicine was applied to the benefit of the lower animals as well as of mankind, and his efforts to provide medical relief for all classes of his subjects demand from us the highest praise. He established hospitals in the villages (one hospital to every ten villages), and appointed to them medical men who were paid from a grain tax of one twentieth part of the produce of cultivated fields. Hostels, furnished with all necessaries, were built along the main roads for the comfort of the lame and the blind.

To other matters of religion and government the king was not indifferent. His reign was one of peace and general prosperity. He gave much encouragement to educated priests by listening to their discourses and providing for their maintenance. For them he extended the Maha Vihara by building the "Peacock" monastery, so called from the bright colours with which it was adorned, and he set apart the revenues of two villages to supply their wants.

In his reign we notice the progress of that intellectual awakening which began in the reign of Jetha Tissa II. Then art schools chiefly were founded; now literature began to be thought of. The "*Suttas*," or Sermons of the Buddha, were in Buddha-dasa's reign translated from Pali into Sinhalese, and the king himself is said to have written a book—the *Sarartha Sangraha*—in which he gave a summary of all that was known at the time about medical matters. A book in Sanskrit, with this name, has survived to this day.

## CHAPTER XV

# Two Famous Visitors

BUDDHA-DASA died A.D. 370 [A.D. 416] after a reign of twenty-nine years, leaving behind him, it is said, no fewer than eighty sons. The eldest of these, **Upatissa I**, succeeded him. This king appears to have been a superstitious monarch, but he built several tanks (one of which was probably the *Topeveva*, near which the city of Polonnaruwa was afterwards built), and both improved and added to the Buddhist buildings which then existed. Images of the Buddha continued to multiply in this reign. A fine palace was erected at Attanagalla, and the roof was covered with copper. The king's wicked queen, however, caused Upatissa to be secretly stabbed to death, and he was succeeded by his younger brother **Mahanama,** who ruled during the years 412 to 434 [458 to 480].

About the year 412 or 413, in the reign of Buddha-dasa, a famous Chinese traveller, named Fa-Hien, visited Ceylon, after he had gone round the principal cities of India searching for Buddhist books. From his writings we obtain ample proof of the greatness to which by this time the city of Anuradhapura had grown. He writes of its temples, monasteries, and statues; of the Bo-tree; of the Tooth which had been recently brought from India, and of the processions held regularly in its honour. There were 5,000 Buddhist priests, he says, in the capital alone, and more than ten times that number dispersed throughout the island. The capital is thus described: "The city is the residence of many magistrates, grandees, and foreign merchants; the mansions beautiful, the public buildings richly adorned, the streets and highways straight and level, and houses for preaching built at every thoroughfare." Fa-Hien lived two years at Anuradhapura, where he employed his time in making copies of the sacred books of Buddhism. His account of Ceylon is important, because it confirms many statements made by the Sinhalese historians.

A more important visitor, however, came from India about seventy years later in the reign of Mahanama. This was Buddhaghosa, an Indian Buddhist priest, who may well be called the second founder of Buddhism in Ceylon; for, besides translating the sacred books he wrote other books in explanation of them, and so gave a fixed and settled meaning to the Buddhist doctrines. Even before he left his native country, Magadha (he was born near the Bo tree at Buddha Gaya), he had composed a work on Buddhism, and coming to Ceylon he re-wrote the *Commentaries* in Pali. In India the Pali version was not to be found at this time. In Ceylon there was only the Sinhalese version which, as we have seen, was first put into writing at Aluvihara, and this Sinhalese version he re-translated into Pali, or it may be even re-wrote in Pali, according to his own judgment. This was done at Aluvihara most probably. He also compiled, at Anuradhapura, the *Visuddhi-Magga*, or the Path to Purity in which the teachings of the *Tripitaka* were briefly summarized. Buddhaghosa, the "Voice of Buddha"—for so he was called on account of his eloquence and learning—stayed in Ceylon three years, and then returned to India.

The kings of Ceylon used frequently to send embassies to foreign countries. In the first century after Christ an embassy was despatched to Rome, in Europe, and another was sent to the same city about the middle of the fourth century. About the same time an embassy was also sent to China. Travelling overland by India it took ten years to reach the capital of China. The next recorded embassy to China was sent in Mahanama's reign. It carried an address to the emperor from the king of Ceylon, together with a model of the shrine in which the Tooth-relic was placed. These facts are worth noticing, if only to shew that Ceylon was in communication with other countries, far distant from it.

## CHAPTER XVI

## Sigiriya

On the death of Mahanama there followed a time of confusion of which the Tamils, as we shall see, did not fail to take advantage. Mahanama's son **Sotthi-Sena,** whose mother was a Tamil, was put to death on the very day of his accession, by his step-sister Sangha. Sangha's husband then became king, but he died within the year. The next king was **Mitta-Sena,** a notorious "plunderer of crops," whom the previous king's confidential minister cunningly placed on the throne to serve his own purposes. After reigning one year, he was put to death by the Tamils, a band of whom invaded the island and held the country for about twenty-five years (436—461). As usual, the Sinhalese chiefs fled to Ruhuna, where several princes of the royal line had settled at the time of Subha's usurpation. During the rule of the Tamil invaders, whose chiefs were six in number, the dagabas and viharas of the Buddhists suffered considerably. But the last three kings were killed one after the other by **Dhatu-sena,** a descendant of one of the old settlers in Ruhuna. Dhatu-sena had for many years carried on an intermittent warfare from Ruhuna against the Tamils. He became king in 461, [516] and the Sinhalese supremacy was thus restored. The Buddhist buildings were rebuilt, improved agriculture was revived, and new tanks were made, of which the *Kala-veva* was the largest. The statues of the Buddha, which the Tamils had damaged and robbed of their ornaments, were restored and again adorned. The king set up a statue also of the *Maitri Buddha*, that is, of a Buddha who was yet to come into the world. Great honour was paid to the memory of Mahinda. A festival was celebrated at the place where the great preacher was cremated. An image of him was carried in procession, and the *Dipavansa* (the oldest history of the island) or, it may be, the new *Mahavansa,* which was then being compiled, was read aloud to the assembled multitudes.

Dhatu-sena's tutor and adviser in most matters was his uncle, a priest named Mahanama whom we must not confuse with the king of that name. During Dathu-sena's reign, this priest Mahanama compiled a history of Ceylon for the period between the arrival of Vijaya and the reign of Maha Sena. It was called the *Mahavansa*, because it referred to the kings of the Great Dynasty. Written

A. D. 449. English kingdoms begun in Britain.

in Pali verse, its very existence was in recent years known to the priests only, and of these but a few were able to understand the Pali language. Further additions, bringing down the history to 1758, were made in later times.* It is from the *Mahavansa* that most of our information regarding the early history of Ceylon is derived. It tells us much about the progress of Buddhism, and very little about the social condition of the Sinhalese. The piety and superstitions of the Buddhist kings, and the successes and misfortunes of the Maha Vihara priests, appear to be the main concern of the writer. But the book is a remarkable one, and of great value in explaining the history of India and Eastern Asia.

Dhatu-sena had two sons, Kasyapa and Mugalan, but by different mothers. The elder son, **Kasyapa**, formed a conspiracy against his father and seized the kingdom. Dhatu-sena was dethroned and imprisoned in a dungeon, where he was afterwards walled up alive, and so came to a terrible end.

Mugalan fled to India where he tried to raise an army to fight against his usurping brother. Meanwhile Kasyapa, feeling that he could not wholly rely upon the support of the people, established his capital at Sigiriya (*the Lion Rock*), a steep and solitary hill some four

* The first part of the *Mahavansa* (that written by Mahanama) was translated into English by Mr. George Turnour, a member of the Ceylon Civil Service, and published in Colombo in 1837. The remaining parts were translated and published, with a revision of Mr. Turnour's work, by Mudaliyar L. C. Wijesingha in 1889.

hundred feet high, at the extreme north of the present Central Province—about forty miles south-east of Anuradhapura. Situated in the midst of the great central forest, this natural fortress was safe from enemies. Water, with all else that was necessary, was provided, and the rooms, stair-cases, and galleries were adorned with carvings and sculptures. The paintings (called *frescoes)* still to be seen in their first bright colours, represent Gupta models. Figures of lions were prominent, and there may still be seen, on the lowest platform, "the claws of the once colossal brick and stucco lion, through whose jaws and body the covered staircase was carried upwards to the summit."*

To this stronghold he removed his treasures, and round it he erected strong fortifications. Within, he built a splendid palace, and lived in great comfort. Remorse for his crime, however, began to creep upon him, and he tried by building viharas and performing acts of charity and piety to quiet the reproaches of his conscience. It was in vain. In the expressive words of the *Mahavansa*, the parricide "made many images, alms-houses, and the like; but he lived on in fear of the world to come—and of Mugalan."

In the eighteenth year of Kasyapa's reign the dreaded Mugalan arrived with a large army from India. Twelve friends of noble birth accompanied him to support his claims to the throne, and confident of success, he

---

*Ceylon *R. A. S. Journal* No. 50. p. 10.

marched towards Sigiriya. About half way, near Kurunegala, "in the country of Ambatthakola," he was met by Kasyapa, and a great battle followed which ended in the defeat and suicide of the usurper. [A.D. 552.]

Anuradhapura again became the capital, and **Mugalan**, (497-515) busied himself in restoring order. He converted the fortress at Sigiriya into a vihara, and bestowed it upon Mahanama, the priest who wrote the first part of the *Mahavansa*. To protect the island from sudden invasion guards were stationed along the sea coast. The king's brother-in-law *Silakala*, who had fled with him to India, is said to have brought over from India a lock of the Buddha's hair, which was treasured as a relic. Silakala ought to be remembered, for he afterwards became king.

Of **Kumara-Dasa** (515-524), [570-579], Mugalan's son, too little is known, for besides being a good ruler, he was distinguished as a poet. One of his poems, the *Jānakiharana*,* relates the story of Rama and of Sita, who was the daughter of king Janaka. The king reigned nine years and then came to an untimely end. On the wall of a house which he used to visit, the king wrote two lines of an unfinished verse, adding underneath them a promise to reward any one who should complete the verse. At this time there lived in Ceylon a poet named Kalidasa. Some believe that he was the

*It is fair to state that this poem is now believed to be the work of a Sinhalese poet of royal blood named Kumaradasa, and not the work of the King.

famous Indian poet of that name, others that he was a native Sinhalese. The latter is more probable; but, whoever he was, he was one of the king's most intimate friends. Kalidasa, happened to pass that way, saw the inscription, and at once wrote the two lines required. A woman of the house who had observed these things, secretly murdered the poet, hid his body, and claimed the promised reward from the king. But Kumāra-Dāsa easily saw through the fraud, for the woman was certainly not able to write poetry; and when enquiries were made it was clearly proved that Kalidasa was murdered. The king's grief was overwhelming; and when the body of his friend was being consumed on the funeral pile, Kumara-Dasa threw himself on it and so ended his own life.

These events are said to have occurred at Matara, where Kumara-Dasa was then residing; but it is more likely that they happened near Anuradhapura.

## CHAPTER XVII

## Growth of Tamil Influence

KUMARA-DASA was succeeded by his son **Kirti Sena,** who reigned nine months only, for then his uncle **Siva** killed him and became king. But Siva reigned twenty-five days only, when his brother-in-law, Upatissa, put him to death and reigned. **Upatissa II** took a great interest in Silakala, of whom we heard before in the reign of Mugalan. He made this man his general, and gave him his daughter in marriage. But Silakala coveted the supreme power for himself and rebelled against his master. Kasyapa, the son of Upatissa, tried bravely to put down the rebellion, but being defeated in battle he killed himself. When Upatissa heard of his son's defeat and death, "he was struck down with grief as if shot by an arrow, and he died."

**Silakala** now gained his object and became king, ruling the country for thirteen years. Toward the close of his reign, however, he became a convert to the Vaitulyan heresy, which was greatly revived through his encouragement of it. On his death, his second son, **Dapulu I** seized the kingdom but was soon defeated by his elder brother, **Mugalan II**, who was very popular with his subjects, both because of his fame as a poet, and because of the liberality and piety he displayed during his reign of twenty years. His son **Kitsirime,** was a weak and indulgent ruler. Bribery prevailed everywhere, and the rich and powerful committed many acts of oppression on the helpless poor. Order was restored by **Mahanaga,** whose gifts to the priesthood were liberal, and who did much to restore the damaged viharas and dagabas. His nephew, **Agbo**, or **Agrabhodi I,** enjoyed a long reign of thirty-four years, (564-598.) He is very highly praised by the historian as "surpassing the sun in glory, the full-orbed moon in gentleness,

---

A.D. 570 Birth of Muhammad.

A.D. 597 The King of Kent converted to Christianity by Augustine.

Mount Meru in firmness, the great ocean in depth, the earth in stability, the breeze in serenity"—with much more of the same extravagant praise. But we shall not be surprised at this language if we consider what a relief it must have been to the people, after all the troubles of the last hundred years, to be ruled again by a king who, besides being devoted to his religion could maintain order, and "free the island from all the thorns of strife." The Mihintale tank was his work, as also the Kurundu Vihara and tank. Poets flourished in his reign, twelve of whom are named in the histories; and the Vaitulyans suffered defeat in a great controversy, when an elder named *Jotipāla* championed the doctrines of the Maha Vihara priests. **Agbo II,** the nephew and son-in-law of the first **Agbo,** built several tanks. The King of Kalinga, "moved with horror at the destruction of the lives of men in warfare, and resolving to lead the life of a recluse," came to Ceylon during this reign, and became a Buddhist priest in Jotipāla's monastery Agrabhodi II. was succeeded by **Sangha Tissa II.** After two months the latter was defeated and slain by **Dala Mugalan,** who, in the sixth year of his reign was killed by Asiggrahaka, who took the name of **Sila Megha. vanna** on his accession to the throne.

And now we begin to find frequent mention made again of the Tamils, who at first assisted various claimants to the throne, and in the end founded a settlement of their own in the north of Ceylon. In Silā Meghavanna's reign a Tamil army landed in the north of Ceylon, to help Sirinaga, a brother of Sangha Tissa II. to obtain the throne. In the fight that followed Sirinaga was killed, the Tamils were defeated, and a number of them were made prisoners and given over as slaves to different viharas. **Agbo III**, also known as **Siri Sangabo II.**, reigned six months and was then defeated in battle by Jettha Tissa son of Sangha Tissa II. **Jettha Tissa III.** reigned six months only: for Agbo fled to India, came back with a large army of Tamils, and fought a great battle near the Kala-veva tank in 624. Here Jettha Tissa, being defeated, killed himself. Agbo then reigned again for sixteen years, but he was constantly disturbed by the rebellion of Dathasiva, the former king's general, who at length ascended the throne as **Dathopa Tissa** I, and, with the assistance of the Tamils, succeeded in dethroning the king. Agbo fled to Ruhuna, where he died while trying to raise an army to recover the throne. During these years of war and confusion the Buddhist viharas and dagabas were shamefully plundered by the Tamils, and even by some of the Sinhalese kings. The images and ornaments of gold were melted down, the jewels carried away, the offerings plundered, and the sacred buildings pulled down. Meanwhile numbers of Sinhalese fled to India to escape from the utter confusion

---

**A.D. 622 Muhammad's flight to Medina (*Hejira*)**

**A.D. 632 Death of Muhammad.**

**A.D. 640 Hiuen Tsang (Chinese traveller) in India**

prevailing to Ceylon. The cities held a large population, but there was no safety for life or property. The land produced rice and fruits in abundance, but the soil could not be cultivated on account of the great disorder everywhere; and famine drove men to rebellion and crime.

Dathopa Tissa I was defeated by **Kasyapa II,** the younger brother of Agbo, and in the latter's reign of nine years there was some attempt made to maintain order. The Tamils were expelled from the offices they held, and **Dapulu I,** who ruled over Ruhuna, was appointed by Kasyapa as his heir. But the Tamils plotted in favour of *Hattha-Datha*, a nephew of Dathopa Tissa I, who without difficulty became king, and reigned nine years under the title of **Dathopa Tissa II,** Dapulu returning to Ruhuna where he died. For one week alone had he reigned at Anuradhapura, though at Ruhuna his reign lasted three years. Hattha Datha was succeeded by his brother **Agbo IV**, who, during his reign of sixteen years "took a right view of things;" that is, he was pious and liberal in his gifts to the Maha Vihara. Several wealthy Tamils are said to have built houses of devotion for the Buddhists, and the Sinhalese chiefs throughout the island built viharas according to their means. Yet the last years of the king's life were spent at Polonnaruva, and we cannot doubt that this was owing to his distrust and fear of the Tamils who were making their power

---

**A.D. 713—710 Muhammadan conquest of Spain.**

**A.D. 731 Bede's Ecclesiastical History finished.**

felt more widely. Indeed, when **Agbo IV** died, it was a Tamil general who really governed the country. This man, named *Potthakuttha*, set up two kings successively at Anuradhapura. These two rulers were called kings, but the real power was in the Tamil general's hands. The second of them was defeated and slain by **Manavamma** (son of Kasyapa II), who had gone over to India, where he first served, and afterwards secured assistance from, a South Indian king named Narasinham. Potthakuttha fled for protection to a friendly chief who, however, poisoned himself to escape from the difficult position in which he was placed; for he feared the king, and yet could not refuse protection to his friend. When the Tamil found this out, he likewise took poison and died. Manavamma reigned thirty-five years and then gave place to **Agbo V**, whose pious example influenced the whole nation, and brought about a more careful observance of Buddhist rules. For a time it seemed as if confidence in the government was restored, for **Kasyapa III**, the next ruler, is said to have compelled not only the priests of Buddhism, but even the Brahmans, to observe their respective religious customs. **Mahinda I**, his successor, was so distressed at the death of a dear friend that he refused to wear the crown, or to take the royal title, though he performed all the duties of a king. His nephew reigned after him and took the name of **Agbo VI** or **Akbo Salamevan.** He was also known as *Silamegha*. His reign of forty years was disturbed by two insurrections of his own subjects, both of which were quickly put down.

The next king was **Agbo VII** (781-787), the son of Mahinda I. He enforced discipline among the priests, and discouraged "false cases" by insisting that law-suits should be decided according to the law. He also was forced to remove his court from Anuradhapura to Polonnaruva, though this removal was only for a time.

We have seen in this chapter how the Tamils steadily increased in power. Their armies took part in the contests between rival claimants to the throne, and plundered the country. Numbers of Tamils settled in Ceylon and acquired wealth and influence. Some rose to high positions in the government, while one at least was in fact, though not in name, the ruler of the island.

CHAPTER XVIII.

## The Rise of Polonnaruva

ON the death of Agbo VII there was some danger of fresh disorder in the island, for the king's son had died before his father. But Agbo's nephew prevented this by hastening to Anuradhapura and taking possession of it. No one had a better claim to the throne than this prince, who now reigned as **Mahinda II**; but it needed all his care and effort to keep the government in his hands. First, the chiefs of the northern districts refused to pay the revenues which they collected; then Agbo's queen treacherously formed a plot to kill Mahinda. These difficulties were easily overcome, but there was much more trouble with *Prince Dapulu*, the governor of Ruhuna. This prince was rich and powerful, and made three separate attempts to wrest the government from Mahinda. On the first occasion Anuradhapura was besieged; but though Dapulu was defeated each time, yet at last, Mahinda found it advisable to come to terms with him. A treaty was made by which the Kalu Ganga was fixed as the boundary between the possessions of Mahinda and Dapulu,—king Mahinda holding all the country north of the river.

Though Anuradhapura was still considered the capital of the Sinhalese kings, the new city of Polonnaruva was by no means neglected. Viharas were erected there, and Mahinda built a splendid palace several storeys high. The sacred buildings were also repaired, and the Tamils had now become so necessary that the king even repaired their devalas, furnished them with images, and provided food for their priests.

**Dapulu II.*** the son of Mahinda, continued to keep order in the country, and to maintain the national religion. But he deserves special notice for the hospital he built at Polonnaruva, and for the code of laws which he directed to

---

* Geiger's Udaya I.

be made. The decisions which had been given in lawsuits were collected and recorded in books, which were carefully kept in the king's house. Disputes were in this way prevented, and there was less chance of injustice and oppression.

Passing over the reign of **Mahinda III,** whose piety caused him to be known as *Dharmika-Silamegha*—"Silamegha the Righteous," we come to **Agbo VIII** who deserves to live in history as a noble example of filial love and devotion. "He was," says the *Mahavansa*, "constant in his attendance on his mother, both by day and night; and he was wont daily to wait on her and anoint her head with oil. The garments also which she had cast off he washed with his own hands, and sprinkled on his crowned head the water in which they were dipped. He made offerings of flowers and perfumes to her as at a shrine, and then bowed himself before her three times, and walked around her with great reverence, and commanded that her servants should be provided with meat and raiment according to their desire. And afterwards he fed her from his own hands with dainty food, and himself ate of the remnants, whereof he scattered a portion on his own head. And after he had seen that her servants were fed with the best of the king's table, he perfumed and set in order her bed chamber, in which he had himself laid out her bed carefully with his own hands. And then he washed her feet and anointed them with soft and sweet-smelling oil, and set himself down by her side until sleep came over her. Then three times walked he round her bed with great reverence, and having made proper obeisance to her, he commanded her servants and slaves to keep watch over her. And when he departed from the bed-chamber he turned not his back upon her, but stepped backwards noiselessly until he could not be seen, and bowed again three times towards where she lay; and bringing to mind oft-times the service he had done unto his mother, he returned to his palace in great joy. In this self-same manner did he serve his mother all the days of his life."

**Dapula III** resided at a place called Beramiṅi-paya, and **Agrabhodi IX** at Anuradhapura again. The Tamils, we may well understand, were not idle during these times, and this becomes certain from the fact that **Sena I** (846-866), [887-907] was obliged to take shelter at Polonnaruva, and here, indeed, he died. In the reign of Sena I occurred another great Tamil invasion, when the king of Pandya came over with a large army, ravaged all the north, and fortified one of the villages. The Tamils in the island flocked to his standard, and the Sinhalese troops were defeated in a great battle. Sena in great terror collected all the treasure he could lay hands upon, and fled to the mountainous Malaya country. Two of the king's brothers, Mahinda and Kasyapa, attempted to keep back the invaders, but they were defeated and Mahinda was slain. The Tamils now ravaged the country. Anuradhapura, the beautiful city, was plundered and left desolate.

The jewels in the king's palace, the golden images which the piety of kings and princes had placed in Buddhist viharas, the golden statue of Buddha that Mahinda II. had made, the gilt covering of the Thuparama dagaba, everything, in short, that was of any value whatever, was carried away by the victorious Pandyans. When at last the city and its neighbourhood had been laid waste, the Tamil king made a treaty with Sena and returned to India, while Sena resumed the sovereignty of Ceylon. But he could not easily forget the ravages of the Tamils, and brooding over them he passed away in the twentieth year of his reign.

It was reserved for his nephew, **Sena II**, to win back the lost honour of the Sinhalese nation. Sena was the son of that Kasyapa who had escaped with his life when Mahinda was killed in battle, but who afterwards fell fighting against the invaders. He was determined on vengeance, and made ready an army to attack the Tamils. It happened at this time that a disappointed prince of the Pandyan dynasty came to Ceylon either for help against his rivals, or for protection from them. Sena seized the opportunity, and sent a large force under the command of his chief general, with instructions to invade Madura, the capital of the Pandya kingdom, and set the exiled prince on the throne. Madura was besieged

---

**A.D. 871—901. Reign of Alfred, king of England.**

and taken by storm; the reigning king of Pandya was killed, and the prince enthroned in his place; the city was sacked, and its inhabitants were put to the sword. The treasures taken from Ceylon were recovered, and immense plunder was brought to the island by Sena's general who had successfully carried out his orders. It is said that the army brought also a new heresy from India, according to which the priests of Buddhism had to wear blue robes instead of the traditional yellow; but this craze did not last long.

There was now rest for a short interval from fears of another Tamil attack, and Sena employed the time wisely in making the country safe against future invasion, in building tanks, and in encouraging agriculture. "He restored to its former condition everything of importance throughout the island . . . . . And the people who had been heavily oppressed under his predecessor, now rejoiced and were glad, as if from the fierce heat they had come to the shelter of a rain-cloud." Nor did he neglect the customary Buddhist festivals or liberal offerings to the viharas.

## CHAPTER XIX.

## Civil Strife among the Sinhalese

SENA II was succeeded by **Udaya I,** whose reign was disturbed by a serious rising under Kitu Akbo, the king's nephew, who tried to form an independent kingdom in Ruhuna. The rebellion was crushed without much difficulty by prince Mahinda, son of the sub-king, who from that time governed Ruhuna himself, and became a very popular ruler. When, however, a king named **Kasyapa IV** succeeded to the throne, Mahinda raised an army to support his own claim. He was defeated, but Kasyapa generously pardoned him and sent him back to Ruhuna as governor of that country.

The Tamils gave so little trouble in those days that the king, or which is more likely, prince Ilanga Sena "the chief captain of his army," was able to build hospitals both at Anuradhapura and at Polonnaruva, as well as dispensaries of medicine at various places. His successor **Kasyapa V** (929-939) is described as both a preacher and a doer of the Buddhist law. He compiled also a Vocabulary with explanatory notes for Buddhaghosa's Commentary on the *Dhammapada*, an old collection of the Buddha's sayings. He rebuilt and adorned the Mirisaveti vihara, originally set up by Dutu-Gemunu, and now falling to decay.

But though free for the time from the Tamils, there was little chance of any lasting improvement in the affairs of the country, for the Sinhalese chiefs were continually warring among themselves. Civil strife did them more harm, perhaps, than foreign invasion. Kasyapa V was evidently well able to keep order in his kingdom, for we read of no disturbances during his reign. He was even strong enough to send a great army to India to help the king of Pandya against his rival, the king of Chola, but the army was forced to return without accomplishing its object, in consequence of a contagious disease that prevailed in the Cholian country, and killed the Sinhalese general and large numbers of his men. Of the next king **Dapula IV**, we know little ; but in the reign of **Dapula V** the Pandyan king fled to Ceylon after a great battle with the king of Chola and was received in Ceylon with every mark of honour. Dapula prepared to give him assistance ; but the fierce dissensions among the Sinhalese chiefs made this impossible, and the Pandyan king returned to his country greatly disappointed. **Udaya II** irritated the chiefs by his cruel conduct, and was for a time a fugitive at Ruhuna. **Sena III** peacefully followed the old customs, restored viharas and tanks, celebrated the festivals, and was liberal in his charity. But **Udaya III** was an indolent man, and *Parantaka*, the king of Chola, took advantage of this to invade Ceylon on the pretence of getting back the crown and robes which the Pandyan king had left behind with Dapula V. The army which should have driven back the Tamils was at this time engaged in putting down a revolt in some of the provinces. When at last it met the Tamils, it was defeated, and the king fled as usual to Ruhuna, whither the Tamils were afraid to follow him. Another Sinhalese army was then raised, and the Tamils were driven back.

**Sena IV** was learned in the doctrines and duties of Buddhism, expounding them on one occasion to all the three viharas assembled together. **Mahinda IV** married a Kalinga princess, but this did not prevent another attack from India. Still, he did not fare badly ; for when the king of the Vallabhas (a South Indian tribe), sent an army to the north of Ceylon, Mahinda's general utterly defeated him, and so made the people of India respect the valour of the Sinhalese forces. Mahinda went a step further than previous kings in his piety ; he made a law that lands belonging to the viharas were henceforth not to be taxed.

But the districts on the borders of the middle country, Maya-rata, were continually in revolt. **Sena V**, only twelve years old when he became king, sent his prime minister (who was also the regent) against them, and when he was away, appointed another chief to be prime minister. This caused the regent to rebel. The king fled to Ruhuna, and the regent allowed the Tamils to plunder the country while he himself stayed at Polonnaruva. Shortly after, the regent and the king were reconciled, but the latter, led away by evil advisers, gave himself up to habits of intemperance, and died a drunkard in the tenth year of his reign.

**Mahinda V** was able to restore the capital to Anuradhapura, where for twelve years (1001-1013) he remained, though in great discomfort. He probably kept the Tamils in his pay ; but since the provinces as usual withheld the revenues which they ought to have paid the king, his treasury was exhausted, and the Tamils rose in arms to demand the wages due to them. On this the king fled secretly to Ruhuna, where he kept up some show of authority for twenty-four years, while the Tamils and others did as they pleased in the surrounding districts. News of this was taken to the king of Chola, who promptly sent a large army to Ceylon. Ruhuna was entered, king Mahinda and his queen were taken captive and were sent with all their treasures to Chola in 1037, where the king died twelve years after, that is, forty-eight years after his coronation ; while throughout the island the devastations of the Tamils went on unchecked. During these twelve years a viceroy of the king of Chola ruled at Polonnaruva, Ceylon thus becoming a part of the Cholian empire. From this time Polonnaruva became the capital of Ceylon.*

## CHAPTER XX

## Ancient Trade of Ceylon

WE may at this point turn aside from the depressing records of civil strife and foreign invasion to learn, from other sources than the Sinhalese books, about the happenings in Ceylon from the sixth century onwards; that is, from about the time of king Kumara-Dasa. Much earlier than the beginning of the sixth century, Ceylon was, as might be expected from its position in the Eastern seas, the centre of a very large trade ; and this trade was carried on chiefly by the Arabs and

* Mr. S. Paranavitane, 1930.

Persians from the west, and by the Chinese from the east. The Arabs had so large a trade that they found it convenient to form settlements at various places on the west coast of India, in towns like the modern towns of Surat, Calicut, and Quilon. This made it easy for them to keep in close communication with the coast towns of Ceylon; and this communication has been kept up to the present day by the Moors, who are believed to be the descendants of these early Arab settlers in India, and who are said to have begun settling in Ceylon about the tenth century of the Christian era.

The Persians appear to have traded chiefly with the districts round Mannar and the pearl fishery; and they were strong enough once to send a fleet against the Sinhalese, who had done some wrong to the Persian settlers in Ceylon. The Chinese were Buddhists, like the Sinhalese, and communication with China was therefore not limited to trade. In the sixth and eighth centuries there were frequent embassies sent to China from Ceylon.

About the beginning of the sixth century, a Greek trader named *Sopater* came from Abyssinia to Ceylon, and a ship from Persia happened to come in at the same time. Sopater and the Persians, one of them an old man of venerable appearance, went ashore and had an interview with the king. During the conversation the king asked them a difficult question: Was the Persian king or the Roman emperor the more powerful? The old Persian at once exclaimed that his king was the king of kings, and so powerful that he could do what he pleased. But Sopater was silent, and the king asked him, "Have you nothing to say?" "What have I to say?" replied Sopater; "but if you wish to know the truth, you have both kings present. Examine them, and judge for yourself." The king did not understand this reply, and he asked in astonishment, "How say you that I have both the kings here?" "You have the money of both," replied Sopater. The king now saw what Sopater meant, and ordered a Roman and a Persian coin to be brought. The Roman coin was of gold—large, bright, and well turned out; the Persian coin was of silver,—small, and of rough workmanship. The king naturally decided in favour of the Roman emperor, and in honour of his victory Sopater was mounted on an elephant and taken in procession round the city.

It is a pretty tale, and the incident may well have happened; but it has been pointed out that a similar story is told about the Sinhalese ambassadors who went to Rome four and a half centuries before Sopater came to Ceylon.

Sopater's account of Ceylon is mixed up with that of Cosmas, a trader from Egypt, and perhaps a Greek by race, who afterwards became a Christian monk. He was surnamed *Inaicopleustes* (the *Indian Voyager*), because he had travelled so widely in India; that is, in Abyssinia and the western coasts of India and Ceylon. Cosmas, who wrote about his travels some thirty years after Sopater's visit, says that in those times there were two rival kings in Ceylon, one of whom possessed a famous gem, and the other governed the coast districts where trade was carried on with foreign nations. Neither of these kings was of the same race as the people of Ceylon. There was also a community of Persians in Ceylon who were Christians, and had a Christian church. The king of Ceylon used to buy horses from Persia, and for that reason the Persians paid no customs duties. The central position of the island between Africa and China, with India neighbouring it in the north, made it a busy seat of commerce.

About the middle of the ninth century a Muhammadan named *Soleyman (Sulaiman)* visited Ceylon and climbed Adam's Peak, round which mountain, he says, were mines of rubies and other gems. Soleyman repeats the statement that there were two kings in Ceylon, and we may gather that in these uncertain days the Tamil kingdom of Jaffna was being established in rivalry with that of the Sinhalese. Another Muhammadan, *Abu-Zeyd*, who wrote sixty years later, by which time Muhammadans had begun to make regular pilgrimages to Adam's Peak, says that the Sinhalese gave much attention to their religion and were particular to have copies made of the Buddhist writings; that the temples were richly furnished, and that some of the images in them were of very great height. The king allowed people of all religions to worship in the way each had been accustomed, and Jews and Muhammadans were among those who freely used this liberty. The Sinhalese are described as a pleasure-loving people, not without a knowledge of arrack flavoured with honey, but especially fond of cock-fighting and gambling. "They play at draughts, and their principal diversion is fighting of cocks, which are very large in this country, and better provided with spurs than cocks ordinarily are; and besides this they arm them with blades of iron like canjiars. Upon these combats they bet gold, silver, lands, and farms; and they venture also great sums on the game of draughts, which they play with such fury, that those who have not wherewithal often play away the ends of their fingers."

The story of Sindbad the Sailor in the *Arabian Nights* is said to be largely founded on Abu-Zeyd's book. In his seventh voyage of adventure Sindbad found himself in Ceylon; that is, on the western coast, for the interior of Ceylon is little referred to by the writers of these times. Some peasants who were at work on their fields took him to the king, who treated him well, and afterwards allowed him to return to Baghdad, his native city, in the company of merchants who were then fitting out a ship for that port. Sindbad's story mentions Adam's Peak, which "is conspicuous from a distance of three days, and it containeth many kinds of rubies and other minerals, and spice-trees of all sorts. The surface is covered with emery wherewith gems are cut and fashioned;

diamonds are in its rivers and pearls in its river-valleys." The king's elephant processions are also mentioned, and when the king rode out on his horse there was a large company of horsemen who attended him.

CHAPTER XXI

## Vijaya Bahu I

WHILE Mahinda V was a captive in India, the Sinhalese, anxious for the safety of the ancient royal line, took his infant son, **Kasyapa**, afterwards known as **Vikrama Bahu,** to Ruhuna, and there hid him from the Tamils. Frequent encounters took place between the Sinhalese and the Tamils in which the latter were sometimes defeated. They were, at all events, obliged to limit their authority to Polonnaruva and its neighbourhood. The Sinhalese had their strongholds in Ruhuna, but prince Vikrama Bahu refused to be anointed king until he had first driven out the Tamils. For twelve years he collected men and money, but just when he was ready for the war, he fell ill and died. The government of Ruhuna then fell into the hands of usurpers, six of whom reigned in succession. King **Kirti** reigned seven days only, and was then put to death by **Mahalana Kirti,** who in the third year of his reign killed himself on being defeated by the Cholians. **Vikrama Pandu** (a prince from Pandya) next ruled for one year, with Kalutara as his capital. He was killed by **Jagatipala,** a prince from Ayodhya (Oudh) in North India, who ruled four years in Ruhuna and was then slain by the Cholians.

After him **Parakrama Pandu** (another Pandyan prince) reigned two years and died in the same way, being succeeded by his general, or prime minister, **Lokesvara**, who reigned six years at Kataragama, and " subdued the pride of Cholians." It will be noticed that none of these usurpers ruled at Anuradhapura or Polonnaruva during the sixteen years 1049—1065.

A determined effort was now made to expel the Tamils and to restore the Sinhalese sovereignty. The movement was headed by *Kirti*, a proud and brave young prince, then only some fifteen years old, who was descended from Mahinda V. In vain did Lokesvara attempt to check the growing power of this new leader, who, at length, on Lokesvara's death after a reign of nearly six years, became king, taking the title of **Vijaya Bahu I.** He had first to defeat a chief named Kasyapa, who for six months had tried to establish himself as ruler of Ceylon.

Vijaya Bahu reigned for fifty-five years (1065-1120), but his reign was not altogether a peaceful one, and, as we shall see, it was followed by another period of disorder in the land.

The king himself was one of the greatest of Sinhalese rulers. He had two objects in view. One was the expulsion of the Tamils; the other, the restoration of Buddhism, which had suffered heavily during the time the Tamils were in power. The Tamils still held Raja-rata, north and west of the Mahaveli Ganga, but the Sinhalese began now to defy the Tamils, and even set out to take Polonnaruva; but on the way, near Anuradhapura, they were met by the Tamils and severely beaten. A large army of Cholians now advanced against Vijaya Bahu; but as he knew that he was yet not able to fight a decisive battle, he retired to Vatagiri, in the Kegalla District, one of his hill fortresses. For one thing, the king had not money enough for a long and difficult war. To supply this want, an embassy was sent to Ramanna (a province of Burma, between Arakan and Siam, now called Pegu) for assistance. As the Burmese also were Buddhists they sent valuable gifts to their brethren by religion in Ceylon. The king had money enough now, and by his example the Sinhalese people were encouraged to resist the Cholians. They began by refusing to pay the taxes demanded by the officers of the Cholian king, and a war followed in consequence. The Sinhalese in Raja-rata were subdued by the Tamils, but Ruhuna was still in Vijaya Bahu's hands, and there the Tamils were defeated. Then the king had to contend against a rebellion among some of his own people. This was put down, and soon after, large forces were raised to attempt once more the conquest of the Cholians. Fortress after fortress fell into Vijaya's hands, and the Cholians in despair

---

A.D. 1066. William the Conqueror invaded England.

collected at Polonnaruva, which, after a long and heavy siege, was at last taken. The king of Chola did not care to make any further attempt against Vijaya. "Now are the Sinhalese powerful," said he when he heard of the destruction of his hosts.

Vijaya Bahu entered Anuradhapura in the fifteenth year of his reign about 1080, but some years later, following the example of the Cholians he made Polonnaruva his capital. The princes of Ruhuna were not always obedient to their king, and Polonnaruva was a suitable "camp city" to repel any attacks from them, or to invade their country. He had great trouble in his efforts to restore order in his kingdom, for more than one serious revolt broke out in his reign. However, justice began to be better administered; taxes were more fairly charged on the people; the defences of the city were set in order; poor people, and even dumb animals, were provided with food. Poets flocked to Vijaya's court and were well rewarded, for the king himself was skilled in making songs.

The havoc made by the Tamils was so great that everywhere in Ceylon Buddhism was fast losing its hold on the people. Vijaya Bahu found that the number of priests in the country was exceedingly small—too small, indeed, for the plan he had in mind of restoring Buddhism. It is said that not ten good

---

* Mr. S. Paranavitana, 1930.

priests were at the time to be found in the island. Another embassy was therefore sent to Burma, not this time to ask for help against the Tamils, but to bring over Buddhist monks of known piety to re-establish Buddhism in Ceylon. These newcomers ordained large numbers of priests, and a great revival of Buddhism followed. Many new viharas were built and many old ones repaired. Offerings of food and land were liberally bestowed on the priests, and neglected festivals were again celebrated with something of the old splendour. The Buddhist doctrines were regularly preached, the *Tripitika*, or "Threefold Collection," and their commentaries being frequently read. We find also that the king granted a village abounding in rice-fields to provide food for those pilgrims who journeyed to Adam's Peak to worship the footprint there. With all this we have to notice that the Hindu *devalas* were maintained as before, and the accustomed offerings to them continued to be given; while Tamil soldiers were still retained in the king's service.

In the thirtieth year of the king's reign an army was prepared to be sent against the Cholians, because the king of Chola had in a fit of anger, ordered that the ears and noses of Vijaya's ambassadors should be cut off; but the Velakkaras, a band of hired Tamil soldiers, refused to fight against Chola, rebelled against the king, and even succeeded in taking Polonnaruva. For a time it seemed as if the king's crown was again in danger. But Vijaya, who was then at Anuradhapura, did not hesitate. Polonnaruva was soon retaken, and the rebel chiefs were seized and burnt alive. Fifteen years later, the king renewed the attempt to make war on the Cholian king, and marched with his army to the coast, waiting for the Cholians; but as the latter did not come to Ceylon, Vijaya returned to Polonnaruva.

The king was twice married—first to the princess Lilavati, a daughter of Jagatipala, the North Indian prince who once ruled Ruhuna. We shall presently meet one of the two grand-daughters (Lilavati and Sugala) of this princess. Vijaya Bahu's second queen was a Kalinga princess who bore the king five daughters and a son who afterwards reigned as Vikrama Bahu I.

## CHAPTER XXII

## A Time of Disorder

BUT when Vijaya Bahu I died, in 1120, his brother, **Jaya Bahu I**, seized the crown, with the assistance of the priests and a party of the nobles who were favourable to the Pandyans. Vikrama Bahu, who was then at Ruhuna, was not, however, to be easily kept out of his rights. He fought six battles against his uncle, whom he at length drove into Ruhuna, and then he himself reigned at Polonnaruva as **Vikrama Bahu I.** 1121-1142.

At this time Ruhuna was governed by the king's cousins, and about them it is necessary

---

A.D. 1096. The First Crusade against the Saracens

that we should know something more. Mitta, the sister of Vijaya Bahu I. and of Jaya Bahu I., was married to a prince of Pandya (thus forming a Pandyan party), and had three sons: (1) *Manabharana*, who married Ratnavali, daughter of Vijaya Bahu I., and was the father of a prince who afterwards reigned as Parakrama Bahu the Great; (2) *Kirti Sri Megha*, who married a sister of Ratnavali; and (3) *Sri Vallabha*, who married *Sugala*, a grand-daughter of Vijaya Bahu I. When Vikrama Bahu became king, Manabharana took over the government of Ruhuna*, with his brothers serving under him as sub-kings.

It must be remembered that Ruhuna was seldom under the actual control of the king of Lanka. There were really two, or rather four, kings in Ceylon in these times of confusion—Vikrama Bahu, and the three kings of Ruhuna—and none of these four kings cared to maintain order in any way in their kingdoms. They broke through all the well-established customs of the country. Vikrama Bahu not only oppressed his subjects with heavy and unjust taxes, but, probably remembering how the priests had tried to

* The *Mahavansa* says: "The sub-king Manabharana with the rest of his brothers brought the southern district and the Rohana country under their yoke." Mr. H. W. Codrington [*Journal of the R.A.S., C.B.* Vol. xxix) makes out an irresistible case for this "southern district" lying outside Ruhuna, and occupying a large portion of the western coast. This would place Parakrama the Great's birthplace and the scene of his early successes in the middle west of Ceylon rather than in the region round Badulla.

prevent his accession, even attempted to destroy Buddhism by plundering the treasures in the viharas and giving away to his favourites the lands which former kings had given over to the priests for religious purposes. The indignant priests took with them what sacred relics they could hurriedly collect, and wandered over the Ruhuna country, lodging wherever they could find shelter. Hired troops, probably Tamils, robbed and plundered whom they could in the villages and on the highways, while families of high rank were compelled to hide themselves to escape being put to death. Tanks were broken down, private quarrels were decided by the sword, and throughout the land of Lanka there was the cry of ruin and destruction. "Thus lived these lords of the land . . . They felt not the dignity of kings; and though placed in high offices of trust wherein they might seek their own good and the good of others, yet lacked they even noble ambition."

In the midst of this confusion Manabharana died, and Kirti Sri Megha became chief ruler of Ruhuna. After a reign of twenty-one years Vikrama Bahu died, and his son **Gaja Bahu II** reigned at Polonnaruva. His first task was to assert his authority by putting down an insurrection raised by the Ruhuna kings. The rest of his reign of twenty-two years (1142-1164) is really the story of Parakrama Bahu's doings, and may be related in connection with that prince.

## CHAPTER XXIII

# Parakrama's Early Life

PARAKRAMA BAHU, the king who became so famous in the history of Ceylon, was born at Sankhatthalai*, in the "southern country." He was the son of Manabharana, and on his mother's side the grandson of Vijaya Bahu I, and cousin to the reigning king Gaja Bahu. At his birth it was foretold, so the historians tell us, that he would be a great conqueror and prosperous in his undertakings, and the name **Parakrama Bahu** *(He whose arm defends others)* was given to him. The prince was ambitious from his very youth. He was vexed at the narrow limits of the kingdom in which he was born, and eagerly desired to be sole ruler, in due time, of the whole island. With all his ambition he was remarkably prudent and cautious. Brave and strong by nature, he practised himself in all the studies and accomplishments of a royal prince—in dancing, music, riding and hunting, in the use of the sword and the bow, and in the science and art of war. He was fond of sport, and dearly loved a jest. He studied grammar and delighted in poetry; he also made himself well acquainted with the doctrines and customs of his religion. These acquirements were very necessary to him, for

---

* See note p. 91.

---

A.D. 1154. Henry II became King of England.
A.D. 1164. The Constitutions of Clarendon.

he had planned a vast design which he was determined to carry out in spite of all difficulties.

The land needed a firm and wise ruler after the troublous times that had passed, and here, if anywhere, the man required was found: a prince whose mind was stirred by the recollection of ancient deeds of chivalry and daring,—of the courage of the Buddha, the valour of Rama, the strength in battle of the five Pandava princes, the wisdom of Canakka the Brahman* ; a prince who knew the weakness of his country and the causes of its decay ; who to the dignity of royal birth added the grace of literary culture ; and in whom was united great personal courage and conspicuous skill in the conduct of war.

But with all his ability, the grandeur of his aims, and the brilliant success of his efforts to improve his native country, it must be confessed that the methods employed by Parakrama were not always worthy of praise. He could be generous and forgiving when it suited him, but he was also unscrupulous and ungrateful when his schemes were interfered with. This will appear as we follow out his history.

On the other hand, Gaja Bahu was too weak a ruler for these troublous times, and he did not inspire confidence in those who knew

* Canakka, or Chanakya, was the adviser of Chandragupta Maurya, a famous king of India, who overthrew the Nanda dynasty in order to establish his own rule (c 316-292 B.C.). This Chandragupta does not belong to the Gupta dynasty referred to in Chapter XIII.

him. His father, Vikrama Bahu, was apparently right in describing him as " nowise able to acquire that which he has not gotten, or to retain that which he has got."

Parakrama's first expedition was against the village of Badalatthalai (said to be Batalagoda, near Kurunegala), which was held by a general named Sangha for Kirti Sri Megha, the uncle of Parakrama, and the chief ruler of Ruhuna. The prince was kindly welcomed, but the general suspected that he had come without Kirti Sri Megha's knowledge, and secretly sent messengers to Kirti Sri Megha to inform him of the fact. Parakrama discovered this and caused Sangha to be slain. The tumult that naturally arose among the general's men was immediately quelled by the prince's troops, and the village was given up to plunder. Large numbers of people now supported Parakrama, whose daring excited their admiration, and the forces sent by Kirti Sri Megha to seize his rebellious nephew were easily defeated. The prince then came to the country which was governed by king Gaja Bahu, and was received by the king at Polonnaruva with affection and honour. But the consideration shewn to him was ill repaid. While enjoying Gaja Bahu's hospitality Parakrama sent his spies into every village to find out the feelings of the people and the condition of the country. Some of his spies went disguised as snake-charmers, others as musicians, as fortune-tellers, as pedlars, as merchants, as physicians, as monks and pilgrims. He himself pretended to be stupid and childish, and he moved freely among the people, gaining their goodwill by lavish gifts and pleasing words. In this way he learnt all that he wished to know.

This went on till Gaja Bahu grew jealous of the praises bestowed by his subjects on the prince. The latter was wise enough to see that nothing could be gained by an immediate conflict, and returned to his uncle, who was readily reconciled to him. Kirti Sri Megha died soon after, and Parakrama succeeded him as ruler of Ruhuna.

## CHAPTER XXIV.

# How Parakrama became King of Lanka

KING Gaja Bahu and Sri Vallabha's son and successor, Manabharana, who ruled a portion of Ruhuna, were duly informed by Parakrama of his own accession to the throne of his father. Parakrama saw that the time had now come for him to attempt the cherished object of his life, and he immediately began to make preparation for war. He first collected a large amount of grain, which he heaped in numerous granaries within his dominions. Extensive tracts of land were brought under irrigation and turned into rice-fields. Old and ruined tanks were cleared and new tanks built. Canals were also cut to keep the tanks supplied with water. Then the army was reorganised. There were regiments of Tamils, and of Veddas, besides the Sinhalese who formed the great body of the army. To train them for the war, Parakrama used to practise the soldiers in mock battles fought in the streets. The treasury required attention, for without money nothing could be done, and the total sum collected in Ruhuna was insufficient for Parakrama's object. By careful supervision of the revenue, and by the export of gems, his ministers were able to amass large sums of money without inflicting oppressive taxes on the people. Lastly, the Malaya district (now known as the Kandyan country) was brought under subjection, and its army and revenue placed under oversight.* The general in charge of that district held his office from Gaja Bahu; but Parakrama persuaded him to be unfaithful to his master.

The war against Gaja Bahu was now openly begun and fiercely carried on. City after city, fort after fort, fell into the hands of Parakrama's captains. Anuradhapura was taken, and so was Polonnaruva, the capital. Gaja Bahu was made prisoner and confined in his palace, but treated with all respect and consideration till a meeting could be arranged between him and Parakrama. However, before the latter could arrive at Polonnaruva, a great riot took place there, caused by the mis-

* "From this period, therefore, probably dates that constitution upon a settled basis of the Kandyan kingdom, with its laws, military and civil organizations." Bell, *Report on the Kegalla District.*)

conduct of the victorious army. Gaja Bahu's ministers were enraged, and invited Manabharana, Parakrama's cousin, to come over from Ruhuna to fight on the king's behalf. He accepted the invitation, and so intense was the anger felt against Parakrama's army that the people rose on all sides and defeated it. Manabharana waited a few days after his victory, and then his real design became plain to everybody. He put to death Gaja Bahu's officers, seized all his treasures, and attempted to kill the king secretly by starvation or by poison. Gaja Bahu himself now implored Parakrama to deliver him. Parakrama sent him assistance and set him at liberty. Then another attempt was made by Gaja Bahu's party to deprive Parakrama of the power he had won with so much difficulty. This new rising was also put down after severe fighting. Lastly, king Gaja Bahu begged the priests to intercede on his behalf. They went to Parakrama and pointed out that the king was old and had no son or brother to succeed him; and they suggested that his life should be spared and that he should even be allowed to continue to reign. Parakrama consented, and Gaja Bahu kept to the agreement that was made. He refused to fight again against Parakrama when Manabharana and others tempted him to do so, offering him their assistance. Indeed, he went to a neighbouring vihara and publicly declared that he had given Rajā-rata to Parakrama; and this declaration he caused to be inscribed on a stone tablet.

When Gaja Bahu died, Manabharana, who had fled to Ruhuna was invited back to the capital by Gaja Bahu's faction. He made one more attempt to seize the throne. The attempt did not succeed, though there was much fierce fighting. Polonnaruva was retaken after a seven days' battle, and Parakrama became king of Lanka, his people "filling the whole heaven with shouts of victory."

CHAPTER XXV

## The Reign of Parakrama

PARAKRAMA was now (1153) the most powerful ruler in Ceylon. He had gained one of the great ends for which he had striven. He was no longer a petty chief in Ruhuna, but, in name at least, the supreme lord of Lanka, fearing no rival or enemy. But he had still other work to do before he could bring the whole Sinhalese country under his sole rule, or as the historian expresses it, "under one canopy of dominion." While he was engaged in restoring the cities of Polonnaruva and Anuradhapura to their former grandeur, the chiefs of Ruhuna were busy stirring up a rebellion in the district. Manabharana was dead, but they found a suitable leader in his mother, the princess Sugalā,* who took a very active part against Parakrama, and stubbornly held out against

---

* See pp 90f.

the royal forces which were sent to put down the rebellion. When this warfare was ended, it became necessary that he should attend to a war of greater consequence.

We have seen that Buddhist priests were invited to Ceylon in the reign of Vijaya Bahu I., when there were very few priests in the island. The foreign priests were from Ramanna, a province of Burma. An ancient friendship existed between that country and Ceylon (both being Buddhist in religion), but in Parakrama's reign this friendship was disturbed by the actions of the king of Ramanna. For some reason or other he began to annoy and ill-treat the Sinhalese people who lived in his country. He forbade the export of elephants from his kingdom and all trade with Ceylon. He plundered the Sinhalese merchants who visited his dominions, and shamefully insulted Parakrama's ambassadors. Besides these hostile acts, he violently seized a princess who was travelling from Ceylon to Cambodia under Parakrama's protection.

Parakrama was not a king who could lightly endure these insults, and he quickly fitted out an expedition to punish his enemy. Kirti Nagaragiri and a Tamil named Adhikaram were placed in command of the forces. They sailed to Ramanna, slew the king (or, it may be, his viceroy), entered the capital in triumph, and proclaimed the supreme authority of

---

A.D. 1189: The Third Crusade.

Parakrama over that country. This happened in the twelfth year of Parakrama's reign about 1165.

Then took place a war with South India. The kingdom of Pandya appears to have been at this time tributary to the Chola king, Kulasekara, who besieged it. According to the Sinhalese records, the king of Pandya could turn to none for help except to the king of Lanka, and Parakrama Bahu, true to the meaning of his name, resolved to help him. "Behold," he exclaimed, "the hare has taken refuge in the moon; what beast of prey can crush her?" He sent his general, Lankapura to India with a large army, but it arrived too late to save the king of Pandya from death, and Madura from being seized by the Cholians. But Lankapura set to work diligently against the enemy. The island of Ramesvaram was captured and made a province of Ceylon. Battle after battle was fought and won in the Pandyan kingdom by Parakrama's general, and city after city fell into his hands. Madura the capital was entered, its king expelled, and another king appointed who was to reign (like the king of Ramanna) as a vassal of the king of Ceylon. The Chola country also was laid waste, a city was founded within its borders in honour of Parakrama, and money was coined bearing the name of the Sinhalese king. Besides, a number of Tamils were brought captive to Ceylon, and made to repair the Ruanveli dagaba which the Cholians had greatly damaged when they were in power.

We must now turn to Parakrama's doings in his own kingdom of Lanka. We have seen in what ways he improved his portion, Ruhuna, when he became its governor on the death of Kirti Sri Megha ; how he drained marshes, cut canals, and changed large tracts of neglected land into valuable rice fields ; and how he built granaries in which rice was stored in immense quantities. Now that Parakrama had succeeded to a much larger government, his improvements were on a larger scale, and they were certainly what we might have expected of so great a king. He made his name famous in foreign countries, but he did not omit to improve and adorn his own kingdom.

The Sinhalese had long been burdened with heavy and unjust taxes that had been imposed on them by former kings. Parakrama gave orders that taxes should in future be collected without loss to the State or oppression to the people. The laws were impartially administered. The poor were liberally fed. Hospitals were built and physicians maintained. The great families, that had been ruined and driven into concealment through the frequent disturbances in the country, were now restored to their former positions. Much was done for the Buddhist religion, and much indeed needed to be done. Heresies had multiplied, the monks had grown selfish and worldly, and the three great brotherhoods—the Maha Vihara, the Abhayagiri Vihara, and the Jetavana Vihara—were divided by bitter differences of custom and doctrine. In 1165

Parakrama called together a council in which a great discussion arose and steps were at once taken to purify Buddhism. The monks who lived evil lives were expelled; and though the brotherhoods could not be fully reconciled to one another, we cannot doubt that a more friendly spirit was established among them.

When we turn to the public buildings by which Parakrama sought to beautify his kingdom we are astonished at the record of their number and greatness. His parks and gardens were royally laid out and supplied with ponds and bathing-halls, with ornamental mansions, and with everything, in short, that was beautiful and pleasant. Images of the Buddha were set up, and viharas were built or repaired in many districts. More than a thousand tanks are said to have been built by his orders, and numerous canals were dug to convey water to them. The "Sea of Parakrama" was a remarkable example of the king's daring and wisdom. A canal starting from the Amba Ganga at Ellahara, near Matale, connected Minneriya, Kantalai, and several other large tanks. This canal was a hundred miles long, and was not only of considerable help to irrigation, but it proved also a convenient waterway for boats conveying goods. The whole extent of water thus united is generally called the "Sea of Parakrama," though the name was probably first given to a tank in Ruhuna.

The principal buildings of Anuradhapura were put into repair, and several other cities were given much-needed attention. But it was Polonnaruva that the king delighted in- most, and that he most zealously sought to enlarge and adorn. By his orders the city was surrounded with fortifications, and with ramparts four leagues long and seven leagues broad. A richly decorated palace, seven storeys high, was built there, and among the other buildings we are told of a theatre, a hall of recreation, and temples for the Brahmans.

Parakrama's reign extended over thirty-three years (1153-1186). It was a reign of peace and progress; and we cannot hesitate to admit that no king of Ceylon more truly deserved to be called "the Great."

## CHAPTER XXVI

## Another Tamil Invasion

FOR forty-three years after the death of Parakrama the Great there was no ruler of Ceylon who can be regarded as a worthy successor to him. Those years were, for the most part, a time of trouble and disorder, and, we need do no more than glance at the most important incidents. **Vijaya Bahu II**, the nephew and successor of Parakrama, was a poet and a Pali scholar of some merit. He was less stern and severe than his uncle in dealing with his subjects, but not less just. He brought about a good understanding with Ramanna, against whom Parakrama had been at war, by writing to the king of that country, "with his own hand, in the Pali tongue, a letter of great merit." This helped to restore the old friendship that existed between Ramanna and Ceylon.

Vijaya Bahu II reigned, however, for only one year, when he was put to death by "a false friend," **Mahinda VI,** a man of Kalinga. "But this foolish man was able to rule the kingdom with great trouble for five days only;" for he was then killed by **Kirti Nissanka Malla,** who was also of the race of Kalinga. Many stone inscriptions have been found in various parts of the island describing Nissanka Malla's deeds and royal proclamations. Some of these inscriptions are boastful in tone, and greatly exaggerated the king's virtues and achievements. Much is attributed to him that was really done by his uncle Parakrama the Great. He claims to have terrified the kings of Pandya, Chola, and other countries into submission to him; but he does not appear to have revisited South India, whence he came originally, except as a guest.

But during his reign of nine years (1198-1207) he shewed himself a liberal-minded and competent, though vain-glorious ruler. The sufferings of the people in consequence of the long wars of Parakrama, compelled him to remit all taxes for five years, and one or two taxes were altogether abolished. He built or repaired many temples and other religious buildings, and canals, tanks, and embankments. He established courts of justice to prevent the oppression of the poor;

and his gifts of money, lands, cattle, clothes, and other things, must have been enormous in amount, if the records are to be taken literally. His charity was extended even to thieves, for he hoped by such means to reform them. He gave them village lands and property so that they should have no excuse for stealing!

He visited many parts of the island.—Anuradhapura, Adam's Peak, Bintenne, Dondra, and Kelaniya. He visited also Ramesvaram, and may have crossed over to South India on the invitation of some of the kings. It was he who began the custom, which existed in South India, of engraving grants of land on copper plates instead of *olas* which were liable to be destroyed by rats and white ants; and he fixed the distance of a *gauwa* (Sinhalese mile), setting up inscribed milestones at proper places.

A great stone lion, on which the king's throne rested, was removed from Polonnaruva in recent times, and is now preserved in the Colombo Museum.

The rulers of Ceylon for the next fifteen years require no special mention. We may note, however, that two queens reigned during that period. One was **Lilavati,** the widow of Parakrama the Great. She reigned three times, and was thrice dethroned. The other queen was **Kalyanavati,** the widow of Nissanka Malla, who reigned for six years. When Lilawati was first dethroned she was succeeded

---

A.D. 1215 Magna Carta (The Great Charter) by king John.

by **Sahasa Malla**, who is described as a lion-hearted king, and who reigned two years. (1200-1202.)

When Lilavati was for the third and last time reigning over Ceylon, the island was overrun by an army of Pandyans, whose leader dethroned the queen, and reigned under the name of **Parakrama Pandu.** But after three years he was in his turn displaced by **Magha** of Kalinga, who invaded Ceylon (1215) with an army of 20,000 men. Magha appears to have been more merciless than any earlier Tamil. So terrible was this invasion of his, that it was regarded by the Sinhalese as the punishment sent upon them by the gods for their previous neglect of religion. This is how the *Mahavansa*, describes the work of Magha's Tamils:—

" Thereupon these mighty men, wicked disturbers of the peace of mankind, stalked about the land hither and thither crying out boastfully, ' Lo! we are the giants of Kerala,' [the Carnatic Country]. And they robbed the inhabitants of their garments and their jewels and everything that they had . . . . They cut off also the hands and feet of the people, and despoiled their dwellings. Their oxen and buffaloes also, and other beasts, they bound up and carried them away forcibly. The rich men they tied up with cords and tortured, and took possession of all their wealth, and brought them to poverty. They broke down the image-houses and destroyed many cetiyas.

They took up their dwellings in the viharas and beat the pious laymen therein. They flogged children, and sorely distressed the five ranks of the religious orders. They compelled the people to carry burdens and made them labour heavily. Many books also of great excellence did they loose from the cords that bound them and cast away in divers places. Even the great and lofty cetiyas, such as the Ratnavalı [Ruvanveli] which stood like the embodiment of the glory of all the pious kings of old, they spared not, but utterly destroyed them, and caused a great many bodily relics to disappear thereby, which were unto them as their lives. Alas! Alas!"

Magha reigned for twenty-one years, but scattered throughout the mountain districts there were yet cities and villages which the Tamil invader could not bring within his power, and fortresses which his armies could not overcome. One of these was Yapahu in the Seven Korales, where a Sinhalese chief built a fort. Another was Dambadeniya, a city fifty miles north-east of Colombo, where **Vijaya Bahu III**, a prince of the Sinhalese royal line, still kept up a show of royal authority. Step by step this prince extended his authority until the Tamils were driven out of Maya-rata and Ruhuna, and forced to confine themselves to the northern parts of the island. Buddhism was once again triumphant in the south. The sacred books were transcribed afresh, disputes among the priests were settled, and many new priests were ordained.

CHAPTER XXVII

# Pandita Parakrama Bahu

VIJAYA BAHU III was succeeded, after a reign of four years, by his son, **Parakrama Bahu II**, (1240-1275) whose extensive learning gained for him the name of "the all-knowing Pandit." But he was not less anxious to free his country from the Tamil dominion. Magha of Kalinga and his lieutenant Jaya Bahu still lorded it in Pihiti-rata, but they soon began to find their position insecure. They were frequently attacked by the Sinhalese, and at length they prepared to flee to India. Parakrama fell upon them at the Kala-veva, where they were routed with great slaughter.

A few years afterwards, in the eleventh year of Parakrama's reign, there was another invasion of Ceylon. A prince named Chandrabhanu came with a number of Malays from the Java Islands, and deceived the people, saying "We also are Buddhists." They landed at various places on the coast and harassed the country with "the fury of a flood of water." This enemy too was beaten after a fierce battle; and Chandra-bhanu was beaten again when he came with a large army of warriors whom he had got together from the Pandya and Chola countries; but the second Malay invasion was defeated by Parakrama's successor, Vijaya Bahu IV. *(See p. 112)*.

Parakrama Bahu II was now able to turn his attention to the improvement of his kingdom. His first care was to restore lands, houses, and fields to their proper owners, and to mark out the boundaries of each. The lands belonging to the priesthood were in the same way restored. New priests were brought over from India, where many from Ceylon had taken refuge during the Tamil invasions, while the priests and students in Ceylon who lived evil lives, or were in other ways unsuitable, were expelled from the monasteries. He directed, further, that those priests who remained should be taught more carefully in the doctrines of their religion, in logic and grammar also, and in other sciences.

The king's buildings are chiefly notable because they were distributed over so large an area. We read of viharas and temples, either newly built or splendidly repaired and enlarged, at places so distant from one another as Kurunegala, Kelaniya, Gampola, Dambadeniya, Bentota, and Dondra. At Attanagalla, where Gothabaya had built a vihara in memory of Siri Sangabo I, Parakrama built a shrine and image-house. Anuradhapura and Polonnaruva were cleared of forest and again made habitable. Dambadeniya, his father's capital, and his own, he fortified and adorned. Afterwards he did honour to his birthplace by building there a great vihara to which he removed the tooth-relic with great ceremony. To this place the title of Sirivardhanapura was given, and for many years it was wrongly supposed that it was the town of Kandy which was referred to by this

---

A.D. 1265. Simon de Montfort killed at Evesham.
,, 1275. Marco Polo received by Kublai Khan of China.

title. But the birthplace of Parakrama was Nambambaraya, a little town six or seven miles from Dambadeniya.

The adornment of cities so far apart from one another proves that Parakrama had gained control over the greater part of the island, while the Tamils had, for the time, to be content with their settlements in the north. That the king was free from their assaults is shewn by the large number of bridges he made in various parts of the country, and by the roads (among them one to the top of Adam's Peak) which he cleared and improved. It is shewn also by the renewed attention paid to Buddhism, and by the great encouragement given to education and literature in those days. About this time, a priest, named Dharmakirti, enlarged the *Mahavansa* by adding to it the history of Ceylon from the death of Maha Sena to the reign of Parakrama Bahu II; and the head of a college of priests wrote the *Pujavaliya*, a work describing the offerings made to the Buddha, and including also a summary of the history of Ceylon.

## CHAPTER XXVIII.

## The Last Phase I.

DURING the last years of Parakrama's reign the government of the country was entrusted to his eldest son Vijaya Bahu, who chose a cousin, Vira Bahu, to be his chief friend and adviser. Vijaya Bahu's principal task was to keep the king's territory safe from attack. Dambadeniya, the capital, was fortified and made safe against Tamil inroads; and Vijaya's brother, Bhuvaneka Bahu, was sent to defend Yapahu, where the danger was greatest. Vijaya himself set out with Vira Bahu and a large army on a march through the country, his chief object being to repair and restore the city of Polonnaruva. He visited Adam's Peak, Gampola, and Kurunegala, and at length came to Yapahu, where he met and defeated Chandra-bhanu, who had added an army of Tamils to his band of Malays. Yapahu was then further fortified, and the prince went on to Anuradhapura and thence to Polonnaruva. This city he nobly adorned, and with splendid ceremonies and festivities he brought here the king his father, and the sacred relics of the Buddha.

When king Parakrama II died, the prince reigned as **Vijaya Bahu IV**, but in the second year of his reign he was treacherously murdered by Mitra, one of his generals, who tried to make himself king at Dambadeniya. Vijaya's brother, Bhuvaneka, escaped from the city to the fortress of Yapahu, soon contrived to secure the death of the usurper, and then himself reigned at Yapahu as **Bhuvaneka Bahu I**. But even Yapahu was not safe now from the attacks of enemies. Kulasekara, king of Pandya, sent an army of Pandyans under the command of a general who called himself *Arya Chakravarti*, a title commonly assumed by the kings of Jaffna. Yapahu was entered, the whole country round about was laid waste, and the tooth-relic was taken away to India with whatever other treasure could be obtained.

The next king, **Parakrama Bahu III,** knew that the Pandyans were too strong a people for him to war against ; but, as he was anxious to get back the tooth-relic, he went over to Pandya, and made himself so agreeable to its king Kulasekera that the relic was returned to him, and it was duly put back into its old place at Polonnaruva. Parakrama was a liberal supporter of the priests, but there is a suspicion that he was jealous of his cousin, Bhuvaneka, and tried to do him bodily harm. The prince escaped from the court, and he afterwards succeeded to the throne as **Bhuvaneka Bahu II.** The most noteworthy fact of his reign is that he made Kurunegala his capital. Thus, after more than four hundred and fifty years, Polonnaruva finally lost its claim to be the royal city, for never again was it the capital of Ceylon.

**Parakrama Bahu IV,** son of Bhuvaneka Bahu II, became king about the year 1295, and during his reign enriched the southern districts of Ceylon with many temples and other sacred buildings. At Kurunegala he built a three-storeyed *maligawa* for the tooth-relic, not far from his own palace. At Totagamuva, a village between Matara and Tangalla, he built and endowed a fine temple in place of that one which the great Vijaya Bahu had built, and which had since fallen into decay. Temples or image-houses were also set up at Dondara, Weligama, and Ratgama. In the Sitawaka district he founded a new city, and there built a *devala* in which he placed an image of Vishnu, one of the Hindu gods, "and made great offerings thereto."

The king was fond of literature, and wrote a book describing the ceremonies for the worship of the tooth-relic. Of more importance was a translation into Sinhalese of the *Jatakas*, a book of the five hundred and fifty "birth stories" of the Buddha. The *Jatakas* were originally written in Pali, and the translation was made by a learned priest who had been invited over from the Cholian country. The *Sidat-Sangara*, the standard grammar of the Sinhalese language, was also compiled in this reign.

Little is definitely known of the next two kings **Bhuvaneka Bahu III** (Vanni Bhuvaneka) and **Jaya Bahu II.** About the year A.D. 1347, **Bhuvaneka Bahu IV** removed the capital from Kurunegala to Gampola.

In the year 1344, the Arab traveller, *Ibn Batuta*, came to Ceylon. Ibn Batuta was born at Tangier, in the extreme north-west of Africa, and when he grew to manhood set out on a course of travels which lasted twenty-four years. He visited countries, so far distant as Sumatra and China in Asia, Astrakhan in Europe, and Quiloa, near Zanzibar, in Africa. That he should have been able to do this shews us how widespread was the extent of the Muhammadan religion and of Arab enterprise by land and sea. On his way from the west to China he came to the Maldive Islands, and sailed thence for India; but an inexperienced pilot kept him nine days at sea, and then they found themselves in Ceylon, having seen "the mountain of Serendib raised in the air like a column of smoke." He landed in the northern part of Ceylon and presented himself before a "Sultan" who called himself Arya Chakravarti, who understood the Persian language, and who was powerful on the sea. Wishing to visit, according to Muhammadan custom, the footprint of Adam, (on Adam's Peak), he entered the territory of the principal sovereign of the island, whose capital was *Conacar*, the town of Kurunegala being probably meant. Ibn Batuta visited also Dondra, Galle, and Colombo, which last he describes as one of the largest and most beautiful towns in the island. He then went back to the king of Jaffna and sailed for India.

Gampola continued to be the capital under the next two kings, **Parakrama Bahu V** and **Vikrama Bahu III**. In the reign of the latter, his prime-minister, Alakesvara, or Alagakkonara, who lived at Peradeniya, built a fort at Rayigama for protection from the Tamils, and built the fort and new city of Jayawardhana-Kotte, now known as Cotta or Kōtte. The Tamils of Jaffna (for by this time the

---

A.D. 1349. The Black Death in England.

Tamil settlements in the North had been formed into a kingdom, with Jaffna as capital) came again under an Arya Chakravarti to harass the Sinhalese. Colombo, Negombo, and Chilaw were occupied, and the Sinhalese were forced to pay an annual tribute to the king of Jaffna. But Alakesvara not long afterwards won a great victory over the Tamils, and there was no more paying of tribute to them.

Vikrama Bahu III was succeeded by **Bhuvanaka Bahu V** who reigned from 1378 to 1398 with his capital at Kōtte. This king may have been no other than Alakesvara (or Alagakkonara) himself, who took the name of Bhuvaneka Bahu V on his accession to the throne. But the point is not quite settled, and it is more likely than otherwise that Alakesvara was the real ruler, for a time, while Bhuvaneka Bahu held nominal authority. Indeed, the history of this period, till the coming of the Portuguese, is full of difficulties. The dates and names of kings, the order of events, and all the main facts, are confused and bewildering.

From the death of Bhuvaneka Bahu V to the year 1410 (or perhaps 1415), when Parakrama Bahu VI came to the throne, we can only guess what actually happened, and the confused records make any accurate, connected narrative almost impossible. If we assume that Bhuvaneka Bahu V died in A.D., 1391, there are twenty four years to be accounted for, 1391—1415. The *Mahavansa* says that *Vira Bahu II* succeeded to the throne, and after him Parakrama Bahu VI. But a king named *Vijaya Bahu* is mentioned in other writings, and in this king's reign there was trouble with the Chinese.

In 1405 a Chinese general came to Ceylon bringing incense and offerings to be laid at the shrine of the Buddha ; for the Chinese also were Buddhists. The general was, however, shamefully insulted by the Sinhalese king, and it was with difficulty he succeeded in escaping to his ship. In 1408 he returned to avenge the insult. The king and queen with many others were taken prisoners to China, but the Chinese emperor compassionately restored them to liberty on condition that the crown of Ceylon should be taken from Vira, or Vijaya Bahu, and given to the "wisest" of the captive king's family. **Parakrama Bahu VI**. was thereupon appointed king, and for the next fifty years Ceylon paid tribute to China.

## CHAPTER XXIX

## The Last Phase II

PARAKRAMA Bahu VI reigned for fifty-two years, 1410—1462. His capital was at Kotte, and here, among other fine buildings, he built a three-storeyed temple for the tooth-relic which was brought here and placed in the innermost of four golden caskets. Buddhism was greatly encouraged in this reign in the customary way; and in addition to the usual gifts to the priests, the king assigned lands for the maintenance and comfort of those who were set apart to make copies of the sacred books. Yet, this king also is said to have had a strong leaning towards Hinduism.

But the reign was not entirely one of peace First came an invasion from Canara a country on the west coast of Southern India. The king of Canara sent a fleet of ships and a large army hoping to establish his power in Ceylon; but the attempt failed, and Parakrama's victory greatly increased his reputation in the East. Next, a trading ship of his, sailing to a South Indian port, was seized and plundered by a Malabar chief of the Chola country. Parakrama sent an army to Chola, many villages of which were despoiled, and from a few of which an annual tribute was exacted.

Then took place a rebellion in the five Kandyan districts of Udunuwara, Yatinuwara, Harispattu, Hewaheta, and Dumbara. These districts were ruled by a prince who now sought to withhold the taxes due to Kotte, and thus to assert his independence. The rebellion was quelled at the cost of many lives, and prince Jayavira of Ambulugala was appointed the new ruler of the Kandyan districts, which were now forming themselves into a separate kingdom.

The Vanniyar, the people who lived in the wild jungles between the kingdom of Jaffna and the Sinhalese territory, defied Parakrama's authority, and were brought under subjection after the capture of their strongholds.

Last came a war with the king of Jaffna, who claimed to be overlord of Ceylon. Parakrama "thought it not right that there should be two seats of government in Lanka," and sent prince Sapumal (elder brother of Jayavira of Ambulugala) bidding him relieve the king of Jaffna of the burden of the new title he had taken. Sapumal's successful invasion of Jaffna was celebrated by the poets of his time. He "created such carnage that the streets of Yapapatuna [Jaffna] were deluged with blood." Jaffna now became subject to Kotte, but it was not subject for long.

The reign of Parakramabahu VI is noted also for the fact that then lived the greatest of Sinhalese poets, *Sri Rahula*, more widely spoken of as *Totagamuve,* from the village of that name. He was a priest, and the principal of a college for priests which the king established near Kotte. He was a favourite with the king, to whose household he belonged before he became a priest, and whom he celebrated in poems shewing the warmest affection. He was famous also as a linguist, knowing thoroughly six eastern languages besides his own. His first and chief poem was the *Kavyasekera*, which was completed in the thirty-fourth year of the king's reign, *i.e.*, about 1444. It describes one

---

A.D. 1428. Siege of Orleans. Henry VI.

of the incarnations of the Buddha, who appeared in this world as a pandit. Other poets and prose writers lived at this time, which must be regarded as one of great literary and religious activity as well as of wars and rebellions.

Parakrama's grandson and successor, **Jaya Bahu II,** called also *Vira Parakrama Bahu*, was murdered in less than two years by Sapumal, the conqueror of Jaffna, who took the title of **Bhuvaneka Bahu VI.** After a reign of seven years he was succeeded by **Parakrama Bahu VII.** who was known as *Pandita*, "the Pandit," because of his great learning. His reign was disturbed by the rebellion of the prince of Ambulugala, in the present Kegalla District, a brother of Sapumal. The rebellion was successful, and the prince reigned as **Vira Parakrama Bahu VIII.** He reigned twenty years, and it was in his reign that the Portuguese came to Ceylon. He was succeeded by his eldest son **Dharma Parakrama Bahu IX.**

## CHAPTER XXX

## The Arrival of the Portuguese

WE have now followed the course of Ceylon history through a period of two thousand years from its known beginnings. We have seen how Ceylon was conquered and peopled by Vijaya; how, some two centuries later, Buddhism was brought into the country; how Buddhist literature was cultivated; how arts and sciences were encouraged; and how a Sinhalese king might make his power felt in Burma and in Southern India. We have seen the Tamils of India attempting time after time to win the Island for themselves, ravaging the country in numberless invasions, forcing the Sinhalese kings from one capital to another, and at length forming a settlement and kingdom of their own in the northern districts. We have seen that Ruhuna and the central districts kept themselves fairly free from intrusion throughout all the changes that occurred elsewhere, furnishing a shelter for kings in their need, and supplying fresh bands of troops with which to repel the Tamil invaders. We have read, too of other invasions,—of the Malays from Java, and the Chinese from their empire farther east. But these invaders were all Asiatics, the people of countries belonging to the same continent as Ceylon itself. We have now to tell of very different races who came to Ceylon, and in the end made it their own; in other words, of the conquest of Ceylon by invaders from Europe,—by the Portuguese, the Dutch, and the English, in turn. The first European invaders of Ceylon were the Portuguese, whom a mere accident brought to our coasts at the very beginning of the sixteenth century.

Ceylon was not unknown to Europeans before this event. The ancient Greeks mention

---

A.D. 1453. Conquest of Constantinople by Turks.

A.D. 1492. Colombus discovered the West Indies.

Ceylon in their writings, and many merchants and travellers carried reports to Europe of the wealth and fertility of the Island. Even in very early times its cinnamon was prized in Europe, and by the sixth century after Christ the island had become a great centre of trade. Ships from China brought silk, porcelain, and cloves; Persia sent horses; India sent musk, pepper, brass, and cloth; while Nubia and Abyssinia sent their gold. It must not be supposed, however, that the Sinhalese owned or manned the ships that carried on this trade: they were not a race of sailors. The trade lay almost entirely in the hands of the Arabs, Persians, and Chinese. The gems, cinnamon, and elephants of Ceylon, together with the other articles of commerce brought into Ceylon from more distant countries, were carried by the Arabs to African ports on the Red Sea, and thence conveyed overland to Europe.

The people of Portugal, in the south-west of Europe, were very anxious to find a way to India, the land from which came the spices and other luxuries they so highly valued. They were a great sea-faring nation, "seamen by nature, conquerors by descent, and crusaders by tradition and creed." They wished to visit the East and bring its treasures to Europe in their own ships. But in the fifteenth century little was known about the coast of Africa, the great continent that lay between Portugal and India. Thanks to the efforts of Prince Henry "the Navigator," a son of the king of Portugal, the western coast of Africa was explored, a little farther each year, till in 1487 or 1488 a brave sailor named Bartholomew Diaz sailed right round the cape at the extreme south of Africa, without knowing that he had done so. The storms he met while doing this were so terrible that he named the cape the "Cape of Storms": but the king of Portugal was so pleased with the result of the voyage that he changed the name to the "Cape of Good Hope," the name it now bears; there was a good hope now of reaching the much desired land of India.

Ten years later, the famous Vasco da Gama was sent by the king of Portugal to find a way by sea to India. He left Lisbon in March or July 1497, sailed along the west coast of Africa, doubled the Cape in November, reached Natal on Christmas Day, and Melinde (just above Mombasa) on the 14th April 1498. Here he was entertained by the king for nine days, and then he sailed north-east for Calicut, which he reached on the 20th of May.

At this time the whole of India south of the river Kistna formed the kingdom of Vijayanagar or Narsinga, and Calicut was the chief town of one of its many provinces. The Arabs had an exceedingly large trade here, as indeed they had throughout the East, their fleets controlling the trade of the whole of the Indian Ocean. The Hindu ruler of Calicut had the title of *Zamorin*, or *Samuri*, and the city was rich owing to the trade of the Arabs. To these Arabs and their descendants in South India, the Moplahs, the Portuguese gave the name of *Moors*, because they were Muhammadans like the true Moors of Morocco in north-west Africa, against whom the Portuguese and the Spaniards had had a long and bitter warfare.

Vasco da Gama was at first kindly received by the Zamorin of Calicut, but the Moors feared that they would no longer be able to keep the trade to themselves if the Portuguese had anything to do with it, and they tried to create ill-feeling between the Hindus and the Portuguese. But the latter succeeded in getting together a valuable cargo with which they returned to Portugal. The Portuguese came again and again, and by 1504 they had won some possessions in India which they began gradually to extend. The carrying trade was now largely in their hands, and the Moors were slowly being driven out of Indian waters.

CHAPTER XXXI

## The Discovery of Ceylon

BOTH the situation and the value of Ceylon were fairly well known to the Portuguese, so that when, early in 1505, Dom Francisco de Almeida, Portuguese viceroy of India, was instructed by his king to "discover" Ceylon, it meant no more than that he was to explore it fully, and to obtain all the information he could. King Manuel of Portugal was so impressed with the advantages to be gained that he wished de Almeida to make his principal residence in Ceylon, as the island was so well suited to be, from its position, the centre of the Portuguese possessions in Asia. Still it was not till about the middle of the year 1506 (but some writers think it was November 1505) that the Portuguese went to Ceylon, and then the visit was not made on purpose; it happened by mere accident.

News was taken to the viceroy in India that the Moors trading between Malacca and the Red Sea sailed south of Ceylon, by the Maldive Islands, to avoid capture by the Portuguese. To prevent this, and to "discover" these islands, whence coir was obtained for the ships, the viceroy sent his son, Dom Lourenco de Almeida, to the Maldives. It was the wrong season for these ships, and the monsoon winds and the currents of the Indian Ocean drove Dom Lourenco to the coast of Ceylon, and he anchored at Colombo. Some writers state that he was driven first to Galle, where he heard that Colombo was the king's residence, and that he then came on to the city. Dom Lourenco found Colombo a crowded and busy port with Moor ships actively loading cinnamon and elephants to be taken to India.

The Sinhalese king, who lived at Kotte, about six miles from Colombo, was at once told of the strange people who had come to his country. Men from the harbour ran to him with the news: "There is in our harbour of Colombo a race of people fair of skin and comely withal. They don jackets of iron and hats of iron. They rest not a minute in one place. They walk here and there. They eat hunks of stone and drink blood. They give two or three pieces of gold and silver for one fish or one lime. The report of their cannon is louder than thunder when it bursts upon the rock Yugandhara. Their cannon balls fly many a *gawwa* and shatter fortresses of granite.*

The Sinhalese at this time knew nothing of guns or gunpowder, and their astonishment may well be understood. The king called his ministers together, and asked them whether he should make peace with the new-comers or attempt to fight them. It was decided that prince Chakra-yuddha should go in disguise to Colombo, and find out the truth about the rumours brought to the king. When Chakra-yuddha returned, he reported that the strangers were certainly dangerous, and that it would be wiser to form an alliance with them than to attack them. Accordingly, the king received an embassy from the Portuguese, and made a treaty of friendship with Dom Lourenco, who then returned to his business of fighting the Moors on the Indian seas.

---

* From the *Rajavaliya*. The passage is held to be an addition of late date, but it summarizes what would be the natural impressions of the people at that time.

There were really two embassies sent by Dom Lourenco, and the first was a small one. The Portuguese were on that occasion led to Kotte, or to a plain near Kotte, not by the usual road, " but through such dense thickets that they could scarcely see the sun, taking so many turns that it seemed to them more like a labyrinth than a direct road to any place." The guides thought that by this trick they would make the Portuguese believe that Kotte was far from Colombo, and three days were spent in this journey! The saying, " As the Portuguese went to Kotte," is still in use. But the strangers were not really deceived.

Meanwhile the Portuguese continued to extend their power in India. They established settlements on the western coast of India and made the town of Goa the capital of their possessions. They went farther east and conquered Malacca. Ceylon which lay midway between these places, was therefore a desirable possession, and the king of Portugal wanted it. At this time, however, cinnamon could be got in India, and though the Portuguese made several visits to the island, it was not till 1518 that they decided upon its conquest.

In the year 1518, seventeen Portuguese ships came under Lopo Soarez de Albergaria, and a factory was speedily built in Colombo, in spite of Sinhalese and Moor opposition; the Portuguese said that permission to build a factory was included in the first treaty. Next a fort was built of mud; but when the

Sinhalese complained that no permission had been given to build a fort, the Portuguese explained that a fort was needed to protect the factory from the attacks of the Moors. The Moors, whose trade was in danger, at length succeeded in stirring up the king to make war against the Portuguese ; but the king's attacks were repelled without difficulty, and he was forced to submit and pay tribute to the king of Portugal. In 1520 or 1521 the fort* was rebuilt, this time of stone though the Sinhalese and Moors did all they could to prevent the work.

## CHAPTER XXXII.

## Extension of Portuguese Influence

THE Portuguese gradually extended their possessions in Ceylon, and in so doing did not spare either the lives or the property of the Sinhalese. This was the way with all invaders in those days. In their anxiety to secure wealth and power they were careless of the rights of the natives of the island, and committed many acts of cruelty and injustice. The Sinhalese, maddened by the oppression which they had to endure, made a vigorous attempt to get back their freedom. A force of twenty thousand men besieged Colombo in 1520, and, but that timely help came from the Portuguese province of Cochin in India, de Brito, who was in command at Colombo, would have been killed with all his soldiers, As it

* See illustration in "Ceylon at the Census of 1911" by E. B. Denham. Page 146.

happened, he was able to drive off the Sinhalese; but he saw that it was necessary to prevent the excesses of his men, and to treat the Sinhalese with more consideration. The fort was demolished in 1524 by the orders of the king of Portugal, but it was strongly rebuilt in 1551. It then included both the present Fort and the Pettah.

With the Portuguese came a new religion to Ceylon. We cannot be quite sure if Christianity had ever been preached before to the Sinhalese, though a Christian community flourished here a thousand years earlier; but when de Albergaria came to Ceylon in 1518, a number of missionaries accompanied him, and tried to convert the Sinhalese to Christianity. The missionaries belonged to the Roman Catholic section of the Christian Church, and there can be no doubt that their teaching, whatever may have been its effect on the Sinhalese people, did a great deal to restrain the violence of the Portuguese soldiers.

**Vijaya Bahu VII.** (1527—1534) was a weak and selfish king, and his rule did not help the Sinhalese to keep their ancient kingdom free, or safe from their enemies. At this time the island was divided into a number of petty governments, each of which was really independent, though all were in name subject to the king of Kotte; and Kotte itself was too

---

A.D. 1517. Luther's theses published at Wittenberg.
" 1529. Fall of Cardinal Wolsey.
" 1535. Act of Supremacy. Henry VIII.

near the Portuguese fort to maintain its independence. In the face of these difficulties, the king increased the disunion among his people by a foolish act. He appointed his step-son as his successor in the government, and shut out his own sons, whom he even tried to put to death. These sons determined upon revenge. They collected an army, plundered Kotte, and hired an assassin to kill their father. **Bhuvaneka Bahu VII,** the eldest of Vijaya Bahu's sons, then became king, while two of his brothers held smaller governments,—*Maya-Dunné*, the most daring and ambitious of the three, at Sitavaka, and *Rayigam Bandara* at Rayigama. But the new king was as unwise as his father had been. He directed that Dharmapala, his grandson, should succeed him as king. This Dharmapala was the son of Vidiye Bandara, called by the Portuguese *Tribuli Pandar.* Vidiye Bandara married Bhuvaneka's daughter, and sided, sometimes with the Portuguese, and sometimes against them. He was killed later on at Jaffna, to which place he had fled to secure assistance against his enemies. Maya-dunnè objected to Dharmapala's succession, and prepared to defend Sitavaka against the king's forces, which he knew would be sent against him. But Bhuvaneka obtained the help of the Portuguese, and Sitavaka was easily taken. Twice after this Maya-dunnè attempted to rise against the king. He was assisted both by his brother Rayigam Bandara and by Moorish trocps from Calicut and Cochin. But the Portuguese were too strong, and Sitavaka was on each occasion invaded and burnt to the ground.

Bhuvaneka now found that if he wished to secure the throne to himself and his family he could not expect enough support from his own countrymen. He was forced to depend more and more upon the Portuguese, and he accordingly determined to keep well with them. To bind them to his cause he did a curious thing. A small statue or image of his grandson and heir, Dharmapala, was sent to Portugal in the charge of a chief named Salappu Arachchi. A golden crown went with it, and Bhuvaneka asked that the king of Portugal should crown the statue. This could only mean that Bhuvaneka considered himself subject to the Portuguese king, and that the latter was acknowledged to have the right to give the crown to any one he pleased. John III, who was at that time (1541) king of Portugal, was, as we may well understand, very pleased to receive this formal acknowledgment of his supremacy. The statue was crowned in Lisbon with great ceremony, and Dharmapala was given the additional name of *Dom Joao—João*, being the Portuguese form of *John*. At the same time John III, required that liberty to preach the Christian religion should be given everywhere in Ceylon, and a number of Christian missionaries accompanied Salappu Arachchi on his return to the island. We must remember that the Portuguese were not only anxious to extend their empire; they were equally anxious to advance their religion.

In 1551 Bhuvaneka Bahu VII died. He was on a visit to Kelaniya, and while walking along the banks of the river was shot in the head, by accident it is supposed, by a Portuguese. Dharmapala succeeded to the throne, Maya-dunné still reigned at Sitavaka, and a prince named *Vira Vikrama* had ruled at Kandy. Dharmapala was in name at least, a Christian, and he owed his crown to the support of the Portuguese. His subjects now found that it was profitable to call themselves Christians, and to worship in the Christian churches, for they might then be appointed to government offices, and "for the sake of Portuguese gold," many natives of all castes professed to be Christians, and took Portuguese names in addition to their own Sinhalese names. On the western coast there were large numbers of Christians—real and pretended.

In 1544 the district of Mannar was converted to Christianity through the eloquence and self-denying zeal of Francis Xavier, an Indian Roman Catholic missionary, but not the well-known saint of that name. Mannar belonged to the Tamil kingdom of Jaffna, and its ruler *Sangkili*, who was a Hindu, did his best to root out the new religion. Six hundred Christians were massacred in Mannar, and other converts were persecuted without mercy. But in spite of this, Christianity spread, and several members of Sangkili's own family were among the converts. To protect them, and to punish the assaults on the Portuguese, the viceroy of Goa determined to conquer the northern kingdom. But the attempt was not made till some years later.

## CHAPTER XXXIII

# The Kandyan Kingdom

MAYA-DUNNÉ of Sitavaka was eager both to drive the Portuguese out of Ceylon and to win for himself the sovereignty of Ceylon. He fortified his capital, Sitavaka, and then began to bring the chiefs of the mountain districts under his authority. The Kandyan Kingdom, whose beginnings we have noted, was growing in strength and independence. Maya-dunne was greatly assisted in the efforts by his son *Tikiri Banda*, the daring warrior who afterwards became King of Ceylon under the name of Raja Sinha I. Even the Portuguese settlements on the southern coast did not escape. The Portuguese in Colombo saw that an effort must be made to check the growing power of Maya-dunné, and in 1552 a combined army of Europeans and Sinhalese, under the command of king Dharmapála of Kotte, marched against Raja Sinha, and a fierce battle was fought in one of the mountain passes leading to the interior of the island. The combined army was defeated and pursued to the walls of Colombo, where they were to a certain extent safe from attack. Kottè was then besieged by Maya-dunné, and its inhabitants were in great danger of starvation ; and in the next year Dharmapála was forced to leave it and to reside in Colombo.

In 1581 Maya-Dunnė, who had planned the murder of his father, was himself murdered by his son Tikiri Banda, who from this time reigned at Sitavaka as **Raja Sinha I.** (1581—1592). He was now the most powerful ruler in Ceylon, for from the time that Dharmapála went to live in Colombo till his death in 1597 he had no influence with his countrymen. On Raja Sinha's accession the Portuguese made another attempt to capture Sitavaka. A large force was sent against it and defeated an army led by one of Raja Sinha's generals. Then Raja Sinha himself took the field. He met the combined Portuguese and Sinhalese forces at Mulleriyava (1561) not far from Colombo, and utterly defeated them. The slaughter was terrible, no fewer than seventeen hundred Portuguese soldiers being killed in the battle. Encouraged by this victory the king marched against Kottė and took possession of it. Meanwhile the Portuguese had received help from Goa, and another army was now sent against Raja Sinha. This time they advanced more cautiously, but Raja Sinha again defeated them and soon besieged Colombo. From this siege, however, he, was, to his great disappointment called away by an insurrection in his own dominions.

---

A.D. 1558. Calais lost to the English. Mary I.

„ 1564. Shakespeare born. (Died 1616.)

„ 1580—1640. The "Spanish Captivity" of Portugal.

„ 1584. Assassination of William the Silent.

„ 1587. Execution of Mary, Queen of Scots.

„ 1588. Defeat of the Spanish Armada.

The Portuguese were more successful in Jaffna which they brought under their power; and here they were able to provide a refuge for some of those against whom Raja Sinha and his father, Maya-dunné, had warred. Vira Bahu was the king of Kandy, and when defeated by Maya-dunné in 1580, he fled with his family to Mannar and sought the protection of the Portuguese. Protection was readily granted; Vira Bahu was baptized and given the name of Dom Philip *(Filippe)* in honour of Philip II., who was at this time king of both Spain and Portugal; and his daughter Dona Catharina remained in the care of the Portuguese at Mannar.

Like all cruel rulers, Raja Sinha was very suspicious, especially of the neighbouring chiefs, whom he compelled to acknowledge his supremacy. One of the princes whom he suspected most was Virasundara Bandara and this man soon fell a victim to the king's distrust. The prince was invited to Sitavaka with the promise of certain districts to be placed under his control as the reward of his former services. On the way two mudaliyars who escorted him pushed him into a pit, at the bottom of which sharp stakes had been fixed, and there he was killed. This murder was afterwards avenged by Virasundara's son, Konappu Bandara, who fled to Colombo and offered his services to the Portuguese. He was baptized, and named Don João, after John, Duke of Austria, one of the greatest generals in Europe at that time. We must be careful to distinguish this Dom João from the Dom João Dharmapála, who was still the nominal ruler of the districts near Colombo, though in fact a dependant on the Portuguese.

Prompted by the Portuguese, Konappu Bandara sailed to Mannar, and thence made his way inland to Kandy, where he successfully raised an insurrection against the king. Raja Sinha was at this time an elderly man. His cruelty had raised bitter enemies against him. Besides, he had given up Buddhism, had become a Hindu, and was doing all he could to destroy Buddhism and to promote Hinduism. Even the Buddhist shrine on the top of Adam's Peak was given over to the Hindus. But in spite of his age and the hatred which he knew was felt against him, he prepared to fight in defence of his crown. The Kandyan districts now refused to acknowledge his rule, and Dom Philip (Vira Bahu) was appointed king of Kandy by the Portuguese. Sitavaka was besieged and the adjoining country laid waste. The southern coast was ravaged by the Portuguese, who gained much plunder in destroying the Buddhist and Hindu temples at Dondra, Matara, and other towns. A decisive battle was fought in 1592 at the Kadugannawa Pass. Konappu Bandara's forces were irresistible. The king's army was routed, and Raja Sinha himself was wounded in the leg. A few days after he died.

Konappu Bandara immediately proclaimed himself king. He threw aside all his former professions of Christianity, declared himself a Buddhist, and took the title of **Vimala Dharma I.** He had not forgiven the Portuguese who had given the throne of Kandy to Dom Philip rather than to him. However, he now took that throne by force. Dom Philip was poisoned, and the Portuguese were treated as enemies. They, on their side, would not recognise Vimala Dharma as king. Now that Dom Philip was dead, they pronounced his daughter, Dona Catharina, to be the lawful sovereign of Kandy; and they made ready to support her claims by force. But they were not strong enough to do anything just then by way of fighting.

About this time a Portuguese ship on its way from Malacca to Goa touched at Colombo, and its commander, Dom Lopez de Souza, was informed of the state of affairs. He was urged to place the matter before the viceroy of Goa and to bring help to Ceylon without delay. De Souza had great influence at Goa, and he succeeded in persuading the viceroy that help was urgently needed. He himself returned to Ceylon in command of a large body of troops; and as he is said to have made it a condition with the viceroy that, when the conquest of Kandy was complete, Dona Catharina should be married to his nephew, de Souza was unsparing in his efforts to destroy the power of Vimala Dharma. Bringing her from Mannar he placed the young princess at the head of his forces and marched towards Kandy in 1594. Jayavira Bandara, the favourite general of Raja Sinha I, was now on the side of the Portuguese, and his army was of great use to them.

This addition to the Portuguese forces was a serious danger to the Kandyan king, but Vimala Dharma cunningly contrived to get rid of Jayavira. He wrote a friendly letter to him reminding him of a pretended plot by which the Portuguese general was to be betrayed, and urging him not to fail in his promise, as the time had now come. There was really no such plot, but the letter fell, as it was intended, into the hands of de Souza, who at once sent for Jayavira, shewed him the letter, and without waiting for any explanation stabbed him to the heart. The Sinhalese who had come to help their princess were naturally indignant, and abandoned de Souza. Many of them joined Vimala Dharma.

De Souza still persisted in his march to Kandy, and there he placed Dona Catharina on the throne. So far he had met with little or no opposition; but at Danture, in the neighbourhood of the Pass, Vimala Dharma's army suddenly fell upon the Portuguese forces and utterly destroyed them. Dona Catharina was taken prisoner, and compelled to marry Vimala Dharma, who by this marriage made himself legally secure on the throne of Kandy.

In 1603 the Portuguese made another attempt to conquer Kandy. They were led by Jeronimo de Azevedo, a brave and skilful soldier, but infamous even in this cruel age for the cruelties he practised on his victims. His army marched to the Balane Pass and took care to avoid being surprised by the enemy as de Souza had been. Vimala Dharma was thus forced to engage in a regular battle, in which he was again victorious, and the remnants of the defeated Portuguese struggled back to Colombo. Azevedo next tried to assassinate the Kandyan king, but the five men he sent for this purpose were murdered at the fatal Pass.

The Portuguese were now obliged to be content with their settlements on the coast. Their chief towns, Colombo the capital, and Galle, were strongly fortified, and became the centres of a large Portuguese population. Trade was carried on with great energy, and churches began to be built. But another European power soon appeared, before whom the Portuguese were finally compelled to give way.

## CHAPTER XXXIV

## Dutch Trade with India

THE king of Spain (Philip II) was at this time king of Portugal also. Spain, was the larger and more important country. Indeed, in the sixteenth century, Spain was, if not the most powerful, at least one of the three most powerful kingdoms of Europe. Among its subject kingdoms were both Portugal and the country now called Holland. In 1568 the Hollanders, or Dutch, as they are commonly called, rose in rebellion against the cruelties and misrule of Spain, and in 1581 they formed among themselves a separate government and declared their national independence. But only one year previously Portugal was conquered by Spain, and for sixty years endured the burden of its "Spanish Captivity."

Until 1594 the Dutch carried on a large trade with the Portuguese, especially in Indian goods. Portuguese ships would bring silks and other articles from India and the Far East to Lisbon. From Lisbon Dutch vessels would take these goods to countries farther north. This trade went on even during the war between Holland and Spain, thougn the king of Spain was also king of Portugal; but in 1594 Philip II. thought to destroy the trade, and in that way the power, of the Dutch, by forbidding the Portuguese to have any dealings with them. More than that, he imprisoned and tortured Dutch captives because they differed from him in their religious beliefs; for though the Dutch, like the Portuguese, were Christians, yet they belonged to the Protestant or Reformed section of the Christian Church.

The loss of this trade made the Dutch only the more determined to make trading voyages in their own ships to India and other eastern countries. They and the other European nations had been prevented all this while from trading with the countries whence came the luxuries they prized so highly. Now they felt free to fetch these luxuries for themselves in their own ships, and the sea-route to India was also now known.

A Dutch company, to trade with "distant lands," was at once formed, and in 1595 Dutch merchant ships (the first of their kind) sailed round the Cape of Good Hope, and were followed very soon by fleet after fleet which visited India and the eastern archipelago. The various Dutch companies that had sprung up were united in 1602 in the *Veerenigde Oost-Indische Compagnie* (V. O. C.), the United East-India Company. Five years later the English formed an English "East India Company," but of this we shall hear more later on.

On the 30th May, 1602, admiral Joris van Spilbergen cast anchor in Batticaloa Bay. His were the first Dutch ships seen in Ceylon, but the Sinhalese, not knowing that there were different races in Europe, thought that the Hollanders were Portuguese, and at first regarded them with much suspicion. The governor of Batticaloa paid a small tribute to the Portuguese and was nominally subject to them; but he was secretly a supporter of Vimala Dharma, king of Kandy. Spilbergen had some trouble in convincing the governor that he was not a Portuguese, but on the contrary an enemy of that nation; all he wanted in Ceylon was to buy pepper and cinnamon.

In a few days he found out that there was a king of Kandy, to whom the surrounding chiefs were subject. Spilbergen resolved to visit the king and to offer him an alliance with Holland. When he arrived at Kandy he was received with honour by Vimala Dharma, who was delighted to find that the Dutch would assist him to drive the Portuguese out of Ceylon. The King and the admiral held long conversations, and the latter was given permission to trade quite freely in and with Ceylon, and even to build a fort in any part of the island. "See," said the king, "I myself, my empress, the prince and princess, will carry on our own shoulders the stones, lime, and all the building materials if the States-General* and the Prince wish to build a fortress in my country."

On the 2nd September, 1602, Spilbergen left Batticaloa for Achin in Sumatra fully satisfied with his visit. Before he left he captured three Portuguese vessels off the east coast, and gave them over to the Sinhalese, thus proving that he was really an enemy of the Portuguese. Next year (1603) Sebald de Weerd, one of Spilbergen's captains, arrived in Ceylon from Achin. On the way he had captured four Portuguese ships, which, however, he afterwards set at liberty. Various reports had then been taken to Vimala Dharma that de Weerd was friendly to the Portuguese. The suspicious and angry king went to meet him at Batticaloa and a quarrel soon took place. To test his fidelity the king directed him to attack the Portuguese at Galle. De Weerd, who had taken too much wine, rudely refused, and is said to have spoken insolently. "Bind that dog," exclaimed the furious king.

---

* The *States-General* was the Parliament or governing body in Holland. The *Prince* was William II, prince of Orange and ruler of Holland. He was the father of William III, king of England.

But de Weerd resisted the officers who tried to bind him, and was killed, and nearly all his crew who had been left on shore were also killed. Then Vimala Dharma returned to Kandy and sent a message to de Weerd's lieutenant. "He who drinks wine comes to mischief. God has done justice. If you seek peace, let it be peace; if war, war be it." The Dutch thought it prudent at this time to take no further notice of this matter. They were not prepared yet to fight in Ceylon. In the next year (1604) Vimala Dharma died, often regretting the murder of de Weerd.

On the death of her husband, Dona Catharina took the government into her own hands, as her son, the appointed heir, was an infant. The Portuguese tried to win her over to their side, but she refused to make any alliance or treaty with them. There were many chiefs who sought to marry the queen and to take over the guardianship of her son; but of these the two principal claimants were the prince of Uva, and Senerat, a priest of the temple on Adam's Peak. Senerat, who gave up his priesthood, at length persuaded Dona Catharina to marry him, and thus strengthen his occupation of the throne.

On the 8th March, 1612, Marcellus de Boschouwer arrived at Kandy as an ambassador from the Dutch Government, and two months later a treaty was made between the Dutch and the king of Kandy. The Dutch promised to assist Senerat in his war against the Portuguese (2) on his side Senerat engaged to build a fort for the Dutch at Kottiyar, near Trincomalee and to allow them full liberty to trade in Ceylon. No European nation except the Dutch was to be allowed any trade at all with or in Ceylon. Senerat was so eager to secure the alliance of the Dutch that he kept de Boschouwer with him in Kandy for more than three years, nominally as Dutch ambassador, but to a greater extent as his private friend and adviser.

The Portuguese were not idle when they heard of these proceedings. In 1611 de Azevedo again set out for Kandy, which he burnt and plundered. In the same year, or the next, Simao Correa, a Christian Sinhalese, whose mother was a Portuguese, with a force of 1000 Portuguese and 3030 natives marched by a secret path to Kottiyar, destroyed the fort, and put to death the Dutch garrison left there by de Boschouwer. But Senerat was true to his bargain ; before the invaders could return to their own territory, a Kandyan army fell upon them. Twenty-three Portuguese and six hundred Sinhalese were killed, and a large amount of plunder was carried to Kandy.

Both sides now began to prepare for a decisive struggle. Senerat collected an army of fifty thousand men and decided to attack Galle and Colombo. The Portuguese got

---

A.D. 1605. Gunpowder Plot.

,, 1608. Virginia, first English settlement in America.

together what troops they could, and invaded Jaffna, where they were defeated; but they were successful in the Seven Korales, where they routed Senerat's army.

The death of Dona Catharina in July 1613 —she died of grief at the death of her eldest son, who had been poisoned by his step-father, Senerat—did not stop the war against the Portuguese. But the latter contrived to establish themselves more firmly in their possessions on the coast and they even approached Kandy. In 1615 Senerat sent de Boschouwer to Holland to ask the Dutch for troops to drive out the Portuguese. But de Boschouwer had by this time become so insolent in his manner (for while he pretended that he was the ambassador of a great foreign king, he forgot that he was still a Dutch subject), that the Dutch refused to have anything to do with him. He then went to Denmark. The Danish king was anxious to have a share in the Indian trade, and readily agreed to send five warships to Ceylon. They reached Ceylon in May 1620, but de Boschouwer had died on the way, and Senerat refused to accept the assistance of the Danes, who returned to their own country greatly disappointed.

The news of the failure of the Danish expedition, and of the death of de Boschouwer, on whom Senerat had so much relied, delighted the Portuguese. They built forts at Trincomalee and Batticaloa, and hoped soon to make their power felt in the Kandyan kingdom. They claimed, further, to be the lawful rulers of the island; for when Dom João Dharmapala died in 1597, he left a will by which he appointed the Portuguese his successors. On his death a "Convention" was held at Malvana on the Kelani Ganga, a few miles from Colombo, where the Sinhalese chiefs acknowledged the king of Portugal as their king and swore to be loyal to him. This assembly met in September 1597, and it is claimed by some that the Sinhalese took the oath of allegiance on the condition that their laws and customs should be maintained.

The Portuguese were not, however, free from heavy anxieties. In 1616, a headman deserted from their service and set up the standard of revolt. He called himself *Nikapitiya Bandara*, though the real prince of this name had been taken to Portugal, where he died eight years before this revolt. Many of the people rallied to the pretender, and an army of two thousand men was sent to his assistance from Kandy. A fierce battle was fought near Alawwa, on the banks of the Maha Oya, in which Nikapitiya was beaten by the Portuguese. He then took service under the Kandyan king, and continued to fight against the Portuguese.

A new governor of Portuguese Ceylon arrived in 1617 This was Don Constantino de Sa de Noronha, a man of distinguished birth and high honour. He had first to restore order among his own troops, and then to face the insurrections of Nikapitiya and of *Barreto*, a Sinhalese chief in Sabaragamuwa. News was also brought to him of risings in Jaffna, where a regent was allowed by the Portuguese to carry on the government. As help for the revolt against their ruler was coming to this regent from South India, de Sa sent Philippe de Oliveira, his captain-major, " renowned as the destroyer of over 500 pagodas," to conquer Jaffna. This de Oliveira did, and he was appointed governor over the re-conquered province.

CHAPTER XXXV.

## The Last Years of Portuguese Rule

THE Portuguese were compelled to invade Kandy sooner than they had intended. The armies of Senerat harassed them by frequent attacks on their possessions, and it was easily seen that the king meant to make a strong effort to expel the Portuguese. For this purpose he was collecting large forces and secretly plotting with the Sinhalese mudaliyars who served under the Portuguese. In 1629 Constantino de Sa found that he had no choice but to declare war, though he knew that the result could at the best be very doubtful. But even though he saw that peace was more necessary than war for the safety of the Portuguese in Ceylon; even though his most experienced advisers pointed out that his

---

A.D. 1618 Thirty Years War begun.
„ „ Petition of Right presented to Charles I.

troops had never been so few, while Senerat had a large army, and occupied a strong position ; yet de Sa felt bound to obey the orders he had received from the viceroy of Goa, and to invade Kandy. Indeed, the viceroy had begun to reproach de Sa with being a trader rather than a soldier, and these reproaches were more than the general's proud spirit could bear. With five hundred Portuguese and about twenty thousand Sinhalese he began the march. The army got safely over the Balane Pass, where there was some fighting, and then advanced to Uva, whither Senerat had cleverly retreated. The Portuguese burned and plundered the villages and towns, including Badulla, on their way, and rested "at Randenivela of Kandapalla" in Wellawaya, in the province of Uva, as the soldiers were worn out with their long march. Suddenly the plain was surrounded by vast numbers of Senerat's troops, and de Sa knew then that he was betrayed and entrapped. It was too late to fight that day, but the night was spent by the Portuguese in religious exercises and in preparations for the morrow. The general went round the camp encouraging his men to do their best, "Before this," said he, "you have battled for glory ; now you must fight for your lives."

There could be only one ending to the next day's battle. The treacherous mudaliyars led the van of the Portuguese army, and when the battle, began, one of them struck off the head of a Portuguese soldier and held it up on his lance. This was the signal for revolt.

The Sinhalese troops—all but one hundred and fifty who remained faithful—faced about and attacked the Portuguese, who now fought desperately, for they saw no way of escape. Raja Sinha, the son of Senerat, commanded the Kandyan army, and continually sent fresh troops to take the places of those who had been slain. The fight continued all day, but the darkness of night brought neither help nor rest to the wearied Portuguese. Rain fell in torrents, and not only prevented sleep but also spoilt their muskets and powder as well as their food. There was still a chance for de Sa to escape, and he was entreated to select fifty soldiers and cut his way through the enemy, but this he nobly refused to do. He said that he had always hitherto done his duty, and if he could not save his brave soldiers, it only remained for him to have the glory of dying with them. Next day (20th August,* 1630) de Sa and his heroic company were destroyed by the hosts of the enemy.

Thus died Constantino de Sa, by far the greatest and the best of those Portuguese leaders whose names are recorded in the history of Ceylon. Others might have equalled him in personal bravery or in military skill and experience, but none of them has left so honourable and pure a name. In an age when every one sought to enrich himself, and was careless whether the means he employed were honest or not, de Sa kept himself free from

---

* 15 September? See *Ceylon Antiquary* vol. II. p. 229.

corruption, did all he could to check and punish evil, and in every way acted as a true gentleman should. "There was no Portuguese in all Ceylon," says Ribeiro,* a fellow-countryman of de Sa's, "but wept on hearing of the deeds and death of Constantino de Sa Noronha, and his memory will be honoured as long as merit and valour are loved. This unfortunate day [the day of de Sa's death] commenced our ruin in the island of Ceylon."

After his victory Raja Sinha went down at once to besiege Colombo, but in spite of repeated attempts failed to take the town, The report of Constantino de Sa's death had reached Goa, and the viceroy, who had all this time "sent his orders but no assistance," hastily despatched six hundred and thirty soldiers, who after being delayed some months by adverse winds, arrived at Colombo in October, 1631. But both the Portuguese and the Sinhalese had troubles of their own, and a treaty was signed at Goa in 1633 by which Senerat consented to pay a tribute of two elephants yearly. In 1634 Senerat died.

**Raja Sinha II.** was now king, his two step-brothers (the sons of Vimala and Dona Catharina) having to be content with the chieftaincies of Uva and Matale. The Portuguese

---

A. D. 1631. Hampden refused to pay ship money.

* Captain Joao Ribeiro came to Ceylon in 1640, was taken prisoner by the Dutch at Jaffna in 1658, and sent to Batavia. He returned to Lisbon in 1680, and in 1685 wrote his "Fatalidade Historica da Ilha de Ceilao"—the fatal history of the island of Ceylon."

thinking that Raja Sinha's accession would be the cause of jealousy and civil war in Kandy, began again their attacks on the Kandyan territories, thus breaking the treaty they had made. It was now quite plain to the king that there would be no real peace until the Portuguese were driven out of the island, and in September 1636 he asked the Dutch governor of Palikat (Pulicat), north of Madras, to help him with troops.

Raja Sinha's application to the Dutch in 1636, which was repeated the next year, was successful. Admiral Westerwold was at this time on his way to Goa to fight the Portuguese, and the Dutch Government of Batavia sent him instructions to come to an agreement with the Kandyan king. These instructions reached Westerwold when he was engaged in a naval battle with the Portuguese off Goa, but immediately after the battle he sent vice-admiral Coster with two or three ships to besiege one or other of the Portuguese forts in Ceylon, and to inform Raja Sinha that reinforcements would be sent in May.

The Portuguese in Colombo got to know of these arrangements between the Dutch and the Kandyans, and in order to thwart them, Diego de Mello de Castro, captain-general of Colombo, set out in March 1638 to invade Kandy. On his march to the capital he was met at the Balane Pass by a Roman Catholic priest from Kandy, whom Raja Sinha had sent to point out to de Mello that he (the king) had kept his part of the treaty, that there was no cause for the

Portuguese invasion, and that if the Portuguese persisted in their unjust proceedings, the God Whom they worshipped would surely punish the guilty person.

De Mello was defiant. He replied angrily that he was determined to punish the king, and ordered his troops to advance. Kandy was taken without resistance, for the city had been abandoned by the Kandyans, and after it was plundered and burnt, the Portuguese were returning to Colombo when, at Gannoruwa (Peradeniya), they were surrounded by Raja Sinha's forces. Many of the Sinhalese lascorins deserted to the enemy, and all but thirty-three of the invaders, who were taken prisoners to Kandy, were slain. De Mello himself lost his life in this attempt.

A few days after this event, Coster arrived at Batticaloa, the port which he had selected for beginning the attack on the Portuguese in Ceylon. Admiral Westerwold, with five ships, arrived from Goa on the 10th May, and Raja-Sinha from Kandy on the 14th. Four days later, the Portuguese garrison surrendered, and on the 23rd May 1638 an important treaty of alliance was signed at Batticaloa between Raja Sinha and the Dutch. By this treaty, the Dutch, in return for expelling the Portuguese and keeping them out, secured the right of free trading in Ceylon, and of alone importing or exporting the products of Ceylon, particularly cinnamon, pepper, wax, and elephant tusks. Captured forts were to be garrisoned by the Dutch, and all the expenses of maintenance were to be borne by

Raja Sinha, who bound himself further not to correspond or to have any dealings with "his and our common enemy the Portuguese." Another article in the treaty required that no Roman Catholic priests should be allowed to remain in the island, since they would be a cause of continual trouble by working for the return of their countrymen.

Westerwold sailed away, and Coster remained at Batticaloa till the end of the year. After a short visit to Goa he came to Trincomalee as second in command, when that fort was taken by the Dutch on the 2nd May 1639. Seven months later, a Dutch naval force on its way to Colombo, cast anchor at Trincomalee, and found that the garrison there had been starved by Raja Sinha, in spite of his promises to maintain them. Raja Sinha was all this time in the neighbourhood of Colombo, the capture of which he was firmly determined upon. In reply to his urgent requests, the Dutch fleet came from Trincomalee to Colombo in January 1640, but there were no signs of the promised Sinhalese forces who were to assist the Dutch, and the admiral (Lucasz) went on to Negombo which, with the assistance of the king's troops, he took by storm on the 9th February 1640. The fort was then garrisoned by the Dutch, and necessary repairs to it were begun. This offended the king, who declared that, according to the treaty of 1638; the fort should be demolished. Lucasz, who was seriously ill, had to sail for Batavia, and Coster now took the command. He conciliated Raja Sinha, and among the new terms then agreed to, it was decided that Negombo and other forts should be occupied by the Dutch until the expenses of the war had been paid.

Coster now sailed for Galle, where a Sinhalese force was to help him in wresting that fort from the Portuguese. Jan Thysz who had succeeded Coster in charge at Batticaloa, arrived at Galle with a Dutch force on the same day (8th March) as Coster arrived from Negombo, and on the 13th March 1640, though without the expected assistance from Raja Sinha, the fort of Galle was stormed and taken, " not without great bloodshed on both sides."

The capture of Galle caused dismay in the Portuguese settlements in India, where the great value of the ports of Ceylon was well understood; and equal rejoicing was caused in Batavia, where the victory was celebrated with "a great military display." Galle was now fixed upon as the headquarters of the Dutch in Ceylon, for by this time they found it necessary to establish a settlement in the island; and from this date, 13th March 1640, we may consider the Dutch occupation of Ceylon to have begun, **Willem Jacobsz Coster** was appointed the first governor or commander, but he is referred to in the early records as " President of the Company's factories in the Island of Ceylon."

Raja Sinha did nothing towards the promised payment of the expenses which the Dutch had incurred in this warfare, and his attitudes towards his allies began to change.

Naturally, he suspected them of seeking to conquer the country, as the Portuguese had done, and the Portuguese themselves may also have encouraged his suspicions. He ceased to reply to Coster's letters, and Coster resolved that he would himself see the king and bring about an understanding. He reached Kandy on the 15th July, and for a whole month was detained there and subjected to indignities. Then seeing that nothing was to be gained by his visit, he left Kandy for Batticaloa. On the way, he was brutally murdered, with eight others of his company, on the 21st August 1640, at the village of Nilgala.

**Jan Thyszoon Payaart,** usually known as Jan Thysz, succeeded Coster as governor of Galle, and a new Portuguese captain-general, Dom Philippe Mascarenhas, arrived with large reinforcements from Goa. Negombo was retaken by the Portuguese on the 9th of November, and even in Galle the Hollanders found themselves hemmed in, and in danger of being overcome. Raja Sinha was giving them no help whatever, and he also kept back the cinnamon and other products which he had bound himself by treaty to give. The truth is evidently that the king was alarmed at the growing power of the Dutch, and suspected that they would behave towards him exactly as the Portuguese had done. He therefore regarded both the European nations as his foes, and took the part of one or the other according as it suited his plans, and he worked against them both impartially with an eye to his own advantage,

He did not, however, cease to ask the Hollanders in Batavia for assistance against the Portuguese.

In 1640 Portugal ceased to be subject to Spain, and became once more an independent kingdom. A truce for ten years was now agreed upon in Europe between Holland and Portugal, but this was not officially proclaimed in Ceylon till October 1642, and fighting went on in Ceylon as before, even after that date. In January 1644 the Dutch re-captured Negombo, but in November of the same year, an agreement was made at Goa between the Dutch and the Portuguese, by which the limits were defined of the territories to be occupied in Ceylon by the two nations; and there was to be peace between them for eight years. It was not to be expected that Raja Sinha could be pleased with these arrangements, and he naturally encouraged his subjects to harass and annoy the Dutch, particularly in the Seven Korales, a district which he greatly desired to keep under his own rule, but which the Dutch now possessed. He also intrigued with the Portuguese. All these circumstances led Thysz in May 1645 to declare war against the king. The Dutch troops were, however, overpowered by the Kandyans, and Thysz was recalled for his imprudence. He was replaced in April 1646 by **Joan Maatzuyker,** who tried to conciliate Raja Sinha, but in vain. He sent Adrian van der Stel to withdraw the Dutch garrison from the Seven Korales, but van der Stel was taken by surprise and killed with nearly all his men, and his head covered with a white cloth, was sent to the captain of the garrison. For three years there was continued misunderstanding, till in 1649 a new treaty was made, by which the Dutch lost their monopoly in cinnamon, and that meant losing half the value of their trade in that spice.

**Jacob van Kittensteyn** succeeded Maatzuyker in 1650, and was warned by him to observe "the necessity for a firm policy in dealing with the king," who, Maatzuyker added, was not to be trusted. The eight years truce came to an end in 1652, and the Dutch and the Portuguese were again at war. The whole country from Galle to Kalutara was occupied by the Dutch, who also planned attacks on Jaffna, Mannar, and Sabaragamuwa. Colombo too, on the capture of which Raja Sinha had set his heart, was to be taken, but this could not be done till more ships and men came from Batavia. When **Adriaan van der Meiden** succeeded as Dutch governor of Galle, in October 1653, he found continual fights going on in the low-country between the Hollanders and the Portuguese and the Sinhalese. The Portuguese had improved their position to such an extent that they were able to regain possession of Kalutara in 1654.

The year 1654 is noteworthy for the death of Vijayapāla, the prince of Uva, and Raja Sinha's step-brother. He had always been

---

A.D. 1642 Civil war begun in England.
,, 1649 Execution of Charles I.

loyal to his brother whom he assisted in his battles. But a quarrel began in 1645 through the king's treacherous murder of Portuguese prisoners to whom protection had been promised, and Vijayapāla went over to the Portuguese. Here he was treated with less respect than he thought was due to him, and his liberty was greatly restricted, for the Portuguese feared that the Dutch would use him for their purposes. He saw, however, that nothing could be gained by complaining, and he spent the remainder of his life in retirement and in the duties of religion. He was taken by the Portuguese to Goa, where he was baptized as a Christian, and where he afterwards died. The death of Vijayapāla removed an obstacle from Raja Sinha's path, for he was now free from rivals to the Kandyan throne, and so he no longer feared to meet the Portuguese when they marched into his dominions.

Preparations continued to be made for the siege of Colombo. **Gerard Hulft,** with a strong Dutch fleet, came from Batavia in September 1655 as commander-in-chief of both the land and sea forces, van der Meiden being thus set free to attend to the management of civil affairs. Hulft took Kalutara in October, and in April 1656 visited Raja Sinha, who honoured him with special marks of regard, and even of an affection which was apparently sincere. Returning to Colombo he resumed his direction of the preparations for taking that city. His camp was on the hill which now bears his name (*Hulfts-dorp*, Hulft's village); but coming down to inspect the works, he was killed near Kayman's Gate by a stray bullet from the Portuguese fort, on the 10th April 1656.

The siege of Colombo had been begun in October 1655, and an assault made by the Dutch in November of that year had been repulsed with great loss. But their final success was only delayed. The ships of the Hollanders threw shells into the town and easily beat down its walls of mud. All Portuguese vessels coming into or going out from the harbour were seized. By land the Dutch, (possibly assisted by Raja Sinha's forces, but that is by no means certain), harassed them and allowed no provisions to be taken to the besieged garrison. The Portuguese suffered severely from want of food. Even elephants, dogs, and other animals were eaten. The heat was unbearable. No rain fell during the siege, and it was difficult to walk in the street even with shoes on. In spite of all this the Portuguese displayed wonderful spirit and bravery; and when at last they found it was impossible to hold out any longer, they wished to place their women in a church, and setting it on fire, to die sword in hand; but this desperate scheme was opposed by their priests. It was not till the 7th May of the following year (1656) that a determined attack was made by the Hollanders on the bastion of Saint Joao, which was at length taken after three unsuccessful attempts. On the 12th May 1656, Antonio de Souza Coutinho, the Portuguese governor of Colombo, signed the terms by which the city was surrendered to the Dutch.

Raja Sinha now demanded that Colombo should be given up to him, for he expected that all fortresses taken by the Dutch should be placed in his hands. But to his surprise and anger the Dutch, who could not trust him, refused the demand, and in a battle fought soon afterwards the Kandyans were defeated. From this time there was continual war between Raja Sinha and the Dutch. The latter did not pay much attention at this time to the anger of the Kandyan king. They were busy with the Portuguese, and went on to the north to expel those Portuguese garrisons, which still held out. Mannar and Kayts were successively taken, and on the 22nd of June, 1658, Jaffna, the last stronghold of the Portuguese, was captured, and the garrison sent as prisoners of war to Batavia.

A few Portuguese, remained in the Kandyan country. Some of them were prisoners of war, and others had come there on Raja Sinha's invitation. They were subject to no restraint except that they could not leave the district where they were placed—at Vahakotté (near Matale), and elsewhere. Here they lived as subjects of Raja Sinha, but enjoying many privileges, especially one privilege which the Dutch had refused them—the liberty to practise their own religion. There are Roman Catholic families still to be found at Vahakotté, who are descended from these settlers.

CHAPTER XXXVI

## Robert Knox in Ceylon

LET us here leave for a moment the record of battles and sieges, and read the story of a remarkable Englishman who lived for twenty years a prisoner in the Kandyan country. One of the first Englishmen, though perhaps not the first, known to have visited Ceylon was Ralph Fitch, a merchant, who landed in Colombo on the 6th March, 1589, when the first Raja Sinha was king. He stayed no more than five days while his ship took in water and provisions. The first English ship to visit Ceylon was the "Edward Bonaventure," which anchored off Galle on the 3rd December, 1592. Neither did this ship stay here any length of time. But in 1660, Robert Knox came to Ceylon, where he remained a prisoner. On his escape he wrote a book, giving an account of what he had seen and suffered, and his *Historical Relation of the Island of Ceylon*, as he called it, is one of the most interesting and valuable books on Ceylon.* It was published in 1681.

The father of Robert Knox was the captain of the frigate "Ann," employed in the service of the English East India Company: for by the year 1600 the English people had, like the Dutch, formed a company to trade with India and the East. In November, 1659, the "Ann" was caught in a severe storm off the Coromandel coast, and took refuge in the bay

A.D. 1660. Charles II king of England.

* It has been suggested that this book was known to Defoe, who published his "Robinson Crusoe" in 1719.

of Kottiyar, near Trincomalee, in April 1660. Captain Knox, his son Robert, and some of the crew were invited by the Sinhalese to come on shore, and there they were surrounded and carried away to the interior. Captain Knox tried, however, to save his son and the ship, and obtained permission to send his son on board. Robert Knox went back to the ship and informed the sailors of what had happened. He added that his father ordered them to leave Ceylon at once, and then he nobly returned to share his father's captivity. He was only nineteen years old at the time.

After some time the prisoners were brought to Kandy, and placed in separate villages until Raja Sinha should be pleased to send for them; "yet God was so merciful," says Robert Knox, "thus not to suffer them to part my father and me." In February 1661 Captain Knox died of an ague and fever, which both he and his son caught in the unhealthy districts where they were forced to live. When Robert Knox recovered from his illness, he wandered in the Matale district attended only by a faithful Tamil servant. He was gradually allowed a little liberty, and the Sinhalese villagers began to treat him with respect. Sometimes, as his stock of money and provisions became smaller, he went fishing in the brooks, "as well as to help out a meal as for recreation." On one of these occasions, an old man who passed by asked the servant if Knox could read; for if so the old man had a book which he got when the Portuguese lost Colombo and he would sell it. Knox hearing this sent the boy to get the book, but was not much concerned about the matter as he thought it was a Portuguese book that the old man had found. The remainder of the story is best told by Knox himself : " The boy having formerly served the English knew the book; and as soon as he had got it in his hand came running with it, calling out to me, ' It is a Bible." It startled me to hear him mention the name of Bible, for I neither had one, nor scarcely could even think to see one, upon which I flung down my angle, and went to meet him. The first place the book opened in, after I took it in my hand, was the sixteenth chapter of the Acts ; and the first place my eye pitched on was the thirtieth and one-and-thirtieth verses, where the Jailor asked St. Paul, *What must I do be saved?* And he answered saying, *Believe on the Lord Jesus Christ and thou shalt be saved and thy house.*

" The sight of this book so rejoiced me and affrighted me together that I cannot say which passion was greater ; the joy for that I had got sight of a Bible, or the fear that I had not enough to buy it, having then but one pagoda [*8 shillings*] in the world ; which I willingly would have given for it had it not been for my boy who dissuaded me from giving so much ; alleging my necessity for money many other ways, and undertaking to procure the book for a far meaner price, provided I would seem to slight it in the sight of the old man. This counsel after I considered, I approved of ; my urgent necessities earnestly craving, and my ability being but very small to relieve the same; and however, I thought I could give my piece of gold at the last cast if other means should fail."

It is pleasing to add that the book was bought next day in exchange for a knitted cap that Knox's boy had made for him.

Knox was a very observant man, and he took careful note of the manners and customs of the Kandyans. He acquired a fair knowledge of the Sinhalese spoken language, and collected as much information as he could about the roads and passes, and in what places the king's guards were stationed throughout the kingdom. He thus found out that his only way of escape was by travelling northwards, and in 1679 he ventured out, and got safely away to Anuradhapura with another Englishman named Rutland. Anuradhapura, which at this time was in ruins and covered with jungle, was on the borders of Raja Sinha's territories; but the guards thought the Englishmen were ordinary traders and allowed them to pass through. After many dangers from elephants, bears, and wild buffaloes in the forests, from crocodiles in the rivers, and from Sinhalese villagers who might betray them if discovered, they reached Arippu on the west coast, which was held by the Dutch. Then they got to Mannar and at length they reached Colombo by sea. Here they were kindly received by the Dutch governor Ryclof van Goens the younger, who was greatly interested in the very useful information which Knox gave concerning the Kandyan country, and who afterwards took both the Englishmen with him to Batavia where they obtained a safe passage to Europe.

From the *Historical Relation* written by Knox we learn a great deal about the state of affairs in the Kandyan Kingdom. Raja Sinha II, whom Knox frequently met, is described as a well-made, corpulent, but muscular man, darker in colour than most of his countrymen, and with sharp active eyes always in motion. He bore his years well. Though between seventy and eighty years old at the time, he was not old either in appearance or in action. His style of dress was peculiar. On his head he wore a high-cornered cap with a feather standing upright before, and a long band hanging down his back after the Portuguese fashion. The body of his coat was one colour, while the sleeves were of another. He wore shoes and stockings and long breeches reaching down to the ankles. A sword with a golden hilt, and scabbard of beaten gold, hung at his side from a belt worn over his shoulder. In his hand he carried a small painted cane richly adorned with gold and precious stones.

The king's palace was, according to Knox, strongly guarded night and day, and even the nobles who kept watch at the doors were so placed that they could not communicate with one another—so little trust had the king in the faithfulness of his people. His own bodyguard consisted of a company of Kaffirs in whom he had more confidence. Nor need we wonder at the suspicions of the king. His cruelty was notorious. "He seems to be naturally disposed to cruelty," says Knox, "for he sheds a great deal of blood without giving any reason for it." There is a story told by Knox that on one occasion while swimming, he pretended to be in danger of drowning. Two young men bolder than the rest went to his rescue, and brought him to land. They were immediately after executed because they had presumed to lay hands on the king's person. They should, it seems, have prostrated themselves before him, so that he might lay his hands on them and in that way gain safety.

In public affairs the king is described as being cautious and cunning; not acting hastily, but considering each matter well, and lying or deceiving whenever he thought it advisable. He was intensely vain. "The Dutch knowing his proud spirit make their advantage of it by flattering him with their ambassadors, telling him that they are his Majesty's humble subjects and servants, and that it is out of their loyalty to him that they build forts, and keep watches round about his country, to prevent foreign nations and enemies from coming up into his Majesty's country. Thus by flattering him, and ascribing to him high and honourable titles, which are things he greatly delights in, sometimes they prevail to have the country they have invaded, and he to have the honour. Yet at other times, on better consideration, he will not be flattered, but falls upon them unawares and does them great damage."

The Kandyan kingdom ruled over by Raja Sinha included the whole mountain region and also a large part of the low-country. The mountain region was so difficult to reach from the low-country that there was no need for the king to maintain strong forts to secure it from invasion. Great, dense jungles, which the king would not allow to be cleared, divided one province from another; and the paths through these were so narrow that only one man at a time could go along them. At various points, gates of the thorn-bush were set, and guards strictly kept, so that no one could pass through unnoticed. Of two districts, Uda Nuwara, where Knox "lived last and had land," and Yatinuwara, in which was the "royal and chief city," Kandy, he makes special mention. They "have the pre-eminence of all the rest in the land. They are most populous and fruitful. The inhabitants thereof are the chief and principal men: insomuch that it is a usual saying among them, that if they want a king, they may take any man of either of these two counties, from the plough, and wash the dirt off him, and he by reason of his quality and descent is fit to be a king."

The chief cities after Kandy were Badulla, then the second city in the land; Alutnuwara, where king Raja Sinha was born; and Nilambe and Digligy (Hanguranketa), two favourite residences of the king. It is worth noting that at this time Anuradhapura and other places which says Knox, "do still retain the name of cities where kings have reigned," were already in ruins. Puttalam, in the low-country, supplied the king with salt and fish, but the Dutch had a fort in that city, which was doubtless a trouble to the king. However, he was able to obtain salt in large quantities from *lewayas* (small lakes of salt water) on the south-eastern coast, near Kataragama.

All the land in the country belonged to the king, who farmed it out in return, not for money, but for service. Those who held land from the king had to serve him as soldiers or as labourers; or they had to give him a portion of the goods they traded in; or to supply his house and table from what they grew on their land. No land-holder was free from paying duty of one kind or another to the king, except only priests, to whom land was given for the maintenance of their viharas and dagabas.

The chief officers next to the king were called *Adigars*. Of these there were two, and Knox describes them as "chief justices," for people could appeal to the adigars if they were not satisfied with the decisions of their provincial rulers. Next to the adigars were the *Disavas,* who were governors of provinces; but all governors of provinces were not disavas. After them came the *Ratemahatmayas* and *Vidanes*, or head of districts. All these officers were responsible that order was kept in their divisions, that the king's taxes and rents were duly paid, and that soldiers were provided when the king required them. But, unfortunately, bribery prevailed among the king's officers to so considerable an extent that Knox reports this as a common saying : " He that has money to fee the judge need not fear nor care whether his cause be right or not."

It is interesting to note the existence in Knox's time of *Gansabhawas*, or village councils. " For the hearing complaints and doing justice among neighbours, here are country courts of judicature, consisting of these officers [the king's], together with the headmen of the places and towns, where the courts are kept ; and these are called Gom sabbi, as much as to say, Town consultations.

The principal occupation of the people was the cultivation of rice, which was the chief food of the country. Their houses were small and low, with thatched roofs and walls. No tiles were allowed, nor lime to whiten the walls. Most houses consisted of only one room, few of more than two rooms. No animal was killed or eaten for food.

Of learning the people had but little, and there were no schools ; nor was it considered a shame to be wanting in education. But the Sinhalese were skilful in the carving of wood and in metal-work, and it is noteworthy that the art of extracting iron from the ore was known to them and practised by them in the time of Knox.

The Kandyans who lived in the mountain regions were more warlike than the dwellers in the low-country ; but they could never be relied on. Of all vices they were said to be least given to stealing.

The general decay of Buddhism in Ceylon is mentioned by Knox. The king himself cared little for any religion, but Christians and Muhammadans and Buddhists were equally allowed to worship in their own ways. Christians were indeed regarded with much respect as being more trustworthy than others. Nor shall we wonder at this when we remember that the king's mother, as Knox points out, was a baptized Christian, no other than Dona Catharina whom Senerat married.

## CHAPTER XXXVII.

# Beginnings of Dutch Rule

IT must be kept in mind that, when the Portuguese forts had been taken, the Dutch did not possess the whole island ; for, besides controlling certain parts of the north-west and south east coasts, Raja Sinha II was still king of the Kandyan country, the natural strength of which, with its high hills, its dangerous passes and its dense, pathless forests, made invasion difficult, and a permanent occupation impossible, unless large numbers of European soldiers were employed for the purpose. But nearly all the coast and especially the west coast, was gradually occupied by the Dutch, in the same way as it was previously held by the Portuguese. It was here that the cinnamon grew, and that was the article of trade which the Dutch valued most

A.D. 1665. The Plague of London ; Charles II.

So long as their trade was safe from foreign invaders the Dutch did not trouble about Kandy. To secure that trade they humoured Raja Sinha, but at the same time took care to protect themselves from his constant attacks.

They did all they could to strengthen their position in Ceylon. They were soon strong enough to forbid devil worship and idolatrous ceremonies among the Sinhalese Christians, as well as, in the early days of their rule, the religious ceremonies of the Roman Catholics, whose priests they regarded as Portuguese spies. From Matara to Jaffna the towns of the western coast were strongly fortified and provisioned lest at any time they should be besieged by the Kandyan king ; and trade was carried on with great vigour. Cinnamon was the chief export, and next to cinnamon in importance came elephants, arecanuts, pepper, cardamoms, and arrack. As traders, the great rivals of the Dutch were the Moors, whom the former tried by harsh measures to suppress. They were scarcely permitted in the island; and when permitted, had to pay heavy and humiliating taxes and to suffer personal hardships ; but no efforts of the Dutch could crush the trade carried on by the Moors.

The rule of the Dutch in this island, has been divided into definite periods.* In the

* R. G. Anthonisz, Introduction to *Memoir of Hendrick Becker*. The writings of Mr. Anthonisz, and the translations of the *Memoirs* of Dutch Governors by Mrs. S. Anthonisz, are of the first importance, and indispensable to students of the Dutch rule in Ceylon. See also *The Dutch in Ceylon*, Vol. I. by R. G. Anthonisz (1929) for a trustworthy summary of the Dutch period.

first period (down to 1697) the Dutch had to fight for the establishment of their authority in the districts which they had won from the Portuguese, and which therefore they were not prepared to surrender to the king of Kandy. The prominent governors of this period were Joan Maatzuyker, Adriaan van der Meiden, the two van Goens (father and son), Lourens Pyl, and Thomas van Rhee. The second period (1697)—1707), during which Gerrit de Heere and Cornelis Joan Simons were governors, was marked by a milder policy. Efforts were made to conciliate the Sinhalese and Tamils, and to win their confidence. Economy was followed in government methods, even when it meant the loss of "good and profitable territory." For, as we might expect from the general character of the times, not in Ceylon only, and not among the native peoples only, the trust placed in subordinate officials was abused, and the Dutch Company's lands and revenues were shamefully mishandled. Hendrick Becker founder of the leper asylum at Hendela, began a third period (1707—1736), which was one of reform. In these reforms he was eminently successful, and his relations with the Kandyan king of his time were also friendly. He was succeeded by Isaac Augustyn Rumpf, another wise and kindly ruler; but the tyranny of Petrus Vuyst belongs also to this period. In July 1736 Baron van Imhoff began a fourth period of Dutch rule.

---

A.D. 1670. Secret Treaty of Dover, Charles II.
,, 1672. William of Orange Stadtholder of Holland.
,, 1685. Edict of Nantes revoked.

CHAPTER XXXVIII

# The First Dutch Period

AFTER the conquest of Jaffna, van der Meiden transferred the Dutch head-quarters from Galle to Colombo. He tried to bring about an understanding with Raja Sinha, who was bitterly disappointed that Colombo was not given into his hands; but the king's only reply to van der Meiden's letters was to do as much damage as he could in the territory held by the Dutch. The ambassadors sent to him by the Dutch were detained in Kandy, without any reason being given, or any reply returned to the requests that they should be sent back. Knox tells us that when he escaped from his captivity in 1679 there were from fifty to sixty Hollanders in the Kandyan kingdom, "some whereof are ambassadors, some prisoners of war, some runaways and malefactors that have escaped the hand of justice and got away from the Dutch quarters. There were also several English, Portuguese, and French captives. The Dutch complained that Raja Sinha behaved badly towards them and could not be trusted to keep his word, but we must not lose sight of the fact that the king was fighting to maintain the territory which he claimed as belonging to him and his people, and which he saw was gradually becoming the possession of foreign powers.

In 1659 Kalpitiya was taken by the Dutch, and fortified, because Raja Sinha's troops had made an attack on it; but it was given back to the king in 1661, though Kalpitiya was a favourable place for the smuggling of cinnamon by the Sinhalese. In 1663, **Rycklof van Goens,** a statesman of exceptional ability, was appointed governor of Colombo, and he held this office practically till 1675, when he was succeeded by his son, who bore the same name. At the end of 1663, Van Goens the elder went to Batavia; then **Jacob Hustaart** was governor for one year; after which Roothaes, the Dutch commandeur of Galle, administered the government till van Goens returned. It was during Hustaart's rule, in 1664, that Sir Edward Winter, British Agent at Madras, sent a mission to Raja Sinha asking for the release of the English prisoners in Kandy. The mission appears not to have been limited to this benevolent purpose. Winter was anxious also to secure the establishment of a factory in Ceylon for the English to obtain cinnamon and thus gain a footing in the island. In Europe, at this time, there was increasing unfriendliness between the Dutch and the English, and war actually broke out between the two nations in February 1665. But Winter's mission was unsuccessful in both its objects. Neither were the prisoners released, nor did the English gain any foothold in the island.

Raja Sinha had his own troubles in Kandy, which drove him to seek the assistance of the Dutch. His cruelty to his own subjects became so unbearable that in December 1664 the Kandyans rose in revolt and forced him to flee to the mountains of Hanguranketa for safety.

Then they proclaimed his young son his successor. But the boy, who was only twelve years old, refused to join the rebels and returned to his father. Thus the revolt broke down, and the conspirators dispersed. Raja Sinha returned in triumph, put to death several chiefs who were suspected of a share in the conspiracy, and, to prevent any similar rising in future, caused his own son to be poisoned.

Meanwhile, van Goens the elder, who had gone to Batavia, returned to Ceylon with instructions to build a fort at Trincomalee and to prevent the open ports of Kalpitiya, Batticaloa, and Kottiyar, from being used by the English to the disadvantage of the Dutch. These instructions were carried out, and by the year 1668 the ports were permanently occupied. They were re-opened to Indian traders the next year for some months, for Raja Sinha's benefit, but closed again, as there was a violent conflict between the Kandyans and the lowlanders.

In 1672 war broke out in Europe between the Dutch and the French, and a French fleet of fourteen ships entered Trincomalee Bay, after being repulsed at Galle. Raja Sinha was delighted to receive the offers of assistance made by the French admiral de La Haye, and the latter was allowed to build a fort in the bay, probably at Kottiyar. But as not enough food could be found in the district for so large a force, de La Haye, leaving some of his men to keep the fort, went to India, promising to return. On his way, however, he was met by van Goens, who captured four of his ships, and scattered the rest of his fleet. Raja Sinha was greatly vexed that de La Haye did not return to fulfil his promises.

During the rule of **Ryclof van Goens** junior (1675-1680), there was still trouble Raja Sinha demanded the restoration of certain lands, and these the Dutch governor was prepared to give over, but the king sent no reply to the governor's letters. The next governor, **Lourens Pyl,** (1680-1692), was engaged all the time he was in Ceylon in trying to arrange a treaty with the Kandyans, but nothing came of the negotiations.

After a long and exciting reign, during which he struggled both to protect the island from foreign intrusion and to secure his authority over his own subjects, Raja Sinha died on the 6th December 1687. He was succeeded by his son *Mahastane*, who took the title of **Vimala Dharma II** (1687-1707) and who, following his father's advice, lived peaceably with the Dutch during the twenty years of his reign. Indeed, the Dutch consented to lend him ships to bring over Buddhist priests from Arakan. Roman Catholics too were benefited in this reign—though this happened in spite of the Dutch prohibitions—by the arrival from Goa of Joseph Vaz, an Indian, and a brave and saintly Catholic priest. Father Vaz came in disguise to Jaffna in 1687, and travelled in the north of Ceylon, ministering to the Tamil Roman Catholics, who hid him from the Dutch. He visited Puttalam, and came to Kandy in 1692. Here he was at first imprisoned by

Vimala Dharma, who suspected him to be a spy. After two years he was set free, and his first work was to build a church on the border of the lake which was then at Bogambara. He afterwards visited several places in Ceylon, returning in the end to Kandy. In 1697 an epidemic of small-pox broke out in Kandy and the neighbouring district, and a large number of people perished. The sick were neglected and allowed to die in the jungles. Those who had not caught the disease fled in terror to escape it. Father Vaz and his nephew, who was also a priest, worked hard and unselfishly for the sick, whom they nursed and fed, assisted greatly by liberal contributions of money from the Roman Catholics in Colombo. The result was that many Sinhalese, rightly admiring such generous conduct, sought Christian baptism. In January 1711, the devoted Father Vaz died at Kandy, and was buried at Bogambara in the church which he had built there.

## CHAPTER XXXIX.

## The Dutch Government of Ceylon

GOVERNOR Pyl discovered that the new king Vimala Dharma's advisers were resolved on preventing peace with the Dutch; and it may well be believed that the king himself was a far more capable and shrewd ruler than the Dutch supposed him to be. But, weary of negotiations, Pyl at length determined to claim the Dutch possessions in Ceylon, not by treaty, or as security for the debts due by the king, but by right of conquest from the Portuguese. It was urged that the Kandyan king was not sovereign over the whole island, or over the low-country, but only over the Kandyan territories, since in 1580 Dharmapala had by will transferred the sovereignty of the island to the king of Portugal.

It will help us to get now some idea of the way in which the Dutch carried on their government in Ceylon. They had much the same system in all their settlements, and their system was found so admirably suited for all necessary purposes that the English, both in England and in India, held it up as a model for their own settlers in India to copy.

The headquarters of the Dutch in all the East was at Batavia in Java, and this town is still the capital and chief port of the Dutch East Indies. It was the Government of Batavia who appointed governors to their Eastern possessions, to whom all reports were sent, and by whom important orders were issued. The full title of the highest Dutch authority in this island was "Governor and Director of the Island of Ceylon and its Dependencies,"—these dependencies including the southern coast of India. The governor was assisted by a Council of not more than ten of the highest officials. Colombo was styled a *Disavony*, and its chief a *Disava*, and there were two *Commandements*, Jaffna and Galle, ruled by *Commandeurs*, the commandeur of Jaffna being higher in rank. The smaller stations of Mannar, Trincomalee, Batticaloa, Negombo, Kalutara, and Kalpitiya, were under *Opperhoofds* (Presidents), while Matara was under the Galle commandeur, though it was sometimes referred to as a separate disavony.

The Dutch rule over Ceylon was mainly for commercial purposes, though they actually gave much more attention to the administration of the country than to its commerce. The Portuguese rule was military in character, and for that reason differed greatly from the Dutch. It is not surprising, therefore, that the titles of the Dutch officials were connected with commerce. The highest class of official was the *Opper-koopman* (Upper Merchant). Then came the *Koopman* (merchant), the *Onder-koopman* (Under Merchant), the *Boek-houder* (Book-keeper), and the *Adsistent* (Assistant). The cadets were styled *Aanquelingen* (apprentices), or *Zoldaat by de pen* (soldier-clerk), or simply *Zoldaat.*

The revenue was obtained chiefly from the export of cinnamon, " the bride round whom they all dance in Ceylon." Other sources of revenue were arecanuts, which were taken in exchange for cotton goods ; elephants, for which buyers could not always be found ; and salt, " which in all countries is considered the property of the lord of the land." Something was got from the occasional pearl fisheries near Mannar. Then there were taxes,—tithes on rice lands, rents and leases of land, tolls, etc. Careful descriptions of lands and their owners were kept in *Thombus* or registers, the word as well as the system being derived from the Portuguese.

In the Public Service there were Military, Naval, Artisan (Public Works), and Ecclesiastical Departments. The last named of these was not the least important. Those clergymen who were ordained in Holland (some of them were natives of Ceylon) were called *Predikants;* and those who were ordained in Ceylon were called *Proponents,* and had less authority. There were lesser clergy, much like our present day "catechists," whose chief business it was to visit the hospitals, teach orphan children, and hold religious meetings during the week. There were many schools, all controlled by School Commissions, or Boards, the chief one being at Colombo, while there were others at Jaffna and Galle. These Commissions had control not only over schools but also over baptisms and marriages among Sinhalese and Tamil Christians. "The educational establishment of the Dutch was one of their greatest contributions to the progress of this Island. The dominions of the Company were carefully mapped out into school circles and schools at which free Vernacular education was provided under a scheme of compulsory attendance."*

Much care was taken that justice was justly administered. The Supreme Court was called the *Raad van Justitie* (Court of Justice), and next to it came the *Landraads* (somewhat like our District Courts), and the *Civiel Raads*, or Courts of Small Causes.

The European community in Ceylon was known as the *Hollandsche Natie* (the Dutch

---

* Mr. E. H. van der Wall. 1932.

Nation, or Hollanders), and included not only those of Dutch origin, but also a small number of Europeans from Germany, France, Sweden, the British Isles, and other countries, who all came as naturalized Dutch subjects, and spoke the Dutch language. The government officials were known as "Company's Servants," and the non-officials as *Burgers*, or *Vryburgers* (Free Burghers). From these Burghers were appointed officers for the *Burgery*, an armed force, composed mainly of *Tupasses*, people of mixed Portuguese descent. When the rule of the Company ceased, in 1796, there could be no "Company's Servants," and all the Dutch people in Ceylon became Burghers.

A study of these matters will shew how many of our modern political and social institutions in Ceylon can be traced back to the Dutch and their rule in this island.

CHAPTER XL

## Conciliation and Economy

WITH governor Pyl and his successor **Thomas van Rhee** (1692-1697), ended the period of uncertainty and of conquest. In the rule of the next two Dutch governors, **Gerrit de Heere** (1697-1702) and **Cornelis Joan Simons** (1703-1707), a new spirit is apparent. "Kindness is advocated, with a view to gain the affection and goodwill of the natives. Expenses are to be cut down as much as possible, in order to make ends meet." On the whole, it may be said that friendliness prevailed between the

Dutch and the Kandyans, and in the lowcountry much was done for the good of the people. It was governor Simons who had a summary made of the Tamil code of laws called the *Thessawalami*. and had it translated into Dutch. It was he also who began building the leper asylum at Hendela, which has since been maintained by the British.

The successor of Vimala Dharma II was his son **Narendra Sinha** (1707-1739), who is known also as *Kundasale Raja,* from the village of that name which he founded four miles from Kandy. A rebellion of his chiefs occurred in his reign, but this was put down. Buddhism made some advance. The king visited Mahiyangana, Anuradhapura, and other places sacred to Buddhists, holding great feasts at each of these places. Kandy, the capital, was greatly improved, the Dalada Maligawa being rebuilt and richly ornamented, while a wall was built round the smaller religious buildings. Learning was encouraged, and several religious and medical works were composed in Sinhalese or translated into that language. The king was, however, unfriendly to the Roman Catholics whose churches he ordered to be destroyed.

Narendra Sinha was the last of the Sinhalese race of kings. He married a princess of Madura, but she bore him no children. On her death in 1721, **Isaac Rumpf**, the Dutch governor of Colombo, sent an ambassador to

---

| | | |
|---|---|---|
| A.D. | 1689. | Declaration of Right. |
| „ | 1707. | Union of England and Scotland. |
| „ | 1713. | Treaty of Utrecht. |
| „ | 1714. | George I. King of England. |

the king to offer him the sympathies of the Dutch Company, Cornelius Takel was the ambassador appointed, and the king was greatly flattered when the Dutchman said that he had been sent to condole with his Majesty on the death of his "high-born, excellent, and accomplished Queen."

Rumpf was one of the Dutch governors who tried to do justice to the people placed under his rule. The officers of the Dutch Company received very small salaries; but on the other hand, they were allowed certain fees, the privilege of private trade, and a few more concessions. By these means, and by lending out money on high interest, many of the Dutch officials become rich, while the Company itself suffered by being thus deprived of much of its proper revenue. There was a good deal of bribery, as there always has been, before and since, and money was extorted from the people whenever possible. Rumpf tried to mend matters, but he could do very little, and towards the end of his rule the cinnamon peelers created a disturbance, which was speedily put down.

In 1726 **Petrus Vuyst** became governor of Colombo. He was a cruel and overbearing ruler. It is said that when he landed in Ceylon he put a blind over his right eye, declaring that his left eye alone was sufficient to govern so small and insignificant a country. Every official whom he suspected of opposition to his will was forced to submit to his cruelty. Many soldiers were tortured and forced to say

---

A.D. 1727 George II. King of England.

that they had committed crimes which they had not even thought of committing. Vuyst actually tried to establish himself in Ceylon as an independent sovereign. But his people had had enough of him. They complained to the governor of Batavia (for Ceylon was under the control of the Dutch Council there), and so great was the terror that Vuyst had inspired, that the complaint was sent away secretly, being stitched into the sole of the messenger's shoe. The Council at Batavia immediately recalled Vuyst (1729 A.D.), and after an enquiry was held, he was beheaded.

**Stephanus Versluys,** the next governor (1729—1732), was very little better. His greed of gain was such that he nearly caused a famine by raising the price of rice to an extent quite beyond the means of ordinary people. After he left Ceylon, two Dutch governors ruled in succession, about whom there is little to be said. In 1736 **Baron van Imhoff** arrived.

Van Imhoff was a ruler of a different stamp. He did not agree with those who thought that if the natives of Ceylon were well treated the Company's revenues would suffer. He found that the Company was being ruined by the thoughtless way in which the Dutch officials behaved, and by the oppressive measures they forced on the people. He found that accounts were carelessly kept in the government offices, and that too many petty officers were employed. The offices swarmed

---

A.D. 1730. The Wesleys at Oxford.

with useless clerks who were kept there simply to please the friends of those in power, and whose cost made it even necessary to reduce the number of soldiers and sailors in Ceylon. Van Imhoff made many useful reforms in these matters, and took care that the taxes due to the Company were not oppressively collected. To increase the public revenue he allowed private persons to trade freely with Indian ports, subject to taxes on all imports and exports. This was the first time such taxes were collected in Ceylon. Agriculture was encouraged, and the land on the south-western coast was planted with coconut palms. Justice was impartially administered, and an effort was made to prevent unnecessary litigation. Education was attended to, and a printing-press, the first in Ceylon, was set up in 1737 to print portions of the Bible and other books for the religious wants of the people.

## CHAPTER XLI

## The Dutch take Kandy

NARENDRA SINHA was succeeded in 1739 by his queen's brother **Sri Vijaya Raja Sinha**. The new king had come from Madura, and was a Hindu; but after his accession to the throne he declared himself a Buddhist, and did a great deal to promote Buddhism during his short reign of eight years. The order of priests had again become extinct, and again foreign priests were invited over from Pegu, Arakan, and Siam; but of the results of this invitation

---

A.D. 1740 War between Frederick the Great and Maria Theresa.
A.D. 1748 Treaty of Aix-la-Chapelle.

we know very little for certain. Either no priests at all came to Ceylon, or too few to be of much use in restoring the extinct order. There is also some mention made of an attack by the Kandyans on the Portuguese who lived in various parts of the country; and this must mean that a persecution of the Roman Catholics took place, for there were now no Portuguese armies or possessions in Ceylon against whom there could be war.

**Kirti Sri Raja Sinha** (1747—1780) was the next king. He also was from Madura and was Sri Vijaya's brother-in-law. The application to Siam for priests was renewed in 1750, for when Kirti Siri began his reign there was, we are told, " not even one priest in this beautiful island of Lanka ;" but this statement cannot be literally correct, for we are shortly after told that while there were some priests who respected the laws of Buddhism, there were "others who made light of sin, and led sinful and wicked lives, maintaining families, and devoting themselves to worldly business;" who " busied themselves with the practice of astrology and medicine and other callings that were not proper for priests." Buddhism was, in fact fallen and neglected, and Kirti Sri resolved to restore it to its ancient influence. The king of Siam was astonished to hear of the continued

---

A.D. 1756. Seven Years' War begun.
,, ,, The Black Hole of Calcutta,
,, 1759. Quebec taken by the English.
,, 1760. George III. king of England.

decay of Buddhism in Ceylon, and immediately sent priests and copies of the Buddhist writings. The mission landed at Trincomalee and was met on its approach to Kandy by king Kirti Siri himself who went forth in royal state at the head of his army.

The order of priests being now restored, other measures were taken to revive Buddhism. Pilgrimages were again made to the principal shrines, festivals were observed, offerings were liberally bestowed, and a number of viharas were built or repaired. In addition to these things, the king ordered the tooth relic of the Buddha to be carried at the head of the procession of elephants and dancers which the Hindus were accustomed to hold annually. This was the beginning of the Perahera procession as it is now observed in Kandy.

While some show of returning prosperity was evident in the Kandyan kingdom, the Sinhalese on the west coast were growing more and more discontented with their Dutch rulers. Baron van Imhoff's wise counsels were disregarded by his successors, and oppressive measures were enforced on the Sinhalese. An exception may be found in **Joan Gideon Loten** (1752-1757) at least, who was "a great lover of birds," and did much for the study of natural history in Ceylon. When he retired, he lived in England and was elected a Fellow of the Royal Society. But in 1760, when **Jan Schreuder** was governor of Colombo, the Sinhalese in the low-country rebelled against the tyranny to which they were subjected, and were readily helped by the Kandyans. At first the Sinhalese gained some slight advantage over the Dutch, but in 1762 Schreuder was recalled, and **Baron van Eck** was appointed governor. Van Eck invaded Kandy in 1765, and the Dutch held the place for about nine months. Van Eck returned to Colombo in a couple of months, appointing Martin Rein commandeur of Kandy. Here the Dutch suffered severely from famine, from sickness, and from the occasional attacks of the enemy. Rein died of fever soon after his arrival, and, after valiantly holding out against vast numbers of the Kandyans, the remainder of the army decided to give up the place and retire to Colombo, where they arrived in September 1765. The sudden death of van Eck in the same year, 1765, of fever brought on by "long marches through unhealthy districts," threw Dutch affairs in Ceylon into great confusion; but governor **Iman Willem Falck** (1765—1785) put an end to the war with Kandy by a treaty made with Kirti Sri on the 14th February, 1766. This treaty was greatly in favour of the Dutch, for it gave them absolute possession of not only those portions of the coast which they held before the war, but of the whole sea-coast round the island. The Dutch now had three times as much territory as they had before, and they held it with more dignity to themselves; for they were acknowledged to be lawful and independent rulers of it, and not even in name subject

---

A.D. 1763. Treaty of Paris.

" 1769. "The Letters of Junius."

as formerly, to the king of Kandy. Kirti Sri was, on the other hand, recognized as king of the remaining districts of the Island, but he was not permitted to make any treaty with other European powers than the Dutch. Complete freedom of trade was established between the Kandyans and the native subjects of the Dutch; but all cinnamon, ivory, pepper, cardamoms, coffee, arecanuts, and wax were to be sold at fixed rates, and to the Dutch Company alone.

Governor Falck thought it inadvisable to occupy the Kandyan kingdom; he saw it would require more money and soldiers than the Company could afford. Besides, there was no need for taking it, since the productions of the kingdom could be bought from the Kandyans at less cost than if the Dutch were in possession.

After peace was made, Falck tried to improve the state of affairs in his government. He encouraged agriculture, and planted so much cinnamon in the low-country districts that he hardly needed any from the Kandyans. He enforced proper methods in the collecting and spending of the revenues of the Company. He was careful not to interfere too much with the customs of the Sinhalese under his government, and so prevented any discontent on their part. After a long and successful rule of twenty years, Falck died in Colombo in 1785, and was succeeded by **William Jacob van de Graaff.**

## CHAPTER XLII

# The End of Dutch Rule

MEANWHILE the English began to consider whether it would not be of advantage to them to take Ceylon for themselves. We have seen that in 1664 an English ambassador visited Raja Sinha II. at Kandy. For a hundred years after that event we read of no further official visit to Ceylon from the English. They had quite enough to do in India, where, by 1763, they had conquered a large part of the country, including Bengal, Bombay, and Madras. They had broken the power of the French in India, and had established themselves there as the principal European power in the country. The Dutch were still their greatest rivals in the trade of the East, and it was therefore thought advisable to take Ceylon, both because that would be a serious blow to the Dutch trade, and because Ceylon was so situated in the Indian Ocean that its possession would be most useful in time of war.

In 1762, the governor of Madras sent Mr. John Pybus to Kirti Sri to offer him the help of the English East India company in his war against the Dutch. Kirti Sri was much pleased, and readily consented to a treaty of alliance; but the English took no further steps in the

---

A.D. 1775. Battle of Bunker's Hill.

„ 1776. Declaration of Independence by the United States.

„ „ Lord George Gordon Riots.

matter. In 1782 England and Holland were at war, and a British force sent by the governor of Madras captured Trincomalee from the Dutch on the 11th January. Early in February Mr. Hugh Boyd was despatched from Madras to ask the Kandyan king for assistance against the Dutch. It was a month before Boyd reached Kandy, for there were scarcely any paths through the dense jungles, and he was delayed a fortnight before he could get a definite answer from the king.

Kirti Sri had died in 1780, and the king who received Boyd was his brother **Rajadhi Raja Sinha** (1780—1798). He had not forgotten the previous English Mission of 1762, and reminded Boyd of it when the latter proposed a treaty. The Kandyan king had then readily accepted the proposals of the English, but the latter had omitted to do anything more in the matter till the present time, when they found themselves at war with the Dutch. It seemed to the king that the English were acting selfishly in the matter, and not, as they professed, from any desire to help the Kandyans. The king therefore declined to make any treaty except directly with the king of Great Britain. With this answer Boyd had to be satisfied ; but when he returned to Trincomalee after his long absence, he found that fort in the possession of the French, for at this time England was at war with France and Spain as well as with

---

A.D. 1786. Impeachment of Warren Hastings
,, 1789. Storming of the Bastille. French Revolution.
,, 1798. War against France.

Holland. During Boyd's absence in Kandy the French admiral Suffrein had surprised the garrison and taken the fort, 31st August, 1782.

Trincomalee remained in the possession of the French till the beginning of the following year, when it was restored to the Dutch, and the English left Ceylon alone till 1795 A. D. During van de Graaff's rule of eight years he had tried to make some reduction in the heavy cost of Ceylon to his Government. On this account he sent away several regiments of European troops. He will be remembered as the first to introduce paper money into the island. In 1793 **John Gerrard van Angelbeek** was appointed governor, and two years later war broke out again between England and Holland, since England was at war with France, and Holland had been forced into an alliance with France.

Stirring events had taken place in Europe. In 1789 the people of France rose against the tyranny of their rulers and set up a government of their own. This led to war with other countries in Europe, and in 1793 France, declared war against both England and her ally Holland. Holland was overrun by French troops, its Stadtholder (king) William was compelled to flee to England, and a republican government (the "Batavian Republic") was formed which was to be in alliance with France. The Dutch people were divided in opinion about this matter, some being for the French, and others for the Stadtholder; but the alliance with France brought about important results in regard to the Dutch colonies in Asia and elsewhere.

The British had now an opportunity of taking Ceylon, and on the 1st August 1795 a strong British force arrived at Trincomalee with a letter from the Stadtholder (who was in England) directing the Dutch in Ceylon to admit the British troops in order that the Dutch possessions should not fall into the hands of the French. While the matter was being discussed, governor van Angelbeek and his council in Colombo were informed of the change of government in Holland, and they decided that they were bound to obey the orders of the new republic, and to defend their possessions against the British. But the Dutch forces in Ceylon were small, and to add to their difficulties, the de Meuron regiment, which they employed, had been induced to transfer its services to the British. Thus they were in no condition to offer any real resistance to the greatly superior British military and naval forces. They were not supported from Holland, and in Ceylon, as in Holland, there was a division of opinion as to whether the Stadtholder or the republic was to be obeyed.

Trincomalee was taken by the British at the end of August 1795, and there was very little fighting after that. Jaffna surrendered at the first summons in September; and on the 16th February, 1796, Colombo was surrendered without a blow being struck in its defence. Shortly before this, van Angelbeek had signed an agreement by which Galle and the other possessions of the Dutch were ceded to the English, who now took the place that the Portuguese first, and then the

Dutch, had occupied in Ceylon. Many of the Dutch "Company's Servants" and Burghers were at their own choice conveyed to Batavia. Others (including van Angelbeek who died in Colombo in 1799) preferred to remain in Ceylon, where they had married or acquired property; some of them afterwards took service under the British.

The Peace of Amiens in 1802 brought to an end the war between England and France, and it was then agreed that Ceylon should be a British possession.

CHAPTER XLIII

## Results of Dutch and Portuguese Rule.

WE may now review the Portuguese and Dutch periods of rule in Ceylon, and examine what was gained or lost to Ceylon by the rule of these nations. We shall try to see how each nation made use of its power, and what traces each has left of its former presence and authority.

The Portuguese held Ceylon—that is, the coast provinces of Ceylon—for one hundred and thirty-four years (1506—1640 A.D.), while the Dutch held it for one hundred and fifty-six years (1640—1796 A.D.) Both nations, therefore, were in possession for nearly the same length of time. They have both disappeared as governing powers. What has each nation left behind to shew that it once existed and governed in this island?

The Portuguese have, first of all, left their RELIGION. They were Christians of the

Roman Catholic branch of the Christian Church, while the Dutch were Protestant Christians – differing from the Roman Catholics in many important matters. In all the conquests the Portuguese made, their object was not only to acquire fresh territory but also to make new converts to their faith. They would allow no other religion to exist where they were rulers. They were ready to help the native princes, but they made it a condition that the native princes must first be baptized and received into the Roman Catholic Church. It is quite true that the Portuguese did not always practise the gentleness and charity which their religion taught. They were often cruel, and thought little of what was due by them to the peoples whose territories they invaded and whose freedom they took away. But people everywhere thought differently in those times from the way in which they think now about the rights of others than themselves. The extension of their religion was nevertheless one of the principal aims of the Portuguese. They were the first to preach Christianity in Ceylon to the masses of the people. Their missionaries came in large numbers. These missionaries preached and taught unceasingly, protected their converts, and braved danger and death for their sakes. The work they did then is still going on. Even at the present day there are more Roman Catholic Christians in Ceylon than all other Christians put together.

The Dutch were as anxious to convert the natives of the Island to Christianity. They did not by any means neglect this duty, for they opened schools ; translated into Sinhalese and Tamil, and printed, a great many portions of the Bible ; and they appointed missionaries to preach the Gospel in the principal towns. The ruins of old Dutch churches are still to be found in every part of the low-country. The religious wants of their own community were not overlooked in making these provisions for the other races. At first they thought to make as much money as they could by trade. It was for that reason they valued Ceylon. It was for that reason some of them patiently endured or ignored the slights of the Kandyan kings. They disliked and distrusted the Roman Catholics, but they thought it would be wrong to make no effort to teach the Christian religion, and the Dutch did very much in their own way to make converts. That laws were passed forbidding natives to hold office under Government unless they had first been admitted by baptism into the Dutch Protestant Church, has been asserted, but never proved. Still numbers of people became Christians in name only, while at heart they remained Buddhists or Hindus ; such things happen everywhere, even in our own times ; and when the Dutch occupation ceased, those who had been nominally converted at once gave up their profession of Christianity. This was not the case with the great majority of Roman Catholics, who adhered to their creed after the Portuguese had left, and in spite of persecution at the hands of the Dutch and of their own countrymen. Dutch Protestantism is now represented by the Dutch congregations in Colombo, Galle, and Matara, and by the great church at Wolvendaal, the building of which was begun in 1749, when van Gollenesse was governor, and completed in 1757.

The Portuguese left behind their LANGUAGE also. The Dutch did all they could at the beginning of their rule to put an end to the use of the Portuguese language in Ceylon and to extend their own; but very soon after they had settled down, they printed books in Portuguese for schools and religious purposes. When the English took over the country the Dutch language gradually fell into disuse, and there are few now in Ceylon who know Dutch. Few speak it. Yet many Dutch words (like the Sinhalese for *potato, hair-pin*, *office-room)* have been taken into the Sinhalese language. But the Portuguese language still survives, though in a corrupt form. It used to be spoken and written till lately by some even of the descendants of the Dutch. Books have been printed in that language. Portuguese words have been freely adopted into Sinhalese (like the words for *almirah*, *shoe*, *lady)* and into English. Thousands of Sinhalese people bear Portuguese names.

Many reasons may, of course, be given for the prevalence of the Portuguese language over the Dutch. The Portuguese came before the Dutch, and the latter found on their arrival that the Sinhalese were already acquainted with a language by means of which the Dutch could converse with them. Then, the Portuguese language is less harsh in sound, and easier of pronunciation than the Dutch. But whatever the explanation may be, it is noteworthy that the Portuguese language remains to this day in Ceylon, while the Dutch survives only in old official documents, and in certain words adopted by the Sinhalese.

But the Dutch are not without memorials of their own in Ceylon. They have left us their system of Law, It is the old Law of the Romans altered and adapted by the Dutch, and therefore called the *Roman-Dutch Law*. To a very great extent that law is recognised and followed by courts of justice in Ceylon at the present day ; but that is not the full measure of its influence. It was of great benefit, before the English came, in improving the social and moral condition of the Sinhalese and Tamils. The Dutch interfered very little with the customs of the people, except in so far as they were contrary to civilized customs. But they did make important alterations in the laws regulating marriage and the succession of property, and in this way they introduced a higher moral tone among their subjects.

Another remnant of Dutch rule may be found in the IRRIGATION WORKS they undertook, and in the encouragement they gave to agriculture by the introduction of many new products. The cultivation of rice was encouraged by grants of land for that purpose. The canal from Colombo to Puttalam, which has been of so much use in our day, is the work of the Dutch; and in various parts of the island they built or restored other works by which agriculture was greatly encouraged and improved.

There was some difference in the way in which the Sinnalese and Tamils were treated by the Dutch and by the Portuguese. The latter in their religious zeal and military ardour, the former in their commercial eagerness, sometimes oppressed the natives by vexatious laws and extravagant demands. Subject races in those times had little liberty, and it is no wonder we read so frequently of rebellions among them. But we should take into account the fact that both Dutch and Portuguese lived at a time when men everywhere were often cruel and generally regardless of the interests of others. It was only in much later times that a gentler and more considerate spirit prevailed, and we should not forget the good done by both Dutch and Portuguese to the Island and its peoples.

## CHAPTER XLIV

## Early Troubles of British Rule

WHEN in 1796 the British became masters of the Dutch possessions in Ceylon a difficulty arose about the future government of these possessions. They had been ceded to the troops of the English East India Company, which had now brought a very large part of India under its rule, and the Company wished to have Ceylon also. The English Government in London preferred that Ceylon should be governed directly by the king of England

(George III.). But as there was a chance that, when the war between England and Holland was brought to an end, Ceylon might be restored to the Dutch, the East India Company was allowed for the time to manage the affairs of the Island. So it happened that Ceylon became part of the territory ruled by the Governor of Madras. Four Military Governors administered the affairs of the Island from February 1796 to October 1798. These were Colonel James Stuart, General Welbore Ellis Doyle, Colonel Peter Bonnevaux (twelve days only), and General Pierre Frederic de Meuron.

Embassies were sent to and from the king of Kandy to arrange a treaty of alliance between the British and the Kandyans, and Mr. Robert Andrews, one of the East India Company's officers, was appointed to superintend the collection of revenue in the maritime districts held by the English. This Mr. Andrews was not a stranger to Ceylon. He had come to the Island before, in 1795, when he went on an embassy from the English in Madras to the Kandyan king. But he and his subordinates thought only of collecting the revenue, and cared nothing about the people of Ceylon and the habits to which they had been so long accustomed. He made an entire change in the existing taxes and in the methods by which the taxes were collected. As he understood only the system of taxation practised in Madras, he directed that that system should be enforced in Ceylon as well.

At the same time he brought over a large number of Indian subordinate officials who took the place of the Sinhalese mudaliyars and headmen. The Indian officials took advantage of the opportunity to plunder and oppress the people. Naturally there was much jealousy and discontent, and this led to an insurrection in 1797. The rising was quieted with some difficulty, and general de Meuron was appointed from Madras in July 1797 to ascertain why the people had revolted, and what measures should be taken to satisfy them. De Meuron reported that the changes so violently and abruptly made by Mr. Andrews were unwise, and that the old system should, for the present at least, be resumed. When Mr. Pitt, the great prime minister of George III., heard of these things, he at once decided to take Ceylon from the East India Company and to govern it directly from England. Accordingly, on the 1st January, 1802, Ceylon was declared to be a *Crown Colony*,* and the Honourable **Frederic North** (afterwards fifth earl of Guilford) entered upon his duties as the first governor of Ceylon. Mr. North resumed the old system of taxation, and dismissed most of the Madras officers whose extortions and inefficiency were ruining the colony.

In the same year, 1798, Rajadhi Raja Sinha died, leaving no children. Pilame Talawwe, his first adigar or chief minister, contrived

---

* *A Crown Colony* is one which is ruled directly by the Imperial Government through a Governor and Legislative Council, the members of the Council being nominated by the Governor, not elected by the people.

to secure the election of a Malabar youth, named *Kannesami*, to the throne of Kandy. Kannesami was a nephew of one of the late king's wives, but he had no right to the throne while nearer relatives of the kings were alive Besides, he was young and had had no proper education; but these very disadvantages made him useful to Pilame Talawwe, who intended the king to be merely an instrument to serve his own purposes. The first adigar aimed at the throne for himself, and sought by his accession to restore the ancient Sinhalese dynasty, for he claimed to be descended from the royal family of Ceylon.

On his accession Kannesami took the title of **Sri Vikrama Raja Sinha.** The nearest relatives of Rajadhi Raja Sinha were imprisoned, and the second adigar, who remained faithful to their cause, was murdered by Pilame Talawwe, while Muttusami, the brother of Rajadhi's principal queen and the lawful heir to the throne, fled to the British for protection. Pilame Talawwe now began a secret correspondence with Mr. North, in which neither party appears to have acted honourably. The Kandyan confessed to Mr. North his hatred of the Malabars and his ambition to revive the Sinhalese dynasty in his own person. He offered to dethrone and kill the king, and, if the British would assist him in his plans, to reign in Kandy as a prince, subject to Great Britain. Mr. North seems to have

---

**1799. Napoleon Bonaparte elected First Consul of the French Republic.**

agreed to these treacherous proposals, but he made it a condition that the king's life should be spared. It was arranged that an ambassador should be sent to Kandy on the pretext of making a treaty ; but he was to be accompanied by a force strong enough to overawe the king, and to carry out Pilame Talawwe's designs.

General MacDowall was appointed ambassador, and in March, 1800, he set out to Kandy with his "escort," as it was called, of about 2,000 armed men. But the king grew suspicious, and, alarmed at the approach of so large a force, refused to allow the general to enter Kandy except with only a few men, too few for the success of the plot. Nothing was done ; no treaty was arranged , and the general returned to Colombo to wait for a more favourable opportunity.

The opportunity soon came, for Pilame Talawwe, had made up his mind to force a war by annoying the British, and in that way compelling them to fight against the Kandyans. If there was war, thought Pilame Talawwe, the king could be put to death and his own authority established. Then he could make his own terms with the British. To bring this about he stirred up the people at Negombo and Mannar to rebel against the British. He spoke against Mr. North to the king, and against the king to Mr. North. Lastly, he seized the property of some Moormen who were returning from Kandy to Puttalam. These Moormen were

British subjects, and Mr. North demanded compensation for the wrongs they had suffered. It was refused. War was then declared, in 1803.

The British troops advanced to Kandy in two divisions, General MacDowall marched from Colombo with one division, and Colonel Barbut with another from Trincomalee. Their united forces numbered more than 3,000 men. They arrived together at Kandy in February, 1803, and found the place abandoned by its inhabitants, the king and Pilame Talawwe having fled to Hanguranketa. General MacDowall thereupon declared Muttusami king, and made a treaty with him by which it was agreed that a strong British force should be kept in Kandy. This bargain really meant that the British were the actual masters of Kandy, and that Muttusami was to act in obedience to them.

Pilame Talawwe kept up a secret correspondence with the British all this time, but it did not suit him at all that Muttusami was appointed king. This was not what he expected, and in his disappointment he determined to revenge himself on the British. He therefore offered to betray the king (Sri Vikrama) if troops were sent to Hanguranketa. Eight hundred men set out under Colonel Baillie for this purpose. They were led through dangerous mountain passes, where

---

A.D. 1800. Act for the Union of Great Britain and Ireland.
" " Austrians defeated by Napoleon at Marengo
" 1802. Treaty of Amiens.

they were attacked by the Kandyans at every point of their march. When they reached Hanguranketa the king had escaped. Colonel Baillie rightly suspected that the adigar intended the destruction of his troops, and returned to Kandy. The adigar next tried to seize the governor, Mr. North. The two men met by arrangement at Dambadeniya ; but the unexpected arrival of Colonel Barbut with three hundred Malays from Kandy to pay his respects to the governor, defeated the adigar's cunning plans.

The British garrison left in Kandy, after the main body of troops had returned to Colombo, soon found themselves placed in a position of great danger. Their numbers were daily diminished by the desertion of many Malays who joined the Kandyans, and by the death of many Europeans from sickness. The hospitals were crowded with patients. On all sides the Kandyans were gathering together in arms, and on the morning of the 24th June, 1803, the British were attacked. By two or three o'clock in the afternoon their resistance was over. Major Davie, who was in command was very unwilling to surrender, but he was forced to do so by his men and, indeed, by the circumstances in which he was placed. Terms were then agreed upon with the adigar. Muttusami and the British troops were to leave Kandy for Trincomalee, but they were not to take with them " a single cartridge, not a grain of gunpowder." The adigar undertook to provide and care for the sick and wounded in the hospital till they could be removed to Colombo or Trincomalee.*

At four or five o'clock in the evening the garrison marched out. There were fourteen British officers, twenty British soldiers, two hundred and fifty Malays, one hundred and forty gun-lascars (also Malays). With them went Muttusami and his attendants. No fewer than one hundred and twenty sick and wounded British soldiers were left behind in the hospital at Kandy.

Major Davie and his troops went but a short distance, and at about seven o'clock they reached Watapulua on the banks of the Mahaveli Ganga. Here they were obliged to halt, till they could find means of crossing, as the river was high through heavy rains, Messengers came to them from the king, asking that Muttusami should be given up, and promising that if this were done, they should be provided with boats. Major Davie at first refused so unreasonable a request, but when he saw that his refusal would end in the massacre of all the troops, he consented, and explained to Muttusami that there was no help for it ; they were not strong enough to resist the king, and the king had promised to treat him kindly. Muttusami was not deceived by the king's assurance of kind treatment, but he was astonished at Davie's consent. "Is it possible," he

* *The Ceylon Expedition of 1803*, by Miss V. M. Methley—to whom, and to Mr. J. P. Lewis, is due the new light thrown on Major Davie's proceedings, substantiating Marshall's account of them.

exclaimed, "that the triumphant arms of England can be so humbled as to fear the menaces of such cowards as the Kandyans?" He was taken by the Kandyans to Kandy with all his attendants, and there he met death with dignity and courage. "I am at the king's mercy," was all he would say in his defence. The promised boats were not supplied, but instead, large numbers of Kandyans surrounded the British and required them to return to Kandy. When they had gone some distance, a halt was called, and the Malay soldiers were asked if they would serve the king. Some of them refused and were at once put to death; the others decided to accept the terms offered to them and were conducted to Kandy. When they were gone the turn of the British soldiers came. They were led out two by two, at a distance from one another, and "after being stripped of every article of value" were mercilessly murdered by the Kaffirs in the service of Vikrama Raja Sinha. Only a few officers were spared in this massacre, and only one soldier, corporal Barnsley, and a Dutch doctor named Greeving escaped. Barnsley had been clubbed with the rest and left for dead, but afterwards recovering, he swam across the river and came to Fort MacDowall (Matale) with the terrible news. It was discovered at the same time that shortly before the massacre of Major Davie's troops, (26th June 1803) the king had cruelly put to death the sick and wounded men left in the hospital at Kandy.

Major Davie and Captain Rumley were taken to Kandy, and then to the king at Hanguranketa. They never returned to their countrymen. Though their lives were spared they were closely watched, and both died in captivity. Nuraddin, the captain of the Malays, and his brother were also taken before the king, and their conduct at this time is the bright spot in this dark picture. The adigar required them to prostrate themselves before the king according to the custom of the country. They refused to do so, saying that they also were of royal blood, and could not stoop to such an act of humiliation. The king was rather pleased with this show of independence. He asked them to enter his service and take command of his Malay troops. This too they refused, because, as they said, they had already sworn allegiance to the British and could not break their word. The king sent them to prison for a month in the hope that imprisonment would break their spirit and induce them to change their minds ; but at the end of the month when they were again led before the king and offered the choice between his service and immediate death, they steadfastly chose the latter, and met their doom like brave and honourable men.

There was astonishment and dismay in Colombo when these events became known to the garrison there. "It was," says one who lived there at the time, "like a clap of thunder, which had been for some time portended by a dark and gloomy sky, and was followed by an awful and overpowering calm."

The British wanted, indeed, to take an immediate and merciless revenge, but this could not be. They had very few soldiers able to take the field, and these were to be soon required nearer home.

CHAPTER XLV

## War against Kandy, 1803

THE hill country was now again in the hands of the Kandyan king, who was naturally very proud of his success in having destroyed the British troops. He was in fact so puffed up that he resolved to attack the British in their own territory and, if possible, to drive them altogether out of Ceylon. He used all his influence to stir up the Sinhalese in various parts of the island to rise against the foreigners, and by the end of July rebellions broke out, at Matara, Chilaw, Puttalam, Kottiyar, Mannar, and other places on the coast. Sri Vikrama Raja Sinha himself, at the head of a large force, marched against Hanwelle (eighteen miles east of Colombo) on the 6th of September, 1803. Captain Pollock, who was in command of the small garrison, at that place, waited till the Kandyan army advanced to within two hundred yards of his house. While they halted here, he sent a detachment under lieutenant Mercer by an unseen path to take them in flank, and shortly after went with the rest of the garrison directly against the enemy. The Kandyans were fired upon by both the British detachments at the same time. For two hours the Kandyans resisted, but when a shot reached the place where the king was stationed, he fled, followed, by the whole army. The slaughter which then took place was terrible. All the roads near Hanwelle were strewed with the bodies of the slain; and if the British had not been quite worn out with the day's work (for some of them had just recovered from fever), the pursuit would have been carried much farther, and most probably the king would have been captured. As it was, he escaped, and in his disappointment and rage at having failed in his attempt, he ordered the execution of numbers of his subjects.

Captain Pollock followed up the enemy later on and routed them again at Ruanwella, where they had rallied, and where large reinforcements had gathered to their support. Hambantota, Batticaloa, Jaffna, and the other places besieged by the Kandyans, were similarly relieved, and the Kandyans were at length driven back to their fastnesses in the mountains. In 1804 the British purposed an attack on Kandy, and arrangements were made by which troops were to start from six different points on the coast and to meet at Kandy. Orders were issued to this effect, and to Captain Johnston among other British officers. Captain Johnston was to march from Batticaloa; but afterwards the attack on Kandy was put off, and by some mistake it happened that Captain Johnston was not informed of the change in the arrangements. He, therefore, on the 20th September marched with three hundred men (of whom eighty-two were Europeans) and fought his way to Kandy, which he occupied for three days. Finding the place deserted, and his position one of great danger, as the other detachments had not come up, he retired to Trincomalee, which he reached on the 20th October with the loss of twenty-six British soldiers. This daring feat made a deep impression on the minds of the Kandyans.

From this time till 1815 A.D. there was no regular war between the Kandyans and the British, as neither party felt strong enough to invade the other's territory. But villages were burned and harvests destroyed by both whenever there was a chance.

Mr. North ceased to be Governor in 1805 and was succeeded by **Sir Thomas Maitland,** who was governor for the next seven years. The severe laws which the Dutch had made against Roman Catholics were repealed in 1806, and the British were gradually introducing order and good government into their possessions. In 1812 general **Sir Robert Brownrigg** succeeded as governor, and further efforts were made to improve the condition of British subjects in Ceylon. Protestant missionaries now began to work in the island, with the conversion of the people to Christianity as their principal object. The Baptist missionaries came in 1812, the Wesleyan missionaries in 1814, the American missionaries (to Jaffna) in 1816, and the Church Missionaries in 1818. In 1812 the privilege of trial by jury was granted to prisoners charged with serious offences, and efforts were made to establish schools for education in English.

But in the Kandyan kingdom all was confusion and horror. The king had entered upon a course of tyranny which his subjects, submissive as they were, found unbearable. He distrusted his chiefs and drove many of them into rebellion. He forced the people to work for him without payment. It was by this forced labour (or *Rajakariya)* that, about the year 1806 A.D., the lake in Kandy and the Pattiripua (the octagonal tower of the Dalada Maligawa) were constructed. They add greatly to the beauty of the town of Kandy ; but they were built at the cost of much suffering to the people, and increased the unpopularity of the king.

At about the same time the disava of the Seven Korales died, and the king made a change in the government of that district. He did not appoint one man to be disava, as was the custom, but divided the district between Ehelapola and Molligoda, his second and third adigars. This change caused serious discontent. The people of the district complained that it was not only contrary to custom, but also needlessly burdensome ; for two disavas would demand double services and double duties. Accordingly the people resisted the change and rose in rebellion. Pilame Talawwe, the first adigar, then promised the king that if the charge of the district was given over to him and his nephew, Ratwatte, the people could be quieted. This was done, and the rebellion ceased. But the king naturally grew more suspicious than before of Pilame Talawwe, and more jealous of his influence with the people; while Pilame Talawwe's hatred of the king grew stronger in proportion. The adigar next proposed a marriage between his son and a grand-daughter of Kirti Sri. Convinced by this proposal that the adigar was scheming to get the throne, the king found some excuse, and in a short time deprived him of all his high offices. Pilame Talawwe on his part, plotted to assassinate the king. The plot failed, and the adigar was beheaded with several members of his family in 1811.

## CHAPTER XLVI

## The Ehelapola Tragedy

EHELAPOLA, the nephew of Pilame Talawwe, succeeded to the office of first adigar, Molligoda being appointed second adigar. The former was from the first suspected of disloyalty by the king. He had probably taken part in the recent plot, and he was quite as cunning and ambitious as his predecessor in office. The king did not, however, shew any ill-will at the time, and Ehelapola did all he could to convince the king of his loyalty. The first sign of hostility between them was shewn on the occasion of the king's marriage, when Ehelapola's presents to his sovereign were returned as unworthy of acceptance.

---

**A.D. 1805. Battle of Trafalgar. Nelson killed.**
**" 1807. Slave Trade abolished in England.**

In his disavony of Sabaragamuwa Ehelàpola was very popular; he tried to rule well and to please his subjects, but his popularity served only to increase the king's fear that Ehelapola was plotting to seize the throne. Certain charges were brought against him and he was ordered to return immediately to Kandy. The order was not obeyed, and the king in anger deprived the minister at once of all his high offices, imprisoned his family, and took away his property. Molligoda (who is thought to have jealously set the king against Ehelapola) was appointed first adigar in his rival's place, and was despatched to Sabaragamuwa against the rebel. In May 1814, after a weak effort at resistance, and failing to receive the help he expected from the British, Ehelapola fled to Colombo and there sought the protection of the governor. Molligoda laid waste Ehelapola's disavony and took large numbers of prisoners to Kandy. The king's rage when he learnt of Ehelapola's flight was terrible. One after another, those whom he suspected of friendship with the fugitive were tortured and put to death.

But for Ehelapola's family was reserved a vengeance that even at this day we cannot recall without a shudder.

The chief's wife and children and his brother and his wife were all condemned to death,—the brother and boys to be beheaded, and the ladies to be drowned. The execution was duly carried out to the horror of those who looked on. The heroic conduct of Ehelapola's second son, nine years old, deserves to be recorded. His elder brother wept when he was to be beheaded and clung to his mother. The second boy "heroically stepped forward; he bid his brother not to be afraid—he would show him the way to die. By one blow of a sword, the head of this noble child was severed from his body."

CHAPTER XLVII.

## The End of Independence

SIR Robert Brownrigg received Ehelapola at Colombo with much sympathy for his sufferings and with promises of assistance against the king. But nothing could be done against Sri Vikrama Raja Sinha until the governor was quite certain that the Kandyan people were fully determined to submit no longer to the king's tyranny. Several Kandyan chiefs followed Ehelapola to Colombo, or secretly invited the British to invade Kandy. The latter expected that the king would very soon make an attack on their possessions, and waited till then; for the king, elated by his success against Ehelapola, and believing that the British were too weak or too frightened to resist him, had begun preparations for a great war.

It happened about this time that ten Moor traders, who were British subjects, were barbarously ill-treated by Sri Vikrama who

---

1814. Napoleon defeated and banished to Elba.

charged them with being spies. They had gone into a Kandyan village to trade with the people as usual, when they were unexpectedly seized and taken to Kandy. Here their arms, ears, and noses were cut off by the king's orders, and seven of them died in consequence of this. The remaining three were driven to Colombo, and on hearing their story the governor decided to declare war at once against the Kandyan king. Another reason for fighting was that the Kandyans had crossed the river of Sitavaka, which was the dividing limit of the Kandyan country, and plundered the inhabitants, who were British subjects.

On the tenth of January, 1815, Sir Robert Brownrigg issued a proclamation setting forth the reasons which compelled the British to declare war against Sri Vikrama Raja Sinha. This proclamation stated definitely that the war was not a war against the Kandyan nation, but against the tyrant who oppressed them ; who had, " by the violation of every religious and moral law, become an object of abhorrence to mankind." The Kandyan people were promised full protection of person and property so long as the British advance was not opposed by them. Their religion should be held sacred, their chiefs should preserve their accustomed ranks and dignities, and their ancient laws and institutions should be maintained.

The British troops marched from Colombo the next day, - January 11, and on the 14th February they entered Kandy in triumph. They met with scarcely any resistance, for the king was hated by most of his subjects, and few would fight on his behalf. Chief after chief revolted from him as the British advanced, and the adigar Molligoda was among those who deserted. But the king would not give up the foolish idea that he was able to overcome the invaders, and those who brought him news of defeat were put to death. At length the near approach of the British roused him from his dream of security, and with a few attendants of his own Malabar race he fled to Dumbara. Here, in a cave near the village of Medamahanuwara, he was captured by Ekneligode disava and some of Ehelapola's men from Sabaragamuwa. The captive king was handed over to Mr. (afterwards Sir) John D'Oyly, of the Civil Service, by whom he was treated with all the respect due to his rank, and brought safely to Kandy.

A convention was held in the Audience Hall (where the Supreme Court now sits) of Kandy, on March 2, 1815. Sir Robert Brownrigg occupied the principal seat, and the Kandyan chiefs came in according to their rank. First and alone entered Ehelapola, who was received with special honour and given a seat at the governor's right hand; for it was he who had begun the revolt against the king, who had urged the British to take Kandy, and who had secured the capture of the king. After him came Molligoda, and then the disavas and other chiefs. A treaty was read

---

1815 March Napoleon's return from Elba.
,, June 18. Battle of Waterloo

both in English and in Sinhalese, and formally agreed to by all present. By this treaty Sri Vikrama Raja Sinha was deposed and the Kandyan kingdom was declared to belong to the British Crown ; Buddhism was to be held inviolable, and its temples and priests were to be protected and maintained as they had always been ; the laws of the country were to remain unaltered and the king's revenues were to be levied as before.

The British flag was then hoisted, and the firing of cannon announced the establishment of British rule in Kandy. The Kandyan independence was now at an end. The ancient rule which had lasted for over two thousand three hundred years now definitely gave place to foreign sway.

The character of Sri Vikrama Raja Sinha, the last king of Kandy, has been the subject of much discussion, and it is not easy to form a definite opinion. He was not so ardent a patriot as Raja Sinha and his immediate successors ; nor did he shew those mental and moral qualities which enabled former kings to hold their own against rebellion and invasion. To say he was cruel does not mean much, for cruel kings and nobles were not rare in those days ; and it is questionable whether all the cruel deeds attributed to Sri Vikrama were of his own devising, or done by his authority. It might be more fair to regard him as a weak tool in the hands of designing chiefs, than as the monster of cruelty which it is an idle fashion with some writers to call him. And it should not be forgotten that he did a good deal to beautify his capital. The lake and the "Octagon" in Kandy have always been considered the work of the king.

CHAPTER XLVIII

## The Rebellion of A.D. 1817-1818.

WE now enter upon the British period of Ceylon history: the history of recent times, when many of the customs and institutions with which we are now familiar began to be established. From March 1815, the British were masters, not of the coast provinces only, but of the whole island of Ceylon—a possession which the Portuguese declared they would "rather lose all India than imperil"; which the Dutch regarded as "a jewel in the Company's coronet"; and which the British prize as the "key of the Indian Ocean, and the great insular outpost of the British Empire in the East."

But, as might be expected, there was no little trouble at first in bringing the Kandyans to understand the nature of British rule, and how it differed from the rule to which the Kandyans had been accustomed for centuries. In January 1816, Sri Vikrama Raja Sinha and his family were taken over to Madras, and thence to Vellore, where the deposed king died sixteen years afterwards. The Kandyan Provinces were placed under the control of a Resident, Sir John D'Oyly, and a small military force was retained in Kandy to keep order. Ehelapola, who expected that, in view of the important services he had rendered, the governor would reward him with the government of the Kandyan provinces, was bitterly disappointed. High office was offered to him, but he declined this as well as large rewards of money. He preferred, he said haughtily, to be known simply as the "Friend of the British Government." Molligoda was thereupon made first adigar.

The Kandyan people were sullenly indifferent to the change of rulers. They were glad to be rid of the Malabar tyrant, but they were not altogether pleased to be governed by foreigners so utterly unlike them as the British. The chiefs, on the other hand, were grievously discontented, because under British rule they found that the greater part of their power was taken away. They could not, as formerly, deal as they pleased with their subjects, and thus they began to be much less respected. The British did not understand all the caste prejudices of the Kandyans, and consequently offended them in various ways, even when no offence was intended. So the chiefs gradually stirred up the people to revolt, and by October 1817, the whole Kandyan country was roused against the British. The first outbreak was in Uva. A pretender was set up, and several chiefs, led by Keppitipola, dissave of Uva, supported him. On both sides the losses were heavy, but the Kandyans naturally suffered

---

A.D. 1816. Bombardment af Algiers by Lord Exmouth.

most. Their villages were burnt down, their plantations were laid waste, their cattle were destroyed, and all persons found with arms in their hands were mercilessly killed. The British troops suffered, on their part, from the hardships and disease that were common in warfare in an unfamiliar and unhealthy country. They almost regretted that they had entered Kandy. Their efforts appeared to be useless, for in every district there was revolt, and no appearance of success in their attempts to establish order. At last, when they were seriously thinking of withdrawing their forces and returning to the coast, they found the Kandyans willing to surrender. The latter had suffered enough, and besides, the chiefs grew jealous of one another and became disunited. Keppitipola was soon defeated and taken prisoner, and the rebellion was at an end in October 1818. Two of the rebel chiefs, Keppitipola, and Madugalla of Dumbara, were beheaded. It was suspected that Ehelapola was concerned in the rebellion and, a few years later, he was banished to the island of Mauritius, where he died in 1829.

The rebellion of 1817-1818 was in effect a breach by the Kandyans of the treaty made at the Convention of 1815, since by agreeing to that treaty the Kandyans had accepted British rule, and now they had rebelled against it. A new arrangement was therefore entered upon. By this, people were released from all forced labour except for the construction of

---

**A.D. 1819. The Six Acts carried in Parliament.**
**„ 1820. Death of George III.**

roads and bridges ; all taxes were abolished, and in their place a single tax of one-tenth of the produce of the paddy lands was substituted. British officers were employed to administer justice, while native headmen were appointed to collect revenue, and chiefs were paid fixed salaries instead of being dependent upon the contributions of the people over whom they were placed. A very important change was also made in the relations between the British Government and Buddhism. By the treaty of 1815 Buddhism was declared "inviolable," and its rites and places of worship were promised maintenance and protection. But it was found that the Buddhist priests were among the chief promoters of the rebellion, and that they were the most bitter of all in their hostility to the British. The new agreement stated merely that "the priests as well as the ceremonies of Buddhism shall receive the respect which in former times was shown to them."

Sir Robert Brownrigg left Ceylon early in 1820. He had governed Ceylon for eight years. For almost exactly the same period (1811 to 1826,) the chief justice of Ceylon was Sir Alexander Johnston, to whose wise and far-seeing counsels this island owes much. It was he who took the chief part in repealing the laws against Roman Catholics in 1816. It was he, too, who introduced the jury system into Ceylon. In 1816 he persuaded the Burghers (Dutch descendants) to set free their slaves, and two years later he induced many of the Sinhalese slave-holders to do the same. How enlightened this policy was may be understood from the fact that it was not till 1833 that slavery was abolished (and then it was abolished by law) in other British Colonies.

Sir Edward Barnes was lieutenant-governor of Ceylon from February 1820 to the same month in 1822, when **Sir Edward Paget** arrived as governor. The latter held office for about ten months (till November) and then left Ceylon. Sir James Campbell was lieutenant-governor till January, 1824, when **Sir Edward Barnes** became governor. Two small risings in 1820 and 1823 were the only events of any importance during these years.

CHAPTER XLIX

## Peace and Progress

WHEN Kandy was taken in 1815, Sir Robert Brownrigg thought of making a road to it from Colombo. The Kandyan Kingdom, surrounded by its high, forest-clad mountains, was still a land of mystery. It had long been comparatively safe from foreign invasion and permanent conquest by the difficulty and danger of marching through the steep and narrow passes that led to its capital. To reach it was no safe or easy task. Sir Robert saw clearly that a good military road from Colombo to Kandy would immensely strengthen the British occupation. Cannon would have no longer to be dragged with endless labour

---

A.D. 1823. Greek War against Turkey.

across the sand or through dense forests. Heavy burdens would no longer need to be carried on men's shoulders. Communication between the hill country and the coast would be easy. But the rebellion of 1817 obliged governor Brownrigg to put aside his plans for the completion of this road.

Sir Edward Barnes made this road the chief business of his administration. There was much to be done. Rivers had to be bridged, and tunnels had to be cut through rocks. The road had to wind upwards, along the irregular course of ravines and the edge of steep precipices. The route lay through uncultivated and malarial districts. But by 1831, after nearly ten years' labour, it was completed, and the Sinhalese were filled with wonder. One of their prophets had foretold that "the Kandyan kingdom would perish when a bullock should be driven through a certain hill, and a horseman ride through a rock." It seemed that the prophecy was now fulfilled, and that the Kandyan independence was indeed at an end.

A monument at the top of the Kadugannawa pass commemorates the services of captain Dawson of the Royal Engineers, who died in Colombo in March 1829, of fever caught while superintending this work. Major Thomas Skinner, then a very young lieutenant in the

---

A.D. 1829. Catholic Relief Bill passed.
„ 1830. Death of George IV.
„ 1830. Revolt and Independence of Belgium.

Ceylon Regiment, had also an important share in the construction of the road. He was afterwards to continue the policy of the governor, and to become the "great road-maker of Ceylon." But to Sir Edward Barnes must be given the chief credit of the work. The cost was naturally very great, and it is said that some one in England declared that the governor deserved to be impeached for his extravagance in making the road. Sir Edward simply replied, "Ceylon's future will determine that point." The after prosperity of Ceylon fully justified Sir Edward's expectation.

But when the great road had been opened Sir Edward resolved to make it much more than a military convenience. He planned to make it serviceable to the island generally. With this object he encouraged, and even began at his own expense, the cultivation of useful plants, and the manufacture of commercial products. Much money was spent in preparing indigo and sugar, but these manufactures had to be given up. Coffee was found more suited to the soil and climate of the hills. This valuable product (as well as tea and cocoa) had been introduced or cultivated by the Dutch a hundred years before; but as they attempted to grow it in the lowlands near Negombo and Galle they were not successful. In 1824 Mr. George Bird opened the first coffee plantation (Sinnapitiya Estate) in Gampola, on land where in former times a Kandyan palace stood. Several other gardens or "estates" followed in the neighbourhood, including the governor's plantation at Gangaruwa, near Peradeniya; and to encourage cultivation, Sir Edward Barnes gave free grants of forest land to intending planters. In 1827 no less than 16,000 cwts. of coffee was exported from Ceylon.

In the same year, Nuwara Eliya, six thousand feet above sea-level, became known to the English, some military officers having got there while hunting elephants. They were struck with the delightful climate and beauty of the place and reported their discovery to the governor. Sir Edward Barnes at once had a road made to it, and houses were erected for himself, and for sick soldiers who required a cooler climate than that of Colombo or even of Kandy. The Pavilion at Kandy, and Mount Lavinia House by the seaside, were also built on the orders of Sir Edward Barnes.

**Sir Robert Wilmot Horton** became governor in 1831, and progress continued to be made in Ceylon. In February, 1832, a company was formed to start a mail coach (the first of its kind in all Asia) between Colombo and Kandy. This was a sign of prosperity, because it shewed that frequent and regular communication between the hills and the low-country was now established. Other signs of prosperity appeared in the opening of a savings bank (1832); in the abolition of the *rajakariya*, or compulsory labour for Government (1832); in the abolition of the cinnamon monopoly, all persons being now allowed to cultivate or trade

---

A.D. 1832. The great Reform Bill passed.

in cinnamon (1833); and in the permission given to Moors and Tamils to own houses and lands in the Fort and Pettah of Colombo (1832), a privilege which had been denied them by the Dutch. In 1832, the government officials started the "Colombo Journal," the first newspaper in Ceylon; but as in it they criticized the actions of the Government in London very unfavourably, they were ordered to discontinue the journal. In 1834 the merchants in Colombo started the "Colombo Observer," which still continues to be issued. In the same year, a Commission was appointed to supervise the schools of the island and to promote education generally. Two years later the Colombo Academy (now the Royal College) was established.

But more important changes have yet to be noted. In 1833 the island was divided into five provinces—the Western, Southern, Eastern, Northern, and Central—with a government agent over each. Two councils—one for making laws, and the other for seeing that the laws were carried out—were formed at the same time. The latter, called the *Executive Council*, consisted of the governor and a few of the highest officials. The former, called the *Legislative Council*, should have had nine official members (besides the governor) and six unofficial members; that is six members who were to speak and act on behalf of all the people in Ceylon. Three of them were to represent

---

**A.D. 1834 Sir Robert Peel Prime Minister.**

British residents, and the remaining three the Burghers, Sinhalese, and Tamils, respectively. But, strangely enough, Sir Robert Horton did not appoint unofficial members till some months after the official members had been appointed. There was a great outcry against the governor on this account.

A Charter, granted in 1833, led to the establishment of new Courts of Justice. A charter is a document granting certain powers, rights, or privileges By authority of this *Charter of Justice* the governor established *District Courts* in various parts of the island. In these courts ordinary cases were tried; but the more important cases were tried before the *Supreme Court*, which had also the right to alter or confirm the decisions of any District Court.

## CHAPTER L

# From A.D. 1837 to 1850.

THE Right Honourable **J. A. Stewart Mackenzie** succeeded as governor in 1837, a few months after the accession of queen Victoria to the throne of England; but he remained in the island for only three and a half years. He did his utmost to improve the condition of the native inhabitants of Ceylon. The tax on fish was taken away. Coffee planting was encouraged. A lunatic asylum was built. Education had up to this time been left to the care of Christian missionaries mainly; but the governor warmly interested himself in the matter, and established several government schools. A few students were even sent to Calcutta to learn medicine. The missionaries and their work found in the governor a valuable friend.

Governor Mackenzie was the first to take a genuine interest in the Veddas. These neglected people lived a wretched life in the forests of the Central and Eastern Provinces, and scarcely any one seems to have thought of doing anything for their good. The governor heard of them, himself visited the districts where they lived, and succeeded in inducing a few Veddas to attend schools and to cultivate paddy. While on this journey he caught a fever which led to his early departure from the island.

In the first year of the government of **Sir Colin Campbell,** the School Commission of 1834 was arranged on a different plan, and there began a steady increase in the number of schools and of pupils. A new province—the North Western—was formed in 1844 with its capital at Kurunegala; at the end of the year slavery, which still lingered in the Kandyan provinces, was totally abolished by law. Police Courts were established in 1844, and Courts of Requests (for settling disputes regarding small sums of money) in 1848, leaving the District Courts free to attend to matters of larger consequence.

---

A.D. 1837. Natal founded by Dutch settlers.
,, 1838. The People's Charter (England.)
,, 1839. Penny Postage established.

Among the European residents and those natives of the island who understood, and to any extent adopted, European ways of thinking, there were many signs of increasing wealth and civilization. The members of the Church of England had grown numerous enough to justify the formation of a diocese separate from Madras, and Dr. James Chapman was appointed first Anglican bishop of Colombo (1845). Efforts were made to secure the construction of a railway to Kandy. Banks were established, and coffee planting was taken up with great enthusiasm. Nearly every European in Ceylon who had money bought land for the cultivation of coffee. Rich men from England and from India spent largely in this new venture, believing that the profits they would gain would make them doubly rich. In 1845 the rush for coffee land was at its height. The result was quickly seen in the changed appearance of the hillsides round Kandy and in the neighbouring districts. Trim, orderly plantations took the place of wild jungle; roads were made through hitherto inaccessible forests; comfortable bungalows were built; the sound of human voices prevailed in regions so long given up to loneliness and silence.

But the first coffee planters in Ceylon were not the experienced and careful men their successors since became. They knew very little

---

**A.D. 1834. Free Church of Scotland Secession.**
**„ 1845-6. First Sikh War.**

about the coffee tree or of the soil best suited for its cultivation. Large tracts of land were consequently bought and cleared for planting, and afterwards found to be quite useless for the purpose. Labour was scarce and very expensive, and few estates could obtain a sufficient numbers of labourers. In two years a disastrous change occurred. The failure of a large firm in England ruined many of those who had invested in coffee and put an end to the remittances liberally sent to Ceylon. Most of those who had been so eager to acquire land now anxiously tried to get rid of it. Estates were sold for anything they would fetch in the market and many estates were abandoned for want of a purchaser. But some planters held on, profited by the lessons they had learnt, and in a few years contrived to recover their position and to make coffee the leading export of the island.

**Lord Torrington**, who succeeded Sir Colin Campbell in 1847, could do little to help the coffee-planters. Graver troubles were soon to occupy his attention. Beneath all the appearance of quiet and contentment, unsuspected, save by one or two men who were more far-seeing than others, there was considerable unrest among the native inhabitants of Ceylon. In 1848 several new taxes were imposed—taxes on dogs, on guns, on boats, the stamp tax, and the road tax. These were strongly resented for

A.D. 1846. Corn Laws repealed.
,, 1848. Revolution in France.
,, 1849. Rebellion in Hungary.

various reasons and a rising (which after all scarcely deserves the name of a "Rebellion") took place in Kandy, Kurunegala, and a few other places. The road tax was the most hateful of the new taxes. Every male in the island between eighteen and sixty years of age (except the governor, the military, and certain others) was required to give six day's labour on the public roads, or to pay three shillings instead. The Kandyans did not care for roads, and thought (wrongly, no doubt) that the tax was for the benefit of the Europeans alone. They suspected also that the tax was a revival of the old *rajakariya* which had been publicly abolished in 1832. The "Rebellion" began in Dambulla, where a number of people assembled under the leadership of Gongalagoda Banda, who pretended to be a descendant of king Raja Sinha. On the 28th July the mob reached Matale and plundered the town. Next morning they were met at Wariapola and driven back by a detachment of European and Malay soldiers. On the 30th July the Kandyans in Kurunegala were put to flight by a few Malays of the Ceylon Rifle Regiment. The District of Kandy was placed under martial law, and application was made to Madras for soldiers. In a week troops landed at Trincomalee and marched towards Kandy. But in less than three months the so-called "Rebellion" was at an end. So much excitement and confusion followed, however, that the Parliament in England ordered an enquiry into the whole matter—with the result that in 1850

Lord Torrington resigned, and Sir James Emerson Tennent, the colonial secretary, was given an appointment out of Ceylon. Sir Emerson Tennent will be remembered as the author of several most valuable and interesting works on Ceylon.

## CHAPTER LI

## From A.D. 1850 to 1865

THESE troublous times of the "Rebellion" were followed by five years of inaction on the part of the government. **Sir George Anderson** did nothing in the way of public works. He explained that the expenditure had all these years been so heavy that he required to save as much money as he could. The railway had to wait, and the introduction of the telegraph system remained under consideration. This waiting policy roused a general feeling of disappointment and dissatisfaction. The coffee planters had by this time grown into a large and important body, and to make their influence felt they formed themselves into an Association in February 1854. Between this Association, which is now one of the most powerful societies in the island, and the government of Sir George Anderson, there were many violent disputes. One important event in this period was that the government put an end to its official connection with

---

A.D. 1853. Gladstone's first Budget.
1854-6 Crimean War.

Buddhism. The famous *dalada* or tooth-relic was handed over to the Diyawadana Nilame (an official of the Maligawa), and the priests were left henceforth to manage their own affairs without the interference of Government.

When in May, 1855, **Sir Henry Ward** arrived in Ceylon as governor it was at once seen that more fortunate times were in store for the island. Progress was the watchword of the new governor's policy. " The question" said he, " is not one of ease or convenience, but of *life*. You must go on, or you must go back." The island did not go back. With an energy and spirit that stirred every one to admiration, Sir Henry Ward studied the needs of the country and supplied its most urgent wants. The suspension bridge at Gampola and the iron lattice bridge at Katugastota ; repairs to the Kirime and Urubokke dams in the Southern Province ; the useful irrigation works at Batticaloa, by which rice crops were saved from destruction, and deserted regions were re-peopled ; telegraph communication opened between Galle and Colombo, and soon extended through Kandy and Mannar to India ; penny postage established within the island ; the Kandyan marriage law amended, and polyandry declared illegal, with the full consent of the Kandyans :—these were the principal benefits gained by Ceylon from Sir Henry Ward's beneficent rule. How real was the contentment among the people may be judged from the fact that troops were sent from Ceylon to India to help the Indian government in putting down the terrible "Mutiny" of 1857. There was no fear of revolt here, and no need to add to the handful of troops which were found sufficient for all local purposes. "It is most gratifying to me," said the governor, "to acknowledge, publicly that my confidence has been repaid by the unexceptionable conduct of the entire population. No man can doubt the Queen's power to vindicate her authority; and a few weeks will shew the fate of those who have braved it in the Presidency of Bengal. But it will be a triumph far more in accordance with Her Majesty's heart to find the ties between the people and the Crown so strongly cemented in Ceylon by kindly feelings and mutual benefits, that even the appearance of political discontent has been avoided."

But the railway question was still unsettled. Public meetings were held in Kandy and Colombo, and angry discussions on this subject were carried on in the newspapers. On the 3rd August 1858, the first sod of the proposed railway to Kandy was turned. A company had undertaken the construction of the line, and to meet expenses the governor imposed a duty on all exports from Ceylon. As the Northern and Eastern Provinces would be very little benefited by the railway to Kandy, a steamer was got out to make regular coasting trips round the island. But meanwhile disputes arose regarding the estimated cost of the railway, and the work was put off, much to the annoyance of the coffee planters and the public generally.

The people of Ceylon were quick to shew their appreciation of Sir Henry Ward's splendid services to the island, in spite of occasional instances in which he fell short of their expectations. Nearly four thousand persons signed a petition to the Queen asking that he might be reappointed governor when his term of office came to an end, and that a special grant of £3,000 a year should be paid to him in addition to his salary. The prayer could not be granted for many reasons, and in June 1860, Sir Henry Ward left Ceylon to be governor of Madras. He died there of cholera in the August following.

The policy of **Sir Charles Justin MacCarthy,** who had previously been colonial secretary of Ceylon, was similar to that of Sir George Anderson. No great public works were undertaken. Roads were neglected, and many of them became impassable, while the money that might have been spent on them was carefully hoarded. But land for planting purposes continued to be sold. The trade of the country had recovered from the depression it suffered in 1845. Sinhalese and Tamil newspapers began to be published. We see, therefore, that progress continued to be made in spite of the inactivity of government. In

---

A. D. 1858. Jews admitted to British Parliament.
" 1860. Victor Emmanuel King of Italy.
" 1861. American Civil War.

at least one matter, however, the government had to act decisively. The costly agreement made with the railway company was cancelled in 1861, and the construction of the line to Kandy was entrusted to a contractor. By 1864 thirty miles of the line had been constructed and the first special train was run in that year to convey a distinguished visitor, the duke of Brabant (afterwards Leopold I, king of Belgium), from Veyangoda to Ambepusse, and on the return journey from Ambepussa to Colombo.

Sir Charles MacCarthy left Ceylon in December 1863, owing to ill-health, and till March 1865 major-general O'Brien, the lieutenant-governor, was in authority. Warm discussions took place at this time in the legislative council, the principal subject being the military expenditure of the island. For many years Ceylon had been compelled to pay annually from its revenue a large sum of money for the troops stationed here. These payments became larger and larger, though the number of troops had been gradually reduced. The legislative council had no control over the expenditure of this money, and the amount of each year's payment was fixed by the secretary of state in London, to whom the governor was directly responsible. The unofficial members argued that the Council, not the secretary of state, should decide how much should be paid on account of the military each year. They thought the present charges excessive, and that important public works in the island were neglected because no money was left to pay for them. They insisted that the control of the military expenditure should be in their hands just as the other expenditure was. These claims the secretary of state would not allow. The unofficials thought that they could then do no good by remaining in Council. They were fewer in number than the official members who voted on the side of the government. Consequently in November 1864, the six unofficials (Messrs. C. A. Lorenz, George Wall, W. Thompson, John Capper, James Alwis, and J. H. Eaton) resigned their seats, rather than by their presence in Council appear to sanction what they thought wrong and harmful to the interests of the island.

This action of the unofficial members was fully supported by public opinion in Ceylon; so much so that a society, named the Ceylon League, was formed in May 1865, to continue the agitation for reforming the legislative council. But in three years the League was broken up from the want of union among its members, and because it was seen that reform was stubbornly opposed by the secretary of state.

## CHAPTER LII.

## From A. D. 1865 to 1877

DURING the government of **Sir Hercules Robinson,** (afterwards known as Lord Rosmead) attention was again paid to the material

---

A.D. 1866. **North Germany united under Prussia.**

„ 1868. **Gladstone Prime Minister.**

improvement of the country. The agitation for a freer legislative council continued, but nothing was gained, and the League was dissolved in 1868. The railway to Kandy was opened for traffic in August, 1867, and from the first it proved so successful that its extension to Nawalapitiya, and from Colombo along the sea-cost to Moratuwa, was strongly pressed upon the government. The former extension was decided upon before the governor left Ceylon. The export duties imposed by Sir Henry Ward were now discontinued. The opening of the Suez Canal in 1869 largely increased the trade of Ceylon, and merchants pointed out the necessity for better harbour accommodation at Colombo. There was then some hesitation whether Galle or Colombo should have the new harbour works, but the decision was made in favour of the latter, and in 1871 an engineer was appointed to report on the matter. In March of the same year the first general census of the island was taken. The Dutch used to number the inhabitants of their maritime provinces occasionally though their dissavas, and in the time of governor van der Graaff the population of the low-country was estimated at 817,000, that of the whole island about 1,500,000. There were other censuses in 1814 and 1824, but the first of the regular decennial (once in ten years) censuses was in 1871. It was found that there were

---

A.D. 1869. Irish Church disestablished.

,, 1870. War declared by France against Prussia.

2,400,380 inhabitants in all—the Western Province, the largest in population, having six and a half times as many as the Eastern, the last in this respect. Colombo had 100,000 inhabitants, nearly three times as many as Galle the next town. Colombo and Kandy were made *Municipalities* in 1865, and given certain powers of self-government, the privilege being extended to Galle in the following year. The foundation stone of the old municipal town hall of Colombo, in the Pettah, was laid by the duke of Edinburgh who visited Ceylon in 1870.

In 1867 there were excited debates regarding education. The number of schools and pupils had increased, and the governor made great alterations in the existing system. The school commission was abolished, and a director of public instruction was appointed, with full power to control the education of the colony. Grants of money were paid to those schools which were not managed by government, according to the progress shewn at the annual examinations. The more advanced pupils were no longer prepared for the Calcutta University examinations, but a scholarship was offered each year sufficient to pay for three years' education at Oxford or Cambridge. All these changes proved very beneficial. But Sir Hercules Robinson went further. The suffering caused by the want of properly trained medical men in outlying districts decided him to establish in Colombo

---

**A.D. 1876. Bulgarian massacres.**

a medical school (1870), for which Dr. James Loos, a member of the government medical service, had pleaded twenty years before, and which Dr. Elliot, the principal civil medical officer of the island, had later on pointed out to be an urgent necessity. Nor was the ancient Sinhalese and Pali literature of the island neglected. Mr. James Alwis was appointed (1869) to collect and report upon such manuscripts as could be found, and a *Descriptive Catalogue* of twenty-three Sinhalese and Pali books was published next year.

From January, 1872, new silver and copper coins were brought into use, and accounts were kept in rupees and cents instead of in pounds, shillings, and pence, which had been introduced by the British.

It will thus be seen that Sir Hercules Robinson's rule was a busy one, and that very much was done by him to advance the interests of the island. His successor, the right honourable **Sir William H. Gregory** was equally active in promoting the material improvement of Ceylon, while his genuine sympathy with the different races, classes, and creeds in the Island, made him perhaps the most popular governor of Ceylon. He himself has left it on record that the great ambition and desire of his life was to be governor of Ceylon, and when he was appointed to that office he proved himself entirely worthy of the trust. In his time occurred the visit of the prince of Wales (afterwards king Edward VII), who was welcomed in all parts of the island with such enthusiastic loyalty as left no doubt in regard to the feeling of the people. At the audience hall, Kandy, in December, 1875, the prince conferred on the governor the honour of knighthood, and returning to Colombo laid the first stone of the breakwater. Sir William Gregory looked upon the improvement of the Colombo harbour as the great work of his rule. But his other acts deserve equal praise. The railway was opened to Panadure and to Nawalapitiya, while its extension to Matale and to Kalutara was arranged for, and great efforts were made to secure the extension of the line from Nawalapitiya to Haputale. In 1873 a new province—the North Central—was formed, with Anuradhapura as its capital. We have seen how hundreds of years ago Anuradhapura was the centre of a well-populated and flourishing district. But, while Kandy and the coast towns rose in importance, the tanks of Anuradhapura had been long neglected and left to decay, its temples and gardens being overrun with weed and jungle. The governor's intention in creating a new province was to clear the country, to rebuild or repair the tanks, and to make things easy for the few people who still lived there. In this way new settlers would be attracted to the place. The wisdom of the attempt has been fully proved. A museum in Colombo, and the water works at Kandy were other important benefits; and the new products (such as tea, cinchona, cocoa, rubber, and Liberian coffee) were encouraged in every way; for there were signs that all was not well with coffee. What was known as " leaf disease " had begun to attack the trees, and much anxiety was felt by the planters and those who were directly or indirectly dependent on the coffee industry.

CHAPTER LIII

## From A. D. 1877 to 1933

THE failure of the coffee crops took place towards the end of **Sir James Robert Longden's** rule. The export of Ceylon coffee in the two years, 1880 to 1882, was over a million cwts each year; in the next two years it fell to half that quantity. The consequence was that many planters were ruined, many estates had to be abandoned, and everywhere people who depended on the coffee industry for employment suffered severely. With an energy and resolution that ought not to be forgotten, the planters, rather than give way, turned to the new products which had here and there been cultivated to some slight extent.

There are but few other important events to record in Sir James Longden's administration. The Church of England and the Presbyterian Churches in Ceylon were disestablished in 1881; that is, their clergy were not in future to be appointed by government, or paid from the public revenues. In 1881 a volunteer corps was enrolled with the prince

---

A.D. 1877. Queen Victoria proclaimed Empress of India.
,, 1878. The Berlin Congress.
,, 1879. Zulu and Afghan Wars.

of Wales as honorary colonel. An ordinance was passed in 1882 for the establishment of postal savings banks. The census of 1881 gave a total population for the island of 2,759,738 persons, an increase of 359,358 from 1871.

**Sir Arthur H. Gordon** (afterwards Lord Stanmore) arrived in December 1883, and in his first address to the legislative council announced a reduction in the military contribution, about which there had been so much trouble in 1864. In the following May the Oriental Bank Corporation, which had existed in Ceylon since 1845, suspended payment, and this brought much confusion and distress to the island, especially as the blow came so soon after the failure of the coffee crops. Merchants and planters were threatened with ruin, and others bitterly foresaw the loss of their hard-earned savings. But Sir Arthur Gordon promptly announced that the government would give silver for the notes issued by the bank, and by this courageous and statesmanlike act he prevented much suffering, especially among the poorer classes. Since that time our currency notes have been in the name of the government and not in the name of any bank.

Two new provinces were created—the province of Uva (capital, Badulla) in 1886, and

---

A.D. 1881. Death of Lord Beaconsfield.
" 1882. Bombardment of Alexandria.
" 1885. Death of General Gordon at Khartum.
" 1886. First Home Rule Bill introduced.

the province of Sabaragamuwa (capital, Ratnapura) in 1889. Irrigation works were vigorously attended to, the most important being the repairs to the Kalaveva and its connected canal, the Yodi-ela. The extension of the railway to Bentota and to Haputale was sanctioned, and the extension to Galle and Matara was discussed. In 1887 the Jubilee of her majesty queen Victoria's reign was celebrated in all parts of the island. In 1889 two unofficial members, one to represent the Kandyans, and the other the Muhammadans, were added to the legislative council.

**Sir Arthur Elibank Havelock** completed the railway extensions to Bandarawela and Matara, and opened a branch line to Kurunegala. In 1893 he established a technical school in Colombo where students were trained for the mechanical branches of the public service. But the most important event of his rule was the abolition in 1892 of the paddy tax, which, though it had existed from time immemorial, was a severe hardship to the village cultivator. The repeal of this tax was, like the establishment of the technical school, mainly due to the efforts of Mr. George Wall, one of the unofficials who resigned in 1864. The census of 1891 shewed that the population of Ceylon had increased to 3,007,789.

**Sir Joseph West Ridgeway** governed Ceylon from 1896, and shewed a liberal and progressive spirit in the measures he adopted. Much of his work lay in the direction of rearranging and establishing on a firmer basis the institutions which he found on his arrival. The civil service and the clerical service, the irrigation department, the survey department, and the technical school bore witness to his keen oversight and desire for improvement. But his most important public work was the beginning of the railways to Jaffna and to the Kelani valley.

Towards the end of the year 1899 war broke out between England and the two Boer republics in South Africa. Over 5,000 Boer prisoners of war were sent to Ceylon and other British possessions. Those in Ceylon were confined mainly at Diyatalawa, in the Uva district, and a few at Ragama and Hambantota. After the declaration of peace in June 1902, these prisoners-of-war were set free.

On the 22nd January 1901, took place the death of queen Victoria, after a long and glorious reign of sixty-four and a half years. Her death was deeply mourned in all parts of her great empire, and nowhere more deeply or more sincerely than in Ceylon. Edward VII (who, as prince of Wales, visited this island in 1876) was proclaimed king in Ceylon in February 1901, and was crowned in London on the 9th August 1902.

Sir West Ridgeway was governor of Ceylon for eight years, a longer period than any former governor enjoyed, except Sir Robert Brownrigg. In December, 1900, he was succeeded by **Sir Henry Blake,** whose government was not so eventful as that of his predecessors;

for so much money had already been spent on various improvements that a time of quiet was again necessary. Sir Henry Blake obtained permission, however, for a railway to Negombo, and he did something to improve the condition of the police. But he will be remembered chiefly by his efforts to improve and encourage agriculture in the island. He started an agricultural society which counted hundreds of members, and which has been a great help.

**Sir Henry McCallum** arrived in Ceylon in 1907 and a number of important engineering works were then begun. One of the most notable of public events was the change made in 1911 in the constitution of the legislative council, which was now to consist of eleven official and ten unofficial members, besides the governor. Four of the unofficials were *elected*, instead of being selected by the governor, and of these, two represented the Europeans, one represented the Burghers, and one those Ceylonese who had attained a certain standard of education. The remaining six unofficials were nominated as before by the governor—two for the Low-country Sinhalese, two for the Tamils, and one each for the Kandyans and the Muhammadans.

A great increase of population was shewn by the census of 1911, when the total population was estimated at 4,606,350. The census of 1901 shewed a population of 3,565,954, so that in 1901 there was an increase of half a million.

The extension of railways was a noteworthy

feature of Sir Henry McCallum's rule, though he was not entirely responsible for all the extensions. A branch line from Madawachchi (on the nothern railway) to Mannar was begun. The line was intended to connect the railways of Ceylon and India, and it has proved useful to the Indian labourers who come in large numbers to work on the tea and rubber estates, but who dislike the rough passage by sea. The line to Negombo was found to pay so well that the demand for its extension to Chilaw could not be resisted. Other extensions which were sanctioned were those from Bandarawela to Badulla, and from Ratnapura to Pelmadulla.

Ill-health compelled Sir Henry McCallum to leave Ceylon in January, 1913, earlier than he expected, and before he could himself carry through several important schemes which he had carefully planned. Among these were an excise scheme for controlling the manufacture and sale of arrack and toddy, and an education scheme making considerable changes in the school system which then prevailed.

On the sixth of May 1910, king Edward VII died. He was known as the "Peace-maker," from his efforts to preserve peace among the nations of Europe. No king of England for a thousand years was greater or more beloved. He was succeeded by his son who now reigns as king George V.

In October 1913 **Sir Robert Chalmers** (now Lord Chalmers) came as governor. He was welcomed in Ceylon as a Pali scholar familiar with the sacred books of Buddhism; but his rule was not to be one of peace. In August 1914 a war broke out between Germany and France, and very soon nearly all the nations of Europe were involved in it, taking one side or the other. England and her colonies fought on the side of France. For a long time it seemed as if Germany and her allies would win, and the nations of Asia, Africa, and America began to take sides; but after four years of hard fighting, causing loss of life and property to an extent unknown before, Germany was beaten. An armistice was declared on the 11th November 1918, and a treaty of peace was signed at Versailles (in France) on the 28th June 1919.

Ceylon was among the British Colonies which sent men and money to help England during those anxious years. Unfortunately, however, in May and June 1915, there occurred in parts of the island a series of riots in which the Moors suffered badly at the hands of some of the Sinhalese. That this should have happened when the empire seemed to be fighting for its very life made the Government take a specially serious view of the matter. Martial law was proclaimed in the troubled districts on the 2nd June, and lasted till the 30th August 1915.

It was afterwards felt in Ceylon that a number of people had been needlessly or excessively punished through being supposed to have taken part in the riots; and when **Sir John Anderson** succeeded Sir Robert Chalmers in April 1916, his first task was to enquire into the whole question. "I come amongst you with an open mind," he said on his arrival, and with an open mind he set himself to the dfficult duty of settling political differences and quieting discontent. In this he was eminently successful. He hoped to do much also in other ways for the good of the country, and he appointed committees and commissions of inquiry into such matters as the excise, local industries, local self-government and the larger employment of Ceylonese in the public service.

But illness pursued him throughout his short rule in Ceylon, and on the 24th March 1918 he died at Nuwara Eliya, and was buried two days later in Colombo. He was succeeded in September 1918 by **Sir William Henry Manning,** who found that there was a loud outcry for reforms in the legislative and executive councils. A large number of people asked for *territorial* instead of *communal* representation; that is, they wanted that members of the legislative council should be elected to represent districts, into which the island was to be divided, rather than communities of men divided by race or religion. They asked also for an *unofficial majority* in the council, *i.e.* that the number of unofficial members should be larger than that of official members.

After a long controversy certain reforms were granted in 1921. The executive council was to consist of four government officials and three unofficial members nominated by the governor. The legislative council was to consist of fourteen government officials and twenty-three unofficial members. Of the unofficials, sixteen were to be elected, and seven nominated, or appointed, by the governor. Eleven of the sixteen elected members were to be "territorial," representing the nine provinces—the Western Province, on account of its large population and commercial importance electing three instead of one; and five representing respectively the Europeans in the towns (the "Urban" electorate), the Europeans outside the towns (the "Rural" electorate), the Burghers, the Ceylon Chamber of Commerce, and the Low Country Products Association. Of the seven nominated unofficials, two were to represent the Kandyans, one the Muhammadans, one the Indians resident in the Island: and three other members were to be appointed at the discretion of the governor. All these reforms were granted as a temporary measure.

Oddly enough, it was in Sir William Manning's time that further reforms were granted. In October 1924 a new and enlarged legislative council came into being. It consisted of twelve officials and thirty-seven unofficial members, all but three of the latter being *elected*. The unofficials represented twenty-three territorial constituencies, or electorates, and eleven communal, the remaining three being nominated by the governor. Further, one of the unofficials was to be elected as vice-president of the council, to preside at its sittings when, as would ordinarily happen, the governor was absent. In the executive council two seats were reserved for unofficial members.

Among the other important events of this rule must be noted the opening of a canal connecting the Colombo Lake with the Harbour (1922), a measure designed by Sir Henry McCallum; the establishment of a statistical department (1921), the need for which was revealed during the census; the extension of the railway from Bandarawela to Ella (1918), and thence to Badulla (1924); and the opening of the University College in Colombo (1921) as the beginning of a future University of Ceylon. The census of 1921 shewed a population of 4,498,605.

In November 1925 **Sir Hugh Clifford** arrived in Ceylon as governor. Like Sir Charles McCarthy, he had been colonial secretary of the island before. Many subjects of stirring interest were debated during the next two years, but in May 1927 Sir Hugh Clifford left Ceylon to be governor of the Straits Settlements, and was succeeded by **Sir Herbert Stanley** in August.

When the Legislative Council of 1924 met, it was understood that the question of further reforms would be considered before it was dissolved in 1929. The government in England appointed, in August 1927, a Commission to visit Ceylon and report upon the whole system of government in the island. This Commission was known as the *Donoughmore Commission*, from its Chairman the earl of Donoughmore,— the other members being Sir Matthew Nathan, Sir Geoffrey Butler, and Dr. T. Drummond Shiels. It began its work in Ceylon in November 1927, and for nearly three months collected information, and heard the statements of people representing all parts of the island and all classes of the inhabitants. The recommendations made in its Report were slightly modified by Sir Herbert Stanley, and again modified by the Government in England, and finally accepted by our Legislative Council.

The new constitution makes an enormous change in our system of government in Ceylon, and gives unusually large powers to the people. These are its principal provisions :—the present Legislative and Executive Councils are both abolished, and a new *State Council* takes their place, consisting of 50 territorially elected members, 8 nominated members, and 3 officials to be known as Officers of State. These officers are the Chief (so long " colonial " ) Secretary, the Financial Secretary ( " treasurer " ), and the Attorney-General, or a Minister of Justice. There will be no communally elected members. When the Council meets for the first time it will elect a Speaker (president) and a Deputy Speaker (vice-president), and then divide itself into seven Committees. Each Committee will elect its own Chairman (to be called the Minister), and will administer the affairs of a group of Departments. These Departments will deal with (1) Home Affairs, (2) Agriculture and Lands, (3) Local Administration, (4) Health, (5) Labour, Industry, and Commerce, (6) Education, (7) Communications and Works. The seven Ministers and the three Officers of State (who will also be in charge of groups of Departments) will form a Board of Ministers, which will practically take the place of the abolished Executive Council. Thus, the Councillors, and through them the people who select them, will not merely advise or criticise the Government, but will take part in the actual government of the country.

A still greater change is made in regard to the *Franchise,* or right of voting for the election of members to the State Council. Up to this time only males could vote, and they had to possess certain qualifications in regard to property, or income, or literacy, *i.e.* being able to read and write. By the new regulations, every man and *every woman* above the age of 21 years is allowed to register as a voter, and to vote at the elections, so long as he or she has resided in Ceylon for at least five years. If the voter can read and write English, he or she may also be elected a Councillor.

Much to his expressed regret, Sir Herbert Stanley was not able to initiate and see at work the new Constitution, in the settlement of which he had taken no small part. On November 1930 he was appointed High Commissioner for South Africa, and he left Ceylon in February

1931. No former governor of Ceylon knew so intimately and at first hand the social life of the people he governed. He was always ready to attend public gatherings, and his tact and geniality disarmed much opposition to government measures. He was unfortunate in coming to Ceylon at a time when the great industries of the island—tea, rubber, and coconut—suffered severely from low prices and a scarcity of markets. Increased taxation appeared to be necessary, and a Bill imposing taxes on incomes was proposed. It was fiercely discussed, and at last defeated in the Legislative Council. There was a great outcry for retrenchment in public expenditure, which resulted in many of those who were employed under Government being dismissed, especially in the lower grades. Railway and postal services were reduced in number, and new schemes (including the establishment of a Ceylon University) were put aside till better times should come. Even the census of February 1931 was a partial one, the city of Colombo being taken in full, as before, but the rest of the island without full detail. The population of the whole island was estimated at 5,306,871, that of Colombo alone being 284,155. The next largest towns in population were: Jaffna (45,708), Galle (38,424), and Kandy (37,147). Before Sir Herbert Stanley left, he appointed a Historical Commission to report on unpublished documents relating to the island, and on the housing and publication of public records. He was succeeded by **Sir Graeme Thomson**, who was once colonial secretary of Ceylon.

Sir Graeme Thomson arrived as governor in April 1931. Within a week of his arrival, the new State Council was proclaimed, and the old Legislative Council was dissolved. The fifty members of the new Council were elected in June. One of the seats became vacant shortly afterwards, and Mrs. A. P. Molamure was elected, —the first lady member of Council. On January 1932 the Income Tax Bill, which had been thrown out by the old Legislative Council in 1930, was passed by the new Council, and became law.

Towards the end of the year 1933 Sir Graeme Thomson left Ceylon, nominally on leave, but it was afterwards known that he was to be appointed to a high official post in London. On the way, however, he fell ill, and died at Aden.

The Chief Secretary Mr. (now Sir) F. G. Tyrrell administered the Government till the arrival in December 1933 of **Sir Edward Stubbs**, who also was a former Colonial Secretary.

More than once has the loyalty of the Ceylonese been publicly referred to in the highest terms ; and in concluding this sketch of our Island's history we may well consider if indeed we have not cause to be loyal. Under British rule we enjoy almost every advantage which an Englishman enjoys in England. We have peace, protection of person and property, the fullest freedom, and equal laws. We have numerous schools which prepare us for our work in life. Every profession is open to us, every trade and occupation is free to all.

Natives of Ceylon have risen and can rise to very high positions in the service of Government. The post, the telegraph, and the steamer have brought us into communication with every part of the world. The literature of Britain, the arts and sciences, the highest ideals of Christian life and thought, and every civilizing influence that makes for peace, comfort, and happiness, have all been placed within our reach. We belong to an empire vast in extent, rich in noble traditions, powerful beyond its rivals, and governed, under the King, by statesmen who are not only prompt to advance its best interests, but sincerely anxious to promote the welfare of all its members. It will be our own fault if we do not so use the advantages we have as to prove that we are not unworthy of them.

## Kings of the Mahavansa

| No. | Name. | Date of Accession B.C. | E.Z. B.C. | Capital |
|---|---|---|---|---|
| 1 | Vijaya ... | 545 | 483 | Tammanna Nuwara |
| | *(Regency of Upatissa)* ... | 505 | 445 | Upatissa Nuwara |
| 2 | Panduvasu-deva ... | 504 | 444 | ,, |
| 3 | Abhaya | 474 | 414 | ,, |
| | (*Regency of Tissa*) ... | 454 | 494 | ,, |
| 4 | Pandukabhaya ... | 437 | 377 | A'pura |
| 5 | (*Gana-pa Tissa*)* ... | — | — | ,, |
| 6 | Mutasiva ... | 367 | 307 | ,, |
| 7 | Devanampiya Tissa ... | 307 | 247 | ,, |
| 8 | Uttiya ... | 267 | 207 | ,, |
| 9 | Mahasiva ... | 257 | 197 | ,, |
| 10 | Sura Tissa ... | 247 | 187 | ,, |
| 11 | Sena } (Tamils) ... | 237 | 177 | ,, |
| 12 | Guttaka } (Tamils) | — | — | ,, |
| 13 | Asela | 215 | 155 | ,, |
| 14 | Elara (Tamil) ... | 205 | 145 | ,, |
| 15 | Dutugëmunu ... | 161 | 101 | ,, |
| 16 | Saddha Tissa ... | 137 | 77 | ,, |
| 17 | Thulathanaka ... | 119 | 59 | ,, |
| 18 | Lanja Tissa ... | 119 | 59 | ,, |
| 19 | Khallata Naga *or* Kaluna ... | 109 | 50 | ,, |
| 20 | Valagam Ba *or* Vatta-Gamini-Abhaya ... | 104 | 44 | ,, |
| 21-5 | *Five Tamil Kings* ... | 103 | 44 | ,, |
| (20) | Valagam Ba (*restored*) ... | 88 | — | ,, |
| 26 | Mahachula Maha Tissa ... | 76 | 17 | ,, |
| | | | A.D. | |
| 27 | Chora Naga ... | 62 | 3 | ,, |
| 28 | Kuda Tissa ... | 50 | 9 | ,, |
| 29 | Anula (*Queen*) ... | 47 | 12 | ,, |

* Said to have reigned 40 years after his father Pandukabhaya who reigned 30 years. See note on p. 15.

E.Z.—Epigraphia Zeylanica.

| | | B.C. | A.D. | |
|---|---|---|---|---|
| 30 | Makalan Tissa ... | 42 | 17 | A'Pura |
| 31 | Bhatiya I. ... | 20 | 39 | " |
| | | A.D. | | |
| 32 | Mahadëliya Mana ... | 9 | 67 | " |
| 33 | Adagëmunu ... | 21 | 79 | " |
| 34 | Kanirajanu Tissa ... | 30 | 89 | " |
| 35 | Chulabhaya ... | 33 | 92 | " |
| 36 | Sivali (*Queen*) ... | 35 | 93 | " |
| 37 | Ila Naga ... | 35 | 93 | " |
| | (*Interregnum of 3 years*) ... | — | — | " |
| (37) | Ila Naga (*restored*) ... | — | — | " |
| 38 | Sandamunu Siva ... | 44 | 103 | " |
| 39 | Yasalalaha Tissa ... | 52 | 112 | " |
| 40 | Subha Raja ... | 60 | 120 | " |
| 41 | Vasabha ... | 66 | 126 | " |
| 42 | Vankanasika Tissa ... | 110 | 170 | " |
| 43 | Gaja Bȧhu I ... | 113 | 173 | " |
| 54 | Mahu'a Na ... | 135 | 196 | " |
| 45 | Bhatiya II ... | 141 | 202 | " |
| 46 | Kanittha Tissa ... | 165 | 226 | " |
| 47 | Kuhun Na ... | 193 | 245 | " |
| 48 | Kuda Na ... | 195 | 247 | " |
| 49 | Siri Naga I ... | 196 | 249 | " |
| 50 | Voharika Tissa ... | 215 | 269 | " |
| 51 | Abhaya Naga ... | 237 | 291 | " |
| 52 | Siri Naga II ... | 244 | 299 | " |
| 53 | Vijaya or Vijayindu ... | 247 | 301 | " |
| 54 | Sangha Tissa I ... | 248 | 302 | " |
| 55 | Siri Sangabo ... | 252 | 306 | " |
| 56 | Gothabhaya or Golu Aba ... | 254 | 309 | " |
| 57 | Jettha Tissa I ... | 267 | 323 | " |
| 58 | Maha Sena ... | 277 | 334 | " |

## Kings of the Suluvansa or Lower Dynasty

| No. | Name. | Date of Accession A. D. | E. Z. A. D. | Capital. |
|---|---|---|---|---|
| 59 | Siri Meghavanna or Kit Siri Mevan ... | 304 | 362 | A'pura |
| 60 | Jettha Tissa II ... | 332 | 389 | ,, |
| 61 | Buddha-dasa ... | 341 | 398 | ,, |
| 62 | Upatissa I ... | 370 | 426 | ,, |
| 63 | Mahanama ... | 412 | 468 | ,, |
| 64 | Sotthi Sena ... | 434 | 490 | ,, |
| 65 | Satgahaka ... | 434 | 490 | ,, |
| 66 | Mitta Sena ... | 435 | 490 | ,, |
| 67–72 | *Six Tamil kings* ... | 436 | 491 | ,, |
| 73 | Dhatu Sena ... | 463 | 516 | ,, |
| 74 | Kasyapa I ... | 479 | 526 | ,, |
| 75 | Mugalan I ... | 497 | 552 | A'pura & Sigiriya |
| 76 | Kumara Dasa ... | 515 | 570 | A'pura |
| 77 | Kirti-Sena ... | 524 | 579 | ,, |
| 78 | Siva ... | 524 | 588 | ,, |
| 79 | Upatissa II ... | 525 | 588 | ,, |
| 80 | Silakala ... | 526 | 590 | ,, |
| 81 | Dapula Sen (or Dapula I) ... | 539 | 603 | ,, |
| 82 | Mugalan II ... | 540 | 603 | ,, |
| 83 | Kitsirime (Kirti Sri Megha)... | 560 | 622 | ,, |
| 84 a | Mahanaga ... | 561 | 622 | ,, |
| (84 b | Lamani Singana...........) | — | — | ,, |
| 85 | Agrabodhi I ... | 564 | 625 | ,, |
| 86 | Agrabodhi II ... | 598 | 658 | ,, |
| 87 | Sangha Tissa II ... | 608 | 667 | ,, |
| 88 | Dalla Mugalan ... | 608 | 667 | ,, |
| 89 | Silameghavanna ... | 614 | 672 | ,, |
| 90 | Agrabodhi III ... | 623 | 680 | ,, |
| 91 | Jettha Tissa III ... | 623 | 680 | ,, |
| (90) | Agrabodhi III (*restored*) ... | 624 | 680 | ,, |
| 92 | Dathopa Tissa I ... | 640 | 692 | ,, |

| | | | | |
|---|---|---|---|---|
| 93 | Kasyapa II ... | 652 | 695 | A'pura |
| 94 | Dapula II* ... | 661 | 703 | ,, |
| 95 | Dathopa Tissa II ... | 664 | 703 | ,, |
| 96 | Agrabodhi IV ... | 673 | 712 | ,, |
| 97 | Datta ... | 989 | 727 | ,, |
| 98 | Hatthadatha ... | 691 | 729 | ,, |
| 99 | Manavamma ... | 691 | 729 | ,, |
| 100 | Agrabodhi V ... | 726 | 765 | ,, |
| 101 | Kasyapa III. ... | 732 | 771 | ,, |
| 102 | Mahinda I. ... | 738 | 779 | ,, |
| 103 | Agrabodhi VI. (Akbo Salamevan)... | 741 | 782 | P'naruwa |
| 104 | Agrabodhi VII. ... | 781 | 822 | A'pura |
| 105 | Mahinda II. ... | 787 | 828 | ,, |
| 106 | Dapula III. ... | 807 | 848 | ,, |
| 107 | Mahinda III. ... | 812 | 853 | ,, |
| 108 | Agrabodhi VIII. ... | 816 | 857 | ,, |
| 109 | Dapulu IV. ... | 827 | 868 | ,, |
| 110 | Agrabodhi IX. ... | 843 | 884 | P'naruwa |
| 111 | Sena I. ... | 846 | 887 | ,, |
| 112 | Sena II. ... | 866 | 907 | ,, |
| 113 | Udaya I. ... | 901 | 941 | ,, |
| 114 | Kasyapa IV. ... | 912 | 952 | ,, |
| 115 | Kasyapa V. ... | 929 | 969 | ,, |
| 116 | Dapulu V. ... | 939 | 979 | ,, |
| 117 | Dapulu VI. ... | 940 | 979 | ,, |
| 118 | Udaya II. ... | 952 | 991 | ,, |
| 119 | Sena III. ... | 955 | 994 | ,, |
| 120 | Udaya III. ... | 964 | 1003 | ,, |
| 121 | Sena IV. ... | 972 | 1011 | ,, |
| 122 | Mahinda IV. ... | 975 | 1015 | ,, |
| 123 | Sena V. ... | 991 | 1032 | ,, |
| 124 | Mahinda V. ... | 1001 | 1052 | P'naruwa & A'pura |
| 125 | Kasyapa (Vikrama Bahu) ... | 1037 | 1078 | Ruhuna |
| 126 | Kirti ... | 1049 | — | ,, |
| 127 | Mahalana Kirti ... | 1049 | — | ,, |
| 128 | Vikrama Pandu ... | 1052 | — | Kalutara |
| 129 | Jagatipala ... | 1053 | — | Ruhuna |

* Commonly reckoned as Dapulu I.

| | | | | | |
|---|---|---|---|---|---|
| 130 | Parakrama Pandu I. | ... | 1057 | — | Ruhuna |
| 131 | Lokesvara | ... | 1059 | — | Kataragama |
| 132 | Kasyapa | ... | — | — | " |
| 133 | Vijaya Bahu I. | ... | 1035 | — | P'naruwa |
| 134 | Jaya Bahu I. | ... | 1120 | — | " |
| 135 | Vikrama Bahu I. | ... | 1121 | — | " |
| 136 | Gaja Bahu II. | ... | 1142 | — | " |
| 137 | Parakrama Bahu I. | ... | 1153 | — | " |
| 138 | Vijaya Bahu II. | ... | 1186 | — | " |
| 139 | Mahinda VI. | ... | 1187 | — | " |
| 140 | Kirti Nissanka Malla | ... | 1187 | — | " |
| 141 | Vira Bahu I. | ... | 1196 | — | " |
| 142 | Vikrrma Bahu II. | ... | 1196 | — | " |
| 143 | Chodaganga | ... | 1196 | — | " |
| 144 | Lilavati (*Queen*) | ... | 1197 | — | " |
| 145 | Sahasa Malla | ... | 1200 | — | " |
| 146 | Kalyanavati (*Queen*) | ... | 1202 | — | " |
| 147 | Dharmasoka | ... | 1208 | — | " |
| 148 | Anikanga | ... | 1209 | — | " |
| (144) | Lilavati (*restored*) | ... | 1209 | — | " |
| 149 | Lokesvara II. | ... | 1209 | — | " |
| (144) | Lilavati (*restored*) | ... | 1210 | — | " |
| 150 | Parakrama Pandu II. | ... | 1212 | — | " |
| 151 | Magha | ... | 1215 | — | " |
| 152 | Vijaya Bahu III. | ... | 1236 | — | D'deniya |
| 153 | Parakrama Bahu II. | ... | 1240 | — | " |
| 154 | Vijaya Bahu IV. | ... | 1275 | — | P'naruwa |
| 155 | Bhuvaneka Bahu I. | ... | 1277 | — | D'deniya & Yapahu |
| 156 | Parakrama Bahu III | ... | 1288 | — | P'naruwa |
| 157 | Bhuvaneka Bahu II | ... | 1293 | — | Kru'gala |
| 158 | Parakrama Bahu IV | ... | 1295 | — | " |
| 159 | Bhuvaneka Bahu III. | ... | — | — | |
| 160 | Jaya Bahu I. or Vijaya Bahu V. | ... | — | — | " |
| 161 | Bhuvaneka Bahu IV. | ... | 1347 | — | Gampola |
| 162 | Parakrama Bahu V. | ... | 1351 | — | " |
| 163 | Vikrama Bahu III. | ... | — | — | " |
| 164 | Bhuvaneka Bahu V. | ... | — | — | Gampola |
| 165 | Vijaya Bahu II. | ... | — | — | & Kotte |

| | | | | |
|---|---|---|---|---|
| 166 | Vira Alakesvara or Vijaya Bahu VI. ... | — | — | Kotte |
| 167 | Parakrama Bahu VI. | { 1410<br>1415 | —<br>— | "<br>" |
| 168 | Jaya Bahu II. ... | 1462 | — | " |
| 169 | Bhuvaneka Bahu VI. ... | 1464 | — | " |
| 170 | Parakrama Bahu VII. (Pandita) ... | 1471 | — | "<br>" |
| 171 | Parakrama Bahu VIII. ... | — | — | " |
| 172 | Parakrama Bahu IX. ... | — | — | " |
| 173 | Vijaya Bahu VII. ... | 1527 | — | " |
| 174 | Bhuvaneka Bahu VII. ... | 1534 | — | " |
| 175 | Don Juan Dharmapala ... | 1551 | — | " |
| 176 | Raja Sinha ... | 1581 | — | |
| 177 | Vimala Dharma Suriya I ... | 1592 | — | Sitawaka |
| 178 | Senerat .. | 1604 | — | Kandy |
| 179 | Raja Sinha ... | 1635 | — | " |
| 180 | Vimala Dharma Suriya II. ... | 1687 | — | " |
| 181 | Narendra Sinha ... | 1707 | — | " |
| 182 | Vijaya Raja Sinha ... | 1739 | — | " |
| 183 | Kirti Sri Raja Sinha ... | 1747 | — | " |
| 184 | Rajadhi Raja Sinha ... | 1780 | — | " |
| 185 | Vikrama Raja Sinha ... | 1798<br>to<br>1815 | —<br>—<br>— | "<br>"<br>" |

## Portuguese Captains General and Governors.

1. Pedro Lopes de Sousa
2. Jeronimo de Azevedo
3. Francisco de Meneses
4. Manuel Mascarenhas Homem
5. Nuno Alvares Pereira
6. Constantine de Sa de Noronha
7. Jorge de Almeida
8. Constantine de Sa de Noronha
9. Jorge de Almeida
10. Diego de Mello
11. Antonio Mascarenhas
12. Philippe Mascarenhas
13. Manuel Mascarenhas
14. Francisco de Mello de Castro
15. Antonio de Sousa Coutinho (*Ribeiro*)

## Dutch Governors.

### At Galle.

| | | From A.D. | |
|---|---|---|---|
| 1. | Willem Jacobsz Coster | March | 1640 |
| 2. | Jan Thyszoon Payaart | August | 1640 |
| 3. | Joan Maatzuyker | May | 1646 |
| 4. | Jacob van Kittensteyn | February | 1650 |
| 5. | Adrian van der Meiden | Oct. | 1653 |

### At Colombo.

| | | | |
|---|---|---|---|
| 6. | Adriaan van der Meiden | May | 1656 |
| 7. | Ryklof van Goens | Sept. | 1662 |
| 8. | Jacob Hustaart | Dec. | 1663 |
| | *Adrian Roothaes* (*acting*) | Nov. | 1664 |
| 9. | Ryklof van Goens | | 1665 |
| 10. | Ryklof van Goens, *Junior* | April | 1675 |
| 11. | Lourens Pyl | Dec. | 1679 |
| 12. | Thomas van Rhee | Jan. | 1692 |
| 13. | Gerrit de Heere | Feb. | 1697 |
| 14. | Cornelis Joan Simons | May | 1703 |
| 15. | Hendrick Becker | Nov. | 1707 |
| 16. | Isaac Augustyn Rumpf | Dec. | 1716 |
| 17. | Johannes Hertenberg | Jan. | 1724 |
| 18. | Petrus Vuyst | Sept. | 1726 |
| 19. | Stephanus Versluys | Aug. | 1729 |
| 20. | Jacob Christiaan Pielat | Dec. | 1732 |
| 21. | Diederick van Domburg | Jan. | 1734 |
| 22. | Gustaaf Willem Baron van Imhoff | July | 1736 |
| 23. | Willem Maurits Bruynink | March | 1740 |
| 24. | Daniel Overbeek | Jan. | 1742 |
| 25. | Julius Valentyn Stein van Gollenesse | May | 1743 |
| 26. | Geraard Joan Vreeland | March | 1751 |
| 27. | Joan Gideon Loten | Sept. | 1752 |
| 28. | Jan Schreuder | March | 1757 |
| 29. | Lubbert Jan Baron van Eck | Nov. | 1762 |
| 30. | Iman Willen Falck | Aug. | 1765 |
| 31. | Willem Jacob van de Graaf | Feb. | 1785 |
| 32. | Johan Gerard van Angelbeek | Aug. | 1794 |

## British Governors.

| | Name | Month | Year |
|---|---|---|---|
| 1. | The Hon. the Governor of Madras in Council | February | 1796 |
| 2. | The Hon. Frederick North (*Earl of Guilford*) | October | 1798 |
| 3. | Lieut-General the Rt. Hon. Sir Thomas Maitland | July | 1805 |
| 4. | General Sir Robert Brownrigg *Bart.* | March | 1812 |
| 5. | Lieut-General The Hon. Sir Edward Paget | February | 1822 |
| 6. | Lieut-General Sir Edward Barnes | January | 1824 |
| 7. | The Rt. Hon. Sir Robert Wilmot Horton, *Bart.* | October | 1831 |
| 8. | The Rt. Hon. James Alexander Stewart Mackenzie | November | 1837 |
| 9. | Lieut-General Sir Colin Campbell | April | 1841 |
| 10. | The Rt. Hon. the Viscount Torrington | May | 1847 |
| 11. | Sir George William Anderson | November | 1850 |
| 12. | Sir Henry George Ward | May | 1855 |
| 13. | Sir Charles Justin MacCarthy | October | 1860 |
| | *Major-General Terence O' Brien* | December | 1863 |
| 14 | Sir Hercules George Robert Robinson (*Lord Rosmead*) | May | 1865 |
| 15. | The Rt. Hon. Sir William Henry Gregory | March | 1872 |
| 16. | Sir James Robert Longden | September | 1877 |
| 17. | The Hon. Sir Arthur Hamilton Gordon (*Lord Stanmore*) | December | 1883 |
| 18. | Sir Arthur Elibank Havelock | May | 1890 |
| 19. | The Rt. Hon. Sir Joseph West Ridgeway | February | 1896 |
| 20. | Sir Henry Arthur Blake | December | 1903 |
| 21. | Sir Henry Edward McCallum | August | 1907 |
| 22. | Sir Robert Chalmers (*Lord Chalmers*) | October | 1913 |
| 23. | Sir John Anderson | April | 1916 |
| 24. | Sir William Henry Manning | September | 1918 |
| 25. | Sir Hugh Clifford | November | 1925 |
| 26. | Sir Herbert James Stanley | August | 1927 |
| 27. | Sir Graeme Thomson | April | 1931 |
| 28. | Sir Edward Stubbs | December | 1933 |

# INDEX.


Abhayagiri 40, 46ff, 102
Abhayaveva 12
Abu Zeyd 83
Abyssinia 81, 83, 122
Adam's Bridge 4
Adam's Peak 10, 17, 83, 85, 89, 111f, 136, 143
Adhikaram 10C
Agricultural Society 248
Alagkkonara (Alakeswara) 115f
Alawwa 146
Albergaria, L. Soarez de 127f
Almeida, L. de 125ff
Alutkuru Korale 46
Alutnuwara 167
Aluvihara 40, 59
Alwis, James, 240, 242
Amba Ganga 108
Ambattha-kola 63
Ambulugala 118f.
American Missionaries 211
Amiens, Peace of 194
Ancient Trade of Ceylon 80
Anderson, Sir G. 235, 238
Anderson, Sir John 251
Andrews, R. 200
Angelbeek, J. G. van 192
Anthonisz, R. G. 171n
Anula, Princess 22f
Anula, Queen 41
Anuradhapura, 12, 14f. 35, 58, 69, 73, 78, 243f. et passim.
*Arabian Nights* 84
Arabs, 2, 81, 115, 112f.
Arakan 87, 176, 185
Arittha, mt. 14
Arya Chakravarti 112, 115f.
Asoka, King 18—23
Asokamala 38
Attanagalla 47, 58, 110
Audience Hall, Kandy, 219, 243
Ayodhya (Oudh.) 4
Azevedo, D. Jeronimo de 138, 144
Badalatthalai 95
Badulla 143, 167, 246, 249, 253
Baillie, Colonel 204
Balane Pass 136, 138, 148, 151
Bali offerings 47
Bandarawela 249
Banks 228, 245f.
Baptist Mission 211
Barbut, Colonel 204f.
Barnes, Sir E. 225
Barreto, 147
Batavia 151, 153ff, 157f, 160, 165, 174f, 178, 184, 194
Batavian Republic, 192
Batticaloa 141f, 145, 152, 175, 179, 210
Batuta, Ibn 114f.
Becker, Governor 172
Belgium, King of 239
Bentota 110, 246
Beraminipaya 74
Bintenne 17
Bird, G. 227
Bishop, first Anglican 231
Blake, Sir H. 248
Boer War 247
Bogambara 177, 216
Bonnevaux, Colonel P. 200
Boschouwer, M. de 143ff.
Bo-tree 22f, 36, 53, 58
Boyd, H. 191
Brahmans 2, 13, 14, 20, 51, 70, 94, 104
Brazen Palace 35, 38, 48f. 53
British Governors, List of, 266
Brito, 128
Brownrigg, Sir R. 211—224
Buddha 2, 5, 12, 15—17, 22, 36, 94, 103
,, Maitri 61
Buddha-Gaya 52f.
Buddhist priests 21—23, 26 36, 39f, 43, 48, 57f., 67, 70, 89f., 100, 108, 110, 176, 185f., 224
Buddhist Writings 40, 57, 58f, 84, 89, 108, 250

Burghers, 181, 194, 224, 229, 249, 252
Burma 3, 87, 89, 100 (See also *Arakan* and *Pegu*)

Calicut 123f, 130
Cambodia 100
Campbell, Sir C. 231
Campbell, Sir J. 225
Canaka, the Brahman 94
Canals 198
Canara 118
Castes 10
Catharina, Dona 135-138, 145, 150, 170
Census 241, 245, 247, 249, 253, 257
Ceylon, names of 2. 9
,, ancient divisions 12, 15
,, modern provinces 221, 229, 231, 243, 246
Chakrayuddha 126
Chalmers, Sir R. 250
Chandrabhanu 109
Chandragupta Maurya 92*n*
Chapman, Bishop 231
Charter of 1833, 230
Chilaw 116, 209, 249
China 2f, 52, 58, 81, 114, 117, 121f.
Chola (*Tanjore*) 9, 19, 26, 45, 78, 80, 86—90, 101, 105, 109, 118
Christianity in Ceylon 83, 129, 131, 170, 194, 211, 224, 230f. 245
Church Mission 211
Cinnamon 3, 122, 125, 127, 141, 152, 170f, 174, 179, 183, 189, 228
Coast steamer 237
Cochin 128, 130
Codrington, H. W. 91*n*
Coffee 227, 232, 244, 246
Coinage 242
Colombo 115, 125—128, 139, 144, 150—153, 157, 159, 173, 193, 228, 241, 243, 253
*Commentaries* 41, 59
Conacar 115
Convention, Kandyan 219, 223
Convention of Malvana 146
Correa, S. 144
Cosmos Indicopleustes 82f.
Coster, W. J. 151—155
Cotta (see *Kotte*)
Courts of Law 230f.
Coutinho, A. de S. 159
Clifford, Sir H. 254
Crown Colony 201*n*

Dagabas 22, 25, 35, 38f. 43, 49f, 68, 107
Dalada Maligawa, Kandy 182, 212
Dan badeniya 108, 112, 205
Dambulla 39, 49, 234
Danes 145
Danture 138
Dappula, prince 72
Dathasiva, general 68
Davie, Major 205—207
Dawson, Captain 226
De la Haye, Admiral 175f.
Denham, E. B. 128*n*
Devil-dancing 47
*Dhammapada* 77
Dharmakirti, Priest 111
Dharmapala King 130—134, 146
Diaz, Bartholomew 123
Dighajantu, General 32
Dighaya 12
Digligy 167
*Dipavansa* 61
"Discovery" of Ceylon 125
Disestablishment, Church, 245
Diyatalawa, 247
Dondra 106, 110, 114f., 136
Donoughmore Commission 254
Doyle, General 200
D'Oyly, Sir J., 219, 221
Dumbara 118, 219, 223
Dutch in Ceylon 194 (*of Holland*)
,, Governors, 265

East India Company, Dutch 141, 161, 181, 183
,, English 141, 161, 174, 190, 199—201
Eck. Baron van 188
Edicts of Asoka 18
Edinburgh, Duke of 241
Edward VII. King 243, 245, 248, 250
Egypt 82
Ehelapola 212—219, 221, 223
Ekneligoda 219
Elara 26—34, 39
Elephants 2, 30, 125, 150, 171, 179, 228
Ellahara 103
English, early visits to Ceylon 161, 173f., 187,
Excise 249
Executive Council 229, 25?, 255
Export duties 237, 241

Fa Hien 58
Falck, Governor 188f
Fitch, Ralph 161
Franchise 255
French 173, 175, 191f

Galle, 115, 125, 139, 154, 157, 161, 173, 175, 179f, 193, 227, 236, 241, 246
Gama Vasco da 123
Gampola 110, 112, 114, 236
Gannoruwa 152
Gansabhawa 169
Gauwa 106, 126
Giri, Monk 40
Goa 127, 133, 134, 137, 150—153, 155, 176
Goens, Ryclof van 164, 172, 175f
Gollenesse, J. V. S. van 197
Gongalagoda Banda 244
Gordon, Sir A. (Lord Stanmore) 245f
Governors, British, 266
,, Dutch, 265
,, Portuguese, 264
Graaf, W. J. van de 189, 192
Greeks, 7, 122
Gregory, Sir W. 243
Guptas in India 50—53, 55
Guttika and Sena 25
Guzerat 6

Hambantota 210, 247
Hanguranketa 167, 175, 204, 207
Hanuman 4
Hanwella 209f
Haputale 243, 246
Harispattu 46, 118
Hattha Datha 69
Havelock, Sir A. 246
Heere, G. de 172, 181
Hendela 172, 182
Hewaheta 118
Hindus 1, 89, 128, 136, 187
Historical Commission 257
Holland (cf *Dutch*) 139, 145—160, 164, 166, 170—199
Horton, Sir R. 228f
Hulft, General 158
Huns 51
Hustaart, J. 174

Ilanaga Sena, 77
Imhoff, Baron G. W. van 172, 184f., 187
Income Tax 256
Indian Mutiny of 1857, 236
,, Representation 252
"Indicopleustes" 83
Irrigation Works 198, 236, 246
Isurumuniya Vihara 44, 51

Jaffna 11, 20, 39, 83, 112, 115, 118, 130, 135, 145, 147, 157, 160, 171, 176, 179f. 193, 210, 247
Jagatipala 54, 90
*Janakiharana* 64

*Jatakas* 114
Java (cf. *Batavia*) 109, 121, 176
Java Bahu 109
Jayawardanapura (cf. *Kotte*) 115
Jayaveva 14
Jetavanarama 49f., 102
Jews 84
Joao, Don (See *Dharmapala* and *Konnappu Bandara*)
Johnston, Sir Alexander 224
,, Captain Arthur 210f.
Jotipala 67
Jury, Trial by 210, 224

Kirti Sir Megha 91—96, 102
Kitu Agbo 77
Kittensteyn, J. van 157
Knox, Robert 161—170, 173
Konnappu Bandara 135f.
Kotmala 31
Kotte (*Cotta*) 115—119, 125—134
Kottiyar 144, 161, 175, 209
Kulesakera of Pandya, 101, 112
Kumara Dasa 64
Kundesale Raja 182
Kurunde Vihara 67
Kurunegala 61, 95, 110, 113—115, 231, 246
Kuveni 8—10

Kadugannawa 136, 226
Kaffirs 165, 207
Kalaveva 61, 68, 109, 246
Kalidasa 52
Kalinga 54, 67, 79, 107
Kalu Ganga 12, 72
Kalutara 86, 157f., 179, 243
Kalyanavati, Queen, 106
Kandapalla 148
Kandula, Elephant, 32f.
Kandy and Kandyans 33, 97, 118, 132, 133—139, 141—143, 161—177, 182., 188—228, 236—238, 243, 249, 252
Kannesami 202
Kantalai tank 49, 103
Kapilavastu 16
Kara Ganga 49
Kashmir 43*n*
Kataragama 86, 168
Katugastota 236
Kavan Tissa 28, 30f.
*Kaviyasekara* 119
Kaymans Gate 159
Kayts 160
Kegalla 118
Kelani Ganga 146, 247
Kelaniya 7, 17, 28, 110, 132
Keppitipola 222f.
Kirime dam 236
Kirti, Prince 86
Kirti Nagaragiri, General 100

Lala 5f.
Lambakarnas 44, 46
Lanka 2, 4, 9
Lankapura, City 4, 7
,, General 101
Lankarama 40
Law, Courts 180, 231f.
,, Roman Dutch 198
Leaf disease 242
League, Ceylon 240
Legislative Council 229, 239f., 245, 246, 248, 252—256
Lepers 55, 172, 182
Lewayas 168
Lewis, J. P. 205*n*
Lilavati. Queen 90, 106f.
Lisbon 123, 131, 140
Lokeswara 86
Longden, Sir J. R. 244
Loos, Dr. J. 242
Loten, Governor 187
Lowa Maha Paya (See *Brazen Palace*)
Lucasz, Admiral 153
Lunatic Asylum 230

Maatzuyker, Governor 156f, 172
MacCarthy, Sir C. J., 238, 254
Mac Dowall, Fort 207
,, General 203
Mackenzie, Rt. Hon. J. A. S. 230
Madras, 174, 190f., 200f., 221, 231, 234
Madugalla 223
Madura (cf. *Pandya*) 9, 76, 101, 182
Magadha 5, 17f., 24, 59
Magha 107
Mahagama 27f.
Mahamega 15, 21, 23
Mahanama, Priest 61
Maha Oya 146
Mahastane 176
Mahathupa (see *Ruanveli Seya*)
Mahavansa, Dynasty 50, 61
*Mahavansa* 61f., 64, 111, 116
Mahaveli Ganga 12f., 26, 31, 87 206
Maha Vihara 22, 24, 46, 48, 50, 57, 62, 67, 69, 102
Minindu, Priest, 18, 21—24, 54, 61
,, Prince 77
Mahiyangana 17, 182
Mail Coach 228
Maitland, Sir T 211
Malacca 125, 127, 137
Malaya-rata 12, 38, 75, 97
Malayas 109, 112, 121, 205—207, 234
Maldive islands 115, 125
Malvana 146
Manabharana 91f., 98f.
Mannar, 26, 81, 132, 135—137, 157, 160, 164, 179, 203, 209, 336, 249
Manning, Sir W. H 251
Mantota 26
Mascarenhas, Governors 155
Matale, 103, 150, 160, 162, 207, 234, 243
Matara 65, 136, 179, 209, 346
Maya Dunne 130—134
Maya-rata 12, 26, 79, 108
Mc Callum, Sir H. E. 248f.
Medamahanuwara 219
Medical School 242
Mello, D. de 151f.
Mercer, Lieutenant 209
Methley, Miss V. 205*n*
Meuron, General de 193, 201f.
Meiden, A. van der Governor 157f., 172f.
Mihintale 22, 43, 67
Military Expenditure 239, 245
Ministers, Board of, 255
Minneriya tank 49f., 103
Mirisveti Vihara 77
Missions, Protestant 211, 230
Mitra, General 112
Molligoda 212—214, 218f., 222
Moors 81, 124—127, 130, 171, 203, 217, 228, 251
Moplahs 124
Moratuwa 241
Mount Lavinia 228
Muhammadans 1, 83f., 170, 246, (cf. *Arabs, Moors*)
Mulleriyava 134
Municipalities 241
Museum, Colombo 106, 224
Mutiny, Indian 236
Muttusami 202—207

Nagadvipa 17
Nagara-guttika 14
Nagas, 7, 9, 17, 28
Nambambaraya 111
Narasinham 70
Nawalapitiya 240, 243
Negombo 153—156, 179, 203, 227, 248f.
Newspapers 228, 238
Nikapitiya Bandara 146f.
Nilambe 167
Nilgala 155
North, Hon. F. 201—211
Nubia 122
Nuraddin 207
Nuwara Eliya 228, 251

O'Brien, Major General T. 289
Octagon, Kandy 212, 220
Ola Grants 106
Oliveira, P. de 147
Oudh (see *Ayodhya*)

Paddy tax 247
Paget, Sir E. 225
Pali, 55, 57, 59, 61f., 105, 114, 242, 250
Palicat 151
Panadure 243
"Pandit," the 120
Panduvasa 11
Pandyans 9, 26, 74—76, 78, 101, 105, 107, 109, 112
Paper Money 192
Parakrama, Sea of, 103
Parantaka, Cholian King 78
Pataliputra 18f.
Pavilion, Kandy, 228
Payaart, Governor 155f.
Peacock, monastery 57
Pearls 19f., 81
Pegu 87, 185
Pelmadulla 249
Penny Postage 236
Peradeniya 152, 227
Perahera 46, 187
Persians 2f., 81, 115, 122
Philip, Don (Vira Babu) 135, 137
Pihit-rata 12, 109
Pilame Talawwa 201
Pitt, William, 201
Planters' Association 235
Police 248
Pollock, Captain 209f.
Polonnaruwa 12, 57, 69, 71f., 79f, 85f., 97f., 104, 106, 100, 110, 112
Population of Ceylon (See *Census*)
Portuguese in Ceylon, 194
" Governors, 264
Potthakutha 69f.
Printing-press 185, 196
*Pujavaliya* 111
Puttalam 7f., 168, 177, 198, 208, 209
Pybus, J 190
Pyl, Governor 172, 176ff.

Quiloa 114
Quilon 81

Ragama 247
Ruhuna, Sri [Totagamuwa] 119
Railways 232, 235, 237f., 240, 243, 240—248, 253
Rajagaha 17
Rajakariya 212, 223, 228, 234
Raja-rata 12, 87, 98
*Rajavaliya* 126*n*
Rama and Sita 1, 4, 64, 94
*Ramayana* 4
Ramanna 87, 100f., 104
Ramesvaram 106
Randenivela 148
Ratgama 114
Ratnapura 246
Ratwatte, Adigar 212
Ravana 4
Rayigam Bandara 130f.
Rebellion of 1817, 33, 222f.
" 1848, 233
Red eyes, Plague of 47
Rein Martin 188
Rhee, van Governor 172, 181
Ribeiro 150
Ridgeway, Sir West 247
Rice 8, 184, 247
Rifle Regiment 234
Riots of 1915, 250f.
Ritigala, 14
Roads 225f., 232,—234, 238
Robinson, Sir H. (Lord Rosmead) 240
Roman Catholics 129, 131f. 159 176f., 182, 186, 194, 211, 244
Roman-Dutch Law 198

Rome 59, 82
Roothaes, Governor 174
Ruvanveli Seya 35, 38, 42, 45, 101
Ruanwella 210
Ruhuna 12, 26f., 43f., 48, 68, 72, 77—80, 85, 90—100, 108, 121
Rumley, Captain 207
Rumpf, Governor 182f.
Rupee Currency 242
Rutland 164

Sa, Constantine de 146—150
Sabaragamuwa 147, 157, 214, 219, 246
Saddha Tissa 36—38
Salappu Arachchi 131
Sali Prince 38
Sangha, General 95
Sanghamitta, Priest 47f.
,, Priestess 22—24
Sangkili 132
Sankhathalai 93
Sanskrit 51, 51
Sapumal, Prince 119
*Sarartha-sangraha* 57
Schools 212, 229—231, 241f., 250
Schreuder, J. Governor 187
Sea of Parakrama 103
Sena and Guttika 25
Serendib 2, 9, 115
Seven Korales 145, 156, 212
Siam 2, 87, 186
*Sidat Sangara* 114
Sigiriya 51, 62
Silakala 64—66
Silamegha, Prince 70
,, Dharmika 73
Simons, Governor 172, 181
Sindbad the Sailor 84
Sinhabahu 5
Sinhapura 5, 11
Siriwardhanapura 110
Sita (see *Rama*)
Sitavaka 114, 130—136, 218
Sivali, Queen 44
Skinner, Major 236
Slaves 66, 197, 224, 231
Soleyman (Suleiman) 83
Somadevi, Queen 38, 40
Somarama 39
Sopara 6
Sopater 81
Souza, D. L. de 137
Southern Country 91*n*, 93
Spain 135, 13f., 156
Spices of Ceylon 122, 140, 152, 171
Spilbergen, Joris van 141
Stanley, Sir H. 254, 256
State Council 255
States General of Holland 142
Stel, A. van der 156
Stuart J. General 200
Stubbs, Sir Edward
Suffrein, Admiral 192
Sugala, Queen 91, 99
Suluvansa Dynasty, 50, 261
Sumatra 144 142
Sumitta 11
Supparoka 6
*Suttas* 57

Takel, C. 185
Tamankaduwa 7*n*
Tambapanni 7
Tamlitti (Tamluk) 20
Tammanna Nuwara 8, 11
Tanjore 18, 26 [of *Chola*]
Taprobane 2, 7
Taxation 54, 79, 83, 87f, 91, 97, 102, 106, 179, 185, 200, 223, 230, 233f., 237, 239, 241, 247, 256
Tea 227, 256
Technical School 246
Telegraphs 235f.
Tennent, Sir J. E. 3*n*, 234
Theraputtabhaya 30, 36
Thesawalamai 182
Thomson, Sir Graeme, 257
Thuparama 22, 75
Thysz (See *Payaart*)
Tikiri Banda (*Raja Sinha* I) 133

Tooth Relic 54, 58. 60, 110
  118f., 187, 235
Topâveva 57
Torrington, Lord 233
Tôtagamuva 113, 119
Trade of Ceylon, Ancient 80
Tradition in Ceylon, Continuity 3*n*
Tribuli Pandar (*Tidiye Ba. dara*) 130
Trincomalee 49, 144, 145, 153, 161, 175, 179, 187, 191—193, 204f., 211, 234
*Tripitaka* 40, 59, 89
Tumpane 46
Turnour, George 62*n*
Tyrrell, Sir F. G. 256

Udunuwara 118, 167
Umbrella Canopy 35
University College 253, 256
Upatissa Nuwara, 9, 11, 14
Urubokke dam 236
Uruvela 42
Uva 143, 148, 150, 157, 222

Vahakotte 160
Vaitulya 46f., 66f.
Vallabhas 79
Vanga 5
Vanniyar 118
Vatagiri 87
Vaz, Father J. 176f.
Veddas 10, 97, 230f.
Velakkara 89
Versluys, Governor 184
Victoria, Queen 230, 246f.
Vidiye Bandara 130
Vihara devi 28
Vijaya 5—2, 15*n*, 39
Vijayanagar 123
Vijapala 157
Vijitagama 12
Vijitapura 9, 32
Vira Bahu of Kandy 135f.
Vira Sandara Banda 135
*Visuddhi-magga* 59
V. O. C. 141
Volunteer Corps 245
Vuyst, Governor 172 183

Wall, G. 240, 247
Ward, Sir H. 235—238, 241
War of 1914, 250
Wariyapola 234
Watapuluwa 206
Weera Sebald de, 142f.
Weligama 114
Wesleyan Mission 211
Westerwold, Admiral 151—153
Wijesinghe, L. C 62*n*
Winter, Sir E. 174
Wolvendaal Church 197

Xavier, Francis 132

Yakkhas 7—10, 14, 17, 49, 97
Yapahu 108, 112
Yatinuwara 118, 167
Yatthala Tissa 28
Yodi Ela 246